WALTZ WITH THE ENEMY

A MOTHER AND DAUGHTER CONFRONT THE AFTERMATH OF THE HOLOCAUST

BY
RASIA KLIOT AND HELEN MITSIOS

PENINA PRESS

Waltzing With the Enemy
A Mother and Daughter Confront the Aftermath of the Holocaust
Text Copyright © 2011 Rasia Kliot and Helen Mitsios

TYPESETTING AND PRODUCTION: Daniella Barak
EDITOR: Sara Rosenbaum

Soft Cover ISBN: 978-1-936068-21-0

First edition. Printed in Israel.

Distributed by:

Urim Publications
POB 52287
Jerusalem 91521, Israel
Tel: 02.679.7633
Fax: 02.679.7634
urim_pub@netvision.net.il

Lambda Publishers, Inc.
527 Empire Blvd.
Brooklyn, NY 11225, USA
Tel: 718.972.5449
Fax: 781.972.6307
mh@ejudaica.com

www.UrimPublications.com

In the living room five or six couples
were dancing to loud music coming
from a gramophone. The German pilot,
smiling happily and without much ceremony,
took my hand and directed me to the dance floor.
I was waltzing with the enemy.

– Rasia

Perhaps everybody has a garden of Eden, I don't know;
but they have scarcely seen their garden before they see the
flaming sword. Then, perhaps, life only offers the choice of
remembering the garden or forgetting it. Either, or: it takes
strength to remember, it takes another kind of strength to
forget, it takes a hero to do both.

– James Baldwin, Giovanni's Room

CONTENTS

PART TWO
HELEN'S STORY

RASIA'S PREFACE

A BRIDGE OF AIR

Procrastination was for years my habitual response to my daughter's insistence to write something about what happened to me during the Holocaust and World War Two.

Little by little, however, I gathered together some scraps and half-written notes. But when I read over the pages, they seemed so strange to me. Who wrote this? Who was the young girl with a wonderful past and bright future? Her story seemed like a novel written by somebody else. And how was this girl related to the woman who had lived in exile and silence all those years since? It appeared to be the story of two people, like conjoined twins, inside of me.

Sometimes when reacting to a situation today, I respond in a way that isn't rational.

"Be careful." I tell my daughter.

"Of what?" she asks.

Such urge for caution is a result of fear and suffering that can't ever be forgotten. Growing up in Vilnius, I had a good life and a promising future, but the Germans tore that away from me and my loved ones when I was only seventeen. In the more than sixty years that have passed since, I never went back to that place, to my roots, to my past. My friends, my uncles, aunts, cousins, were all killed. The senseless brutal killing of my father broke my heart forever. But these people will always be alive in my memory.

I sometimes forget what I did yesterday, but things that happened years ago continue to flash before my eyes. I see my young handsome father taken away from our lives in the darkness of night, never to appear again. I try not to dwell on the past, but the visions happen again and again. They are deeply embedded in my heart and mind and have become an unwelcome part of me. It is painful to write and relive the suffering of the past, but I have decided now, so many years later, that I had to rescue the memories and identities of my family and friends, and write them down. I am taking my daughter's advice and giving them a voice in our lives.

Sometimes at night when sleep won't come, I recount the names of my closest friends. I see their faces in the mirror of my mind, the color of their hair, their eyes, as if tomorrow my loneliness will disappear with the darkness of the night. Carla, Mira, Frida, Paula, Rosa and others are still waiting for my call to meet at the coffee house, go to the movies or theatre and later join up with the rest of the bunch.

My call will never reach any of them. All killed. Life interrupted and vanished as if they never existed.

Why did they disappear and I survive? I firmly believe that for some unknown reason an external force directed and watched over my life. Time and time again I was saved during the Holocaust from certain death by a miracle. One moment, one look, one word, a slight hesitation or an ounce of fear that could be noticed would have pushed my life into the murderers' hands. I must have played my part very well. Happy, relaxed, appearing to be entirely at ease. Smiling and looking the killers straight in the eyes – a mask covering a soul distorted with horror and fear.

My life could have been erased in the blink of an eye. Many times during the darkest years I happened to be one step ahead of disaster. My being alive helped my mother and brother survive, as when the final liquidation of the Vilnius ghetto approached in September 1943, I had found a place for them to stay and work on a farm in Lithuania. It was like being in the jaws of the wolf. Nobody could imagine a Jewish woman and boy posing as Polish farmhands surviving in Lithuania. The smallest suspicion that we were Jewish and had escaped from the ghetto would have meant someone immediately turning us in to the Lithuanian police who cooperated with the Germans in getting rid of the Jewish population.

All my emotions and feelings were frozen deep inside me during the years of my struggle. Not one tear escaped my eyes until a sunny day in April 1945, when the Soviet army entered Vienna. Like a dam suddenly opened up I was unable to stop sobbing. The women I lived with at the

Viennese labor camp thought I had gone insane when my knees gave out and I collapsed on the floor. They were ready to pour a bucket of cold water on me to stop my convulsions. How could they know my pain? In their eyes I was one of them. They were happy and going back to their families, friends and former lives.

The incident was forgotten and one by one, the women quickly left the camp. The room emptied, the iron beds exposing skeletons of wire netting void of life. Only I remained. I didn't have a home. I didn't have anywhere to go. I didn't know if any member of my family was alive.

For a long time while I was in and out of the ghetto I had a dream that often repeated itself. I dreamed that there was semi-darkness around me and I could see a big storm approaching. I could see a bridge suspended in the air made out of thin glass squares alternating with empty spaces in between where the water was rushing beneath me. I had to cross the bridge immediately or huge dark waves would swallow me. I was slowly, systematically and very carefully moving across the bridge on my toes so as not to lose my footing. One wrong move and I would fall into the fast current of the black muddy water below. Despite my fear I managed to reach the safe shore. I felt there was an invisible hand helping me. Reaching solid ground, I looked back at where I had started. The water had turned into enormous black wheels almost touching the sky, rolling behind me, completely devastating everything in their path. There was nothing left. I took this as a good omen. "I crossed the bridge. I'll make it. I might stay alive."

When my daughter told me she wanted to visit Vilnius, I was a little surprised, but I thought it would be interesting for her to see the city where my family lived for generations. I still have no desire to travel there. In a way, the dream foretold my future. There is nothing left for me there. And I don't need to go back to my hometown for closure. There is no such thing as closure for me. Closure is a label that well-intentioned therapists use to help people. The only closure for me will be when I am dead.

HELEN'S PREFACE

A WORLD OF GHOSTS

Did I want to enter a lost world full of ghosts? It didn't occur to me to even ask the question when my mother and I started writing this book. I hadn't expected to encounter a world full of relatives and strangers who would become alive to me. I didn't realize that I would hear the vibrant Yiddish language in the context of my mother's storybook childhood, walk the streets of Vilnius with her, and hold my breath every time she risked denouncement as a Jew. I thought I could come and go as I pleased, not knowing a person can become a captive of someone else's past. But I also learned that a captive can become a guardian – and I am a proud guardian of all that my mother and I could reclaim in telling these stories.

When my mother and I started writing this memoir, I believed I could detach myself emotionally from the pain of hearing and writing about lives culled from the black hole of absence and loss. I thought I could step aside from the knowledge that the enormity of the Holocaust affected not only one generation, but also the second generation, the children of survivors, who often experience secondary post-traumatic stress. I wanted to write about overcoming tragedy, about people who brush themselves off and pick up the pieces, and like the cowboys in movies, keep heading toward the next new horizon. The script in my head insisted on a happy ending. It still does. But I've also learned that sometimes the only happy ending is survival itself, and just being alive is enough to ask for.

My mother's stories of the Holocaust end with her survival. Like an action hero in a movie she defied the enemy and enormous odds, emerging from the rubble, battered but still courageous and relatively intact. How difficult then could it be to write about her life, and mine as her daughter? Much harder than I ever anticipated because on this journey I began to learn about my mother and my inherited past in a new way. I discovered anger as strong as my love, and resentment that equaled my admiration. Instead of continuing to hero-worship my mother and holding her up as an impossible yardstick with which to measure myself, I found a person emotionally battered by her experiences who would never fully recover. I faced the helplessness and realization that love is not always enough – just as my mother's love could not protect me from the world, my love could never heal her pain. And I acknowledged parts of myself that were shaped by her fears and sadness. Writing this book together risked what my mother had spent decades overcoming – letting the Holocaust become the defining factor of her life, and my life too. But this is what we did and here it is. Her story…and mine.

PART ONE
RASIA'S STORY

FORBIDDEN LOVE

Sometimes when my mother took me for a walk in the neighborhood, people would pass us and occasionally glance at me again. This wasn't because I was the most beautiful little girl in the world, but because I was so fair. They must have thought I was "colorless" as my mother used to happily say since I had very light, thin, blondish white hair, and light blue eyes without distinguishing lashes or brows.

I resembled my father's side of the family. My paternal grandfather was very fair, had blond hair, but I remember him with a few wisps of hair left and deep blue smiling eyes. We used to visit him often and I had a great time playing with his daughter and son from his second marriage. He was generous and kind. He was fortunate and died just before the start of World War II, in his own bed, surrounded by family.

I never knew my real grandmother. She died a short time before I was born and I inherited her name, Rasia, which was unusual, and didn't sound right to my ears. I think that most children would choose a different name if given the chance.

I heard a story about my grandmother from my Aunt Lisa, my father's younger sister. My grandmother grew up in a small town close to the city of Grodno, in a Polish neighborhood sprinkled with a few Jewish families. Missionaries from the Roman Catholic church had a big estate outside the village in a green forest of pine trees with a small creek of crystal-clear water that flowed next to the assembly hall. Jewish children from poor families were invited to come and stay there, enjoy good food and play together. Religion lessons were part of the entertainment. Given the continuing missionary effort, some of the Jewish boys and girls were converted to Catholicism. One of the new Christians happened to be my grandmother's childhood friend whom she grew up with and who was sent away by the missionaries for more education. He came back to the village as an ordained priest and lived in the rectory next to the church and cemetery.

My grandmother was very fond of this young man she had known since childhood. He often visited his family and would stop at my grandmother's house for a short time. This didn't last too long and in no time he was sent away to another parish. The villagers accused him of being too close to his Jewish roots, and my grandmother of being responsible for his departure. In those days, a priest had tremendous influence and was regarded as a holy man. As a result of this "scandal," the village authorities ordered my grandmother's family to leave the village in twenty-four hours or pay the consequences. In those days a small incident like this could easily ignite a pogrom, a killing spree by the peasants. My grandmother's family quickly packed their belongings and moved to the city of Grodno where they had relatives and tried to build a new life.

The event was a big topic of conversation. The news spread like wildfire through the nearby Jewish communities. Her parents tried to marry her off as soon as possible before her name could be permanently blemished. She was introduced to my future grandfather and they were soon married. From what I heard, it wasn't a happy union, since Rasia had been torn away from her true love and now forced to marry my grandfather. Nevertheless, she dutifully had children and raised a family. My father was the oldest of their five children. When he was twenty-two he married my twenty-one-year-old mother in Kaunas on April 12, 1919.

When my grandmother, Rasia, passed away at a young age, my father took this very hard. Even in his later years when I asked him about my grandmother, I could tell it made him very sad to talk about her. There was a photograph of her on the wall in our living room, and I remember her as a beautiful young woman with her hair piled on top of her head and a heavily embroidered dress reaching to her ankles. I also asked my mother about the tragedy of my grandmother's life, and when she told me the story I already knew by heart, tears would come to my eyes as I imagined the love of two young people, the priest and the Jewess torn apart by circumstance. It sounded like Romeo and Juliet to me. When I was young, my romantic idea was that people in love should leave everything behind and elope for the sake of their happiness. How little I knew about real life.

A Young Girl

I'm playing hide and seek with my brothers in the beautiful formal living room of our home in Vilnius. I am the only girl, the second oldest of four children. It's dark in the room, my parents have gone out for the evening and the maid, Ancia, is smart enough to leave us alone. We jump on the couch, turn over a few chairs, hide under the table. Suddenly the big chandelier is turned on and we are exposed to a flood of bright lights. My parents and Ancia are at the door, our dog, Lalka, is barking happily while we stand there looking guiltily at the floor. We are reprimanded and promise not to do it again. We have a whole big house to play in, but not the formal living room with the exquisite new furniture that was a surprise from my father when we returned one time from the country where we spent our summers.

Our summer residence was about fifteen to twenty kilometers from Vilnius, in a place called the Black Forest, Czarny Bor in Polish. It was always a lively place full of friends and family coming and going. My father's two younger brothers, Leon and Sholem, often came to visit with their wives and stayed with us over the weekend. My father commuted daily to the country by the electric fast train, and Mr. Ladowski, the farmer who lived close by, picked him up from the train station with a horse and buggy carriage. Each of us children would take turns riding with the farmer who sometimes let us hold the reins on the straight road. Even for a few minutes, holding the reins was a big adventure for us. It was fascinating and magical to see the huge iron locomotive slowing down and coming to a sudden stop in the station. People poured out of the compartments in a hurry, like ants out of an ant hill after a rain, and disappeared in all directions. But this time, who was following my father on a short leash? It was a little white dog that looked like a tiny down pillow turned inside out, with a tiny black button nose and beautiful dark eyes. My father had brought us a new pet! We called her Lalka, a Polish name for doll, and she became our constant companion right up to our days in the ghetto.

Our country house was on a small hill overlooking the river and a big meadow full of wild flowers with a thousand aromas and a rainbow of colors reaching to the riverbank. The river was about thirty feet across and flowed peacefully toward the Baltic Sea. In some places the river was shallow, the water clear, and we could cross to the other side and then run back before our maid would get scared and come after us. When I was older I liked to go there by myself for a swim, accompanied just by Lalka. Then I'd lie down on the soft green wildflower bed and listen to the lively sound of the river and the chirping of birds. After a while Lalka would become restless or hungry and run home and I knew it was time for me to follow her.

I would often invite my best friend, Frida, to the country. We had met in the third grade and discovered we were almost neighbors and our families each had four children, ours three boys and I the only girl, the second oldest. Her family was the opposite. They had three girls and a brother, Misha. Our parents also knew each other. Frida's parents owned one of the best and most popular coffee houses in the city. It was down the street about three blocks from our home and I used to go there very often and enjoy the best ice cream in town or have a light lunch, waited on by nice waiters who looked handsome in their uniforms. Sometimes to look grown up, I used to order a small coffee that was very much in vogue. I sipped it slowly even though I didn't like the taste because it was bitter and strong. I felt welcome there and was considered a friend of the family by everyone.

In the evening, on weekends, there was a very nice female orchestra that entertained the patrons with music and songs. The atmosphere was always relaxed, elegant and intimate. Some professors from our school used to go there with their dates. Seeing them was an unexpected treat for us. The next day we could tell our schoolmates who we saw and who they were with, what they wore and how they looked. Most of us girls were in love at one time or another with the bachelor professors and curious to hear the stories about their activities outside the schoolroom. By the time we were fifteen, we observed the scene and pretended to know it all.

* * *

A few hundred yards from our country house the forest stretched for miles. My brothers and I would run around the forest to our liking under the watchful eyes of Ancia. We knew every mushroom, what tree it grew under, and when was the best time to pick it – soon after a short, intensive summer rain. In some places the forest was so dense that even in the brightest days full of sunshine there was an eternal darkness. Green moss covered the small yellow mushrooms we called *lesniki*, which meant "plain forest grown" that grew in clusters. The forest held an abundance of all kinds of berries: blueberries that grew on short bushes, small sweet strawberries nourished by the sun in a clearing, raspberries and what we now call granberries – small sour berries, medium to dark red that were prepared with some sugar and small apples and kept for the winter as a relish with meat or fowl.

I possessed a rich imagination that goes back to the years as far as my memory can reach. It was infused in me at a very young age by my father's storytelling as a special treat for us children. I associated the sparks of firewood bursting in the fireplace with the burning bush and the voice that spoke to Moses. And I heard a voice, but it was my father asking me why I had my eyes closed when he told us stories.

"I can see better," was my reply.

The tales were never boring and we always asked for more. The only thing that I remember irritating me was my oldest brother's constant interruptions and questions. Years later I realized that every tale my father told us in simple words had a very deep social and moral meaning. I also liked my grandfather's stories, but they were different. His stories were about kings and queens and full of rewards and punishments that happened to our ancestors.

After a while I had enough and tried to escape with different excuses, but nevertheless we had learned about God, the prophets, the sages and angels that gave meaning to our lives.

21

EARLY YEARS IN VILNIUS

We lived in Vilnius, on Wielka (Wide) St., the second building northwest of the Holy Kazimir Catholic Church and across from the old renovated baroque City Hall. The entrance to the courtyard was through two huge doors that were locked by the janitor at 10:00 PM. Though distant, a mixture of Jews and Christian families lived in the building in harmony and tolerance. I became acquainted with some of the Christian children, played games with them and exchanged visits. There was one girl, Irene, who I especially liked and felt at ease with.

Irene was the daughter of a Christian family who owned an elegant store where you could buy ice cream and halvah. The halvah was displayed in the huge windows in big blocks, almost any flavor imaginable. It was my favorite store. I loved sweets and visited quite often. Irene's mother was a fashionable woman with dark blond hair that she wore twisted in a bun and dark brown eyes that always seemed sad to me. She was very friendly, paid me compliments, and never forgot to send greetings to my parents. But I didn't feel at ease in the presence of her father. Something about him bothered me. I don't know if I felt rejection or some kind of scrutiny, even when he smiled at me with tightly shut lips. At the time I didn't know that he belonged to the *endecja*, an anti-Semitic political party. Years later I was told of the fights he had with his wife and daughter because of our friendship.

Irene had straight dark brown hair, brown eyes, a darkish complexion, thin lips and a nice smile. We were about the same age. Ironically, it was I who looked typically Polish, and it's possible that this was partly the reason why when her father saw us together, he greeted me with, "And here is your friend Raszka." As long as I can remember I hated that name. Maybe it was because in the country when we played with the village children, they made fun of my name. To them Raszka meant a washing board, and to tease me they repeatedly called me Raszka, until I got mad and hit some boy, who ran home screaming as if he were being killed.

For a time I thought that Irene's father didn't approve of me just because of my name. I was a naïve child who wanted to be accepted. Mother told me that she heard Irene's mother was descended from Jews, but then so was Jesus, I thought. I liked Irene and wished she were my sister.

Christmas Eve was a special treat at Irene's home. The big pine tree stood in the middle of the room all decorated with candy and cookies, wrapped in colorful paper. I don't remember exchanging presents, but eating all kinds of sweets and not wanting to leave. I used to stay on a little longer after my parents left, and then Irene and her mother would bring me to our door, sometimes come in for a while or stand at the threshold and with a smile on her face, Irene's mother would say, "Here is your sweet daughter. If you don't want her, we'll take her back."

I almost wished they would, as I didn't want to part from Irene. Years later our paths diverged when I went to Dr. Czarny's private Hebrew school, and we didn't see each other very often. School was out at 3:00 PM, then homework and a little free time. We also attended school on Sunday and had Saturday off. I made some friends at Dr. Czarny's school but didn't like the subjects taught in Hebrew and resented going to school on Sunday since it was the only day I could visit with Irene.

Little did I know that Irene would be the first person to give me her Christian ID and help save my life during the Nazi regime.

THE GATHERING STORM

On September 1, 1939 we were in the country when a general mobilization was called and the radio was hysterically announcing, "Germany provoking an attack on Poland. The German army has crossed the Polish border; Poland will defend its borders and the enemy will soon be eliminated and driven back by our patriots."

I heard my parents talking about the negotiation that was going on between England, Germany and Russia and we hoped the war would be avoided. We read in the daily Yiddish newspaper, *Der Vilner Zeitung*, that in Germany the Nazis confiscated Jewish businesses and hooligans were harassing Jews and looting Jewish property, but there was nothing about killing people or concentration camps. It's possible that the people in the government were aware of it, but for the general public both the radio and newspapers were strictly censored. We had heard on the radio that Germany "wasn't behaving well toward the Jewish population," but what awaited us was beyond the scope of our imagination.

Unfortunately, the Polish army soon realized that patriotism and love of the country were no match for the mobilized armed forces of the strongest army in Europe at the time.

I was amazed and disappointed at all the commotion, and sad that we had to leave the country a few days earlier than anticipated. I had just come in from my morning swim, water dripping from my blue bathing suit and trying to dry my long hair that was turning the color of ripe wheat from the water and sun. I heard my mother calling me through the open door from the dining room, "Come, something very important is happening."

"Yes mother, I'm coming," I said. With a few steps, and a little annoyed and curious, I asked my mother what happened. Lalka, my dear companion, was barking, tail wagging, expressing her devotion by jumping all over me and trying to get my attention. All I wanted to do was take a leisurely walk in the woods with my dog, and hear and watch life going on in the shadow of the trees.

"Can't we talk later?" I asked. Mother seemed irritated and impatient with my tone of voice, her words were strange and the usual smile on her face vanished. In a shaky voice she told me to pack my things.

"We're taking the next train back to the city," she said.

"Why? I want to stay. I can take the train back tomorrow. Let the boys go with you, I'll even take Lalka with me." I said this without conviction as I knew perfectly well it was impossible to be left alone. Why not try and have my way? But of course my plea didn't work.

At the train station, I waited with my mother and two younger brothers for the train to come in. Ancia, our maid, would come the next day by horse and buggy with the farmer's son, Janek, and bring our dog, Lalka, and some of our clothes to the city. I had never before seen so many people at one time coming from all directions: fathers, friends, families accompanying their sons, some families holding onto each other, young men with their head high trying to keep up morale with mobilization orders in their hands, going to fight the enemies wherever they might be.

"Poland must stay free," people were saying. An older lady we knew from the village stood at the platform, a rosary in hand, and with the cross, blessed the departing men. It all looked like a movie, but the music was missing. Slowly a little fear crept into me. I turned to mother who looked kind of solemn.

"Don't worry, Father won't be drafted. He's an old man and just young men go to war," I assured her with the wisdom of my experience.

"Old?" My mother turned, looked at me and said, "He's not even forty years old and in emergencies the army can draft any able-bodied man."

Slowly the train moved away from the station. I stood at the open window in the hall with the wind blowing my hair away from my face, absorbing the beauty of the passing green forest, the lush landscape and, as the train gained speed, the runaway blue cloudless sky. From farther away the field in the distance reminded me of the Persian carpet in our living room interwoven with greens and gold, and of the sea captain, a friend of my father's, who either sold it or gave it to him as a present. He visited us once in a while, and I had never thought to ask him where he came from or how he and my father met. He was handsome and charming, and I was thrilled when he nonchalantly kissed my hand in the Polish manner and, half-smiling, whispered, "I wish you were a few years older." With my eyes cast down I smiled. He didn't know how I wished the same. If only I could speed my growing up. I remembered him occasionally when I saw a handsome young man that resembled him a little. But I never forgot the twinkling in his eyes and imagine that he fell as a hero in battle fighting for the honor of his beloved country.

The train was slowing down and the sudden stop brought me back to reality. Vilnius was swarming with people coming and going without any definite direction. Everybody was excited and in a hurry. The minute we jumped into his cab, our cab driver, a middle-aged man with a big reddish mustache, started talking about the coming disaster and the vulnerability of our city, being right between the two big powers of Russia and Germany.

"Two wars in one lifetime, two wars," he repeated under his breath, reminiscing years past. "It's too much. All we want is to be left alone." He felt sorry for his country and the young men going to war.

At the time, we didn't know about the secret pact of non-aggression the Germans signed with Stalin. Two deadly enemies aligned with each other for their own temporary interests. The Poland I knew was divided between the cold-blooded despot, Stalin, who killed millions of his own people, and a racist killer and megalomaniac, Hitler. Hitler, who believed in the superiority of the Aryan race, partitioned Poland as a prize, and demanded Russia's non-aggression so that it wouldn't get involved in a war with Germany. The east of Poland went to Russia and the west to Germany.

Just a few days later, after we returned to our apartment in Vilnius, my little brother, Leo, who had been visiting his friend next door, came running back home screaming, "The soldiers are coming. They're wearing long coats and have guns on their shoulders. Come look. There are a lot of people on the street." He ran over to the window and pulled the drapes apart. We saw people down the street packing the small park.

"I'll be right back. Nobody leave the house," Father said and hurried out the door with a strange look on his face I'd never seen before. In the meantime my other younger brother, Hershel, who was two years younger than me, took out a book and, as if nothing was going on, sat at the table, poured himself some tea and buried his face in his reading. Something must have been bothering him. After a while he gave me the honor of his explanation, "Many armies passed our city before and we survived. I can't predict the future or read father's face, but let's just wait and see what happens. I'm sure everything will be fine. Just don't fantasize too much," and pushing himself calmly from the table, went to his room and brought me a book with a red cover.

"Read this," he said. "It's a story about love and war. You'll find it interesting." I had seen this book, *Gone With the Wind*, on display at my friend Luba Wakier's bookstore.

"I'll read it, but not right now," I said. "I'm curious about what Father found out. Who are the soldiers? Germans? Russians? Or maybe Turks?" Right then my father came in.

"It's the Russian army," he said. "They look like hungry, tired peasants that suffered famine after years of drought. A few of them on motorcycles and in cars almost look like real soldiers." Slowly, as if still observing the strange army, he pulled a chair up to the table and reached for his coffee. "I can't believe my eyes. What I saw made me sick. Some people were waving flags, welcoming the Red Army, and there were some of our workers in the welcoming party too, screaming like mad men, 'Long live Stalin, our liberator.' Don't they know what Stalin is doing to his own people? He's the sole judge and jury and sends yesterday's friends to death. He wants to take over the whole world and infect it with his Communist dictatorship."

My father was a successful businessman. He owned the Ch. Kliot Factory for leather gloves and coats, and a suede tannery where he employed both Jewish and Polish workers. We had representatives in large Polish cities like Warsaw, Krakow and Poznan who took orders for large department stores in those places, and we also exported goods to England and South Africa through a company called Kaznwill.

My mother looked at her husband with concern and worry on her pretty face. "Some of the people really are idealists and believe in a worker's paradise," Mother said, looking at us children who didn't care much about politics. I felt secure and protected. Whatever happened, my father would take care of everything.

My father was horrified by the open arms extended to the Russian Communists by the Jewish working class and by the poor element that existed in Vilnius as well as other Polish cities. Vilnius had its narrow alleys and old quarters occupied by poor Jews, except for the janitors who for some reason always seemed to be Christians. We had private organizations that supported the people who couldn't help themselves, but for a large segment of the middle class life was quite good. For a stranger coming from afar to Vilnius for whatever reason before World War II, it most likely looked like a second Jerusalem, a remark that Napoleon made. When he encountered the flourishing Jewish scholarship and culture in Vilnius, he called it the "Jerusalem of the North," Jerushalayim de Lita.

THE RUSSIANS IN OUR HOME

School started a few weeks later in September 1939, and soon after, two Russian families moved into our house. First, a short, broad-shouldered man dressed in a military uniform drenched in medals accompanied by a pretty youngish-looking heavy-set woman. I disliked him from the moment he jumped on the bed to try it out in a vulgar manner and happily laughed. I was embarrassed and left the room. Whenever I happened to come face to face with him in the hall, I turned my face away as if he didn't exist. At the time I didn't know what an important part he would play in our lives.

The other two rooms, the big living room with the six tall windows and beautiful furnishings, as well as the adjoining room, were also confiscated and occupied by two military men. One about my father's age and the other, his son. I couldn't guess his age since for me anyone older than myself or my brother, two years my senior, I considered old. The Russians didn't pay attention to me, which pleased me in one way as I didn't like any Russians and knew my parents' dislike of Communism and what it stood for. On the other hand, I didn't want to be ignored by people who forced themselves into our lives. It made me feel self-conscious and insecure. It affected my self-esteem when my mother told me I was getting skinny. I assured her and promised to buy lunch instead of sweets in the future. I liked my school and was pleased that we didn't have to adhere to the strict uniform code. Underneath the required jacket, I took the opportunity to show off the assortment of my beautiful blouses.

My friend Frida and I were the only Jewish girls in our class, as the whole school had no more than four Jewish students. I made new friends and often included my friend Irene in our company. I became one of the best students in my class. I studied hard, and helped other gentile students who later helped me survive the German extermination of the Vilnius Jewish population. It was also my good luck that my Polish improved tremendously since I was exposed to Polish-speaking people the whole year. We attended parties at different homes, played music and danced.

The brother of one of my friends invited me to the movies. We met in front of Kino Pan, and then went inside and sat in the last row. After accompanying me to the door before saying goodnight, he gave me a quick kiss on the cheek. It was so sudden and unexpected that I rapidly turned my head and accidentally hit his nose. The poor kid grabbed his face in pain. But despite this, my "love life" was starting to be on the right track. I liked school parties and meeting new people. The world was a charming place to be and, like most adolescents, I felt like it revolved exclusively around me.

Our home was large and my father managed to bribe the Russian NKVD man (People's Commissariat for Internal Affairs, which was the leading secret police organization of the Soviet Union) with expensive presents like fur or leather coats and jackets for him and his plump girlfriend. Some of our holdings were confiscated, but with my father's good connection to the commissar, we were warned any time we were on a new list to be arrested and deported to Siberia as capitalists. As soon as we heard of such a listing, we were separately dispersed to the homes of some of our devoted employees for a day or two. Then after everyone on the list had been rounded up and sent away, we returned quietly to our apartment until another list might appear.

Once in a while, I saw the two Russians, father and son, emerging and disappearing like shadows from the part of the house they occupied. They were both very polite when we met face to face, with usually just a light nod of the head and not a second look.

On one Saturday night, however, there was a difference. I was wearing my new dress, a light green silk outfit with narrow pleats reaching to my knees, black silk stockings and high-heeled pumps. We were having a party in my high school auditorium, with an orchestra supplying music for the event. I was finishing a dance with one of my new classmates, when

I noticed somebody staring at me. To my surprise, it was the young Russian, Paul, who lived with his father in our house. Paul was standing there with another young man, both in military uniforms. Paul introduced me to his friend, who was in his unit and from the same town in Russia. The music started to play. Paul bowed from the waist, and asked me to dance, taking my arm gently and directing me to the dance floor. I felt like I was floating on air. The music changed, but our dance continued until it was time to go home. We left separately. I left first and he followed me later so we wouldn't be seen walking together. Nina, my beautiful Polish friend, who later gave me her sister's ID, joined us for a short while and then left with her boyfriend. At home after that, whenever I saw Paul, he smiled at me and his short greetings intrigued and flattered me. A few times as if by accident, he was waiting for me after school. Sometimes out of nowhere I saw Paul's father observing me. I understood Paul must have told him about our friendship.

One Friday night during dinner, we heard some commotion in the entrance hall and a knock at the door. It was Paul, his father and an older lady, standing next to a girl about my age with a small suitcase at her side, and a soldier bringing in some bags. We were introduced to Paul's mother and sister, Mrs. and Miss Chernienko. I knew from Paul that his mother was a physician and his sister was studying music and was nineteen years old, four years younger than Paul.

On a chilly afternoon, I was walking toward home. I noticed a man approaching me swiftly from across the street. A little scared, I stepped back but to my relief it was Paul, with his bright smile and shining eyes, dressed in civilian clothes. We walked toward the Wilia River (the Neris River in Polish) that flows through Vilnius, and then we continued to walk through the Bernardin Park, an oasis in the center of the city. Paul described his good life in Russia, his town, their country house in the Crimea, and of all the privileges that Russia offered. He grew up in a well-to-do family, was educated and had a bright future. For me it was like a storybook fairy tale – a faraway world with its own laws, traditions and ideas. Not that I didn't believe him, but for me his country had always been portrayed as a depressed, miserable place ruled by rootless despots.

Nevertheless, I felt an indescribable fascination when he put his arms around me and gently kissed me on the lips. I wanted to bury my head in his arms, forget the world around us, reconcile our different ideologies and overcome all the obstacles confronting us. We couldn't

31

afford to be seen together entering my home, so I walked home alone up the busy street and away from the eternal river, my mind occupied by dreamy thoughts. My parents' instructions regarding the Russians were well known to me: be polite, reserved, no personal association and no political discussions. I agreed, but Paul was different. With him I could talk about anything. He understood that I came from a different environment, was brought up in a traditional Jewish home and was not very politically inclined. Sometimes I met Paul's sister in the hall. We exchanged few words. I didn't know how close she was to Paul and we decided for the time to keep our romance secret.

It was a white Sunday. The city looked like a wonderland. It snowed for days, diamonds falling from heaven, covering the roads and chimneys with a thick white-blue blanket creating a huge horizon united with the sky, my own magic snow world. Paul and I decided to visit my grandfather who lived in the suburbs and whom I loved dearly. We walked hand in hand. Some places were covered with ice where water was spilled and looked like a shiny mirror, slippery to walk on, but great to slide on while holding on to each other. After deciding it was too late for an unexpected visit to my grandfather's, we turned back toward home and started running just for fun, the fresh snow falling, cracking under our boots. I slid and fell with my face down and was buried for a moment in the soft snow, losing consciousness for a split-second. Two strong arms reached toward me holding me tight, kissing my frozen face, wet with the melting snow. Before we reached home the snow stopped falling and the sky assumed the softness and deep color of blue velvet.

Not long after, Mrs. Chernienko invited me through Paul for afternoon tea. I told my mother who said it wasn't polite to refuse her, especially as it was in our own house. I showed up with a jar of homemade raspberry jam, a traditional Russian addition to hot tea. It was a short visit. Paul's sister and mother and another Russian woman who resembled a prison matron, were there. I hadn't expected the strange woman, lost my voice, and felt like turning back, but Paul took my hand and we both sat on my favorite green velvet sofa. I had to get away, feeling like an object to be assessed and judged. By this time, I knew that Paul told his family he was in love with me and wanted to propose marriage. But we were like Romeo and Juliet. My parents would never accept him.

Somehow I made it through the tea. But in order to see Paul I had to invent all kinds of excuses to get out of the apartment and meet him secretly. That made me feel guilty, but in my mind it was all justified. His confession of true love added a layer of excitement, adventure and secrecy, but was also a strain. When he told me that he wanted to marry me, I didn't and couldn't take him seriously. I didn't have the heart to tell this beautiful human being that I could never see myself tied to one person for the rest of my life. I was seventeen years old. Nonetheless, I had to admit the idea fed my ego and made me feel very desirable.

The winter months went by quickly. I was busy with schoolwork and preparing for end-of-the-year exams. Paul had been called back to Russia for a few months. When he finally returned early in May, he came in after dinner, and for the first time in my parents' presence, asked me to go out with him for a walk. We went over to the small park about a block from the City Hall, the majestic building that was erected at the liberation of Poland after the First World War. Now it was occupied by the Russian military. We found a bench under a tree, the branches alive with deep green young leaves, facing the sun and ascending toward the cloudless sky after a long icy winter. I felt like a bolt of lightning struck me when he said that his father received orders for the family to leave for Russia in ten days, and that war was imminent.

"It is a secret known only to high-ranking military personnel," he told me. He begged me to talk to my parents, to join his family in their exodus. But I already knew no matter what the political situation was, my father had no intention of ever leaving our beloved city, family and friends.

I could never leave without my parents. Whatever happened, we would be together. When a big van stopped in front of our house a few days later, and soldiers started hastily loading the Chernienko's luggage, Paul came into my room, begging me to go with them, warning me of the perils of war, asserting his love. Crying, holding on to each other, the tears flooded our grim faces. But by the time my family realized the mistake we had made by not leaving with them, it was too late.

June 22, 1941. The city was in an unprecedented turmoil. Russian soldiers, some with loaves of bread under their arms, ran in the middle of the street trying to jump on moving vehicles to get out of the city. Cars and trucks drove by without stopping. Everyone for himself. No time to lose. The Germans were already at the outskirts of the city. Soon their airplanes started dropping bombs that scared us with a whistling roaring noise. Many Jewish natives and refugees from German occupied territories also tried to leave the city. But it was too late; the road to the east was cut off.

No escape, just chaos everywhere. An unorganized herd, a cloud of people hanging in the air between the sky and Hades. Now we had the house to ourselves after the man from the NKVD and his girlfriend had packed up all their belongings and accumulated all the merchandise they could get their hands on. In the early morning they said goodbye and left. Like Paul's father, they too had asked us to leave the city and escape to Russia with them.

My parents couldn't imagine that life under German rule could be worse than living under Russian occupation. My father fondly recalled living and working in Emden, Germany, as a young man. He didn't believe the Jewish refugees who came to Vilnius from the western part of Poland occupied by the Germans, who told us of the atrocities committed by the German occupation. We thought they were trying to improve their lot, not trying to escape persecution by coming to our city which was under Russian rule and considered safer. Now they tried to run toward Russia, but were forced to return to Vilnius, as they were cut off by the German army advancing like a hurricane toward Russia, taking city after city with very little resistance and spreading their deadly might.

The house seemed unreal, empty and quiet. Some kind of indescribable fear and intuition of an imminent loss crept over me. Something out of my control was going to happen. I also realized how much I missed Paul, and even the other couple who I never really cared for much.

Many times in the coming months and years I wished that we would have taken Mr. Chernienko's advice and left with them, or had even been arrested and deported to Siberia. With all the gold and jewelry my parents had, we might have survived the war far away from the front. Unfortunately, most of our fortune was stolen and after the war I became homeless, stateless and almost destitute.

MY FATHER

After the Russians left in a hurry and the Germans occupied the city, it became a very dangerous time for us. Jewish men were afraid to walk on the streets, as the Germans, with the help of some Lithuanians who pointed them out, were arrested and disappeared. We were shocked when we found out my mother's brother who came from the provinces to see a doctor was caught on the street, arrested and killed. My parents realized too late that they should have left Vilnius. Now there was no escape. My mother went out sometimes to buy food and other necessities, but I was the one who left the house on a regular basis. We were completely cut off from the news. The Lithuanians had confiscated the radios of Jewish people. The *Vilner Tog*, the Vilnius daily Yiddish newspaper, was no longer being printed. We were left to sit in the house and wait, hoping this was a dark storm that would soon pass over.

It was a very depressing time in our house because of my brother Hershel's death from typhoid. Hershel, two years my junior, had died in the typhoid epidemic that spread throughout the city and killed many young people just before the Germans entered the city. The day of his funeral, the city was bombed and the Germans were advancing toward Vilnius. My parents were in mourning, depressed, crying for their son whose death may have been avoided if we could have brought our personal physician to see him. Unfortunately, the Russians locked the doors of the hospitals and didn't allow any outsiders to come in. Finally, when my brother was dying, they let my mother and our doctor go in. After he examined my brother, he told my mother, "If I could have seen him a few days ago, I might have been able to save his life."

My other brother, Benjamin, who was two years older than me, belonged to Betar, the Zionist Revisionists' youth movement. His decision to leave Vilnius was made after an experience at the flight school where he took private lessons. There he was the only Jewish boy in the midst of elite Polish boys from military and wealthy families. He thought they considered him one of the group until one day they got drunk and jokingly said, "Let's go beat up some Jews." He had to take his final exam the next week. When he got to the plane, the engine wouldn't start, and the Polish boys stood around laughing at their prank. This was the last straw for him. Disregarding my parents' warnings and pleas, he made preparations to leave for Palestine, just six months before WWII started. One day, shouldering a heavy backpack and wearing a leather coat and high boots, he left for the train station accompanied by the whole family. As he was getting ready to board the train, my mother asked, "How are you going to carry such a heavy backpack?" He turned to her and said, "One day you won't be able to take even this much with you."

On the 15th of July, 1941 at about 2:00 AM my parents heard some commotion in the courtyard and woke us up. I was half asleep, a little surprised, but unaware of what was coming next. Suddenly, we heard knocking at the door.

"Open up or we will break down the door and kill you all. We're the authorities, the police, we have to talk to you."

Not having much of a choice, the door was opened, and like a swarm of beasts, about four or five men wearing uniforms and swastika armbands rushed in. One of the intruders came over to my father who was wearing my favorite light beige suit and ordered him to hand over his gold watch. With their guns pointed they forced my father to walk out of the house, down the steps to the courtyard. I followed him and started to cry.

My father turned toward me and said the words that will live in my memory the rest of my life, "My child, don't cry. I will be back." And they took him into the night, into a darkness from which he never returned.

I was left with only my mother and baby brother, Leo. We felt scared, bewildered and empty, like a roof was suddenly torn off from above our heads, with four walls left, but no shelter. On the second day we had new visitors again. This time two Germans in brown uniforms came in and demanded money, saying our father told them we had it hidden in the house.

"You better come up with it," they said. They started looking around and shouted, "We'll kill you. Hand over the money." As I had a little money on me, my mother said, "Give it to them." They demanded more, but I said, "This is all I have." As they were turning toward the door, I asked them where my father was and when he'd be back. One of them turned sharply toward me and answered ironically, "*Du wirst dort auch gehen, nur warte ein wenig*" (You'll go there too, just wait a little), slammed the door and left.

The day before, my friend Frida's father and brother two years my senior were also arrested in the middle of the night and taken away. Also, Rosa Feigelson's father and brother, who lived one floor below us, were arrested at the same time as my father. So were other Jewish men who lived in the building. It was a calculated move by the Germans to first get rid of the influential and wealthy Jewish men, since women and children would be easy prey.

Sister Teresa

A few days after my father was taken away, we heard a light knocking at the door. Our dog, Lalka, ran toward the door wagging her tail and barking. Somebody she knew was behind the door. I always recognized it by her behavior. My heart stopped beating. My father! Father was coming home. I ran toward the door, mother right behind me, but our happiness died the minute we saw it wasn't my dear father, but instead a Polish acquaintance accompanied by a young woman.

The young woman was a nun. She wasn't wearing a habit, but was dressed in a simple skirt and blouse. The Russians had closed all the nunneries and monasteries. After a short introduction, we understood that she had been asked by our Polish friend to come to our house with the idea of re-educating us and converting us to the Christian faith. Jewish persecution was hardly lessening, and my mother decided it might be useful in some way for us to learn about the Catholic religion. So we learned the basic prayers and how to cross ourselves, with the hope that some day it might help us. The nun's name was Teresa. She seemed very nice, friendly, and sincerely concerned about our welfare.

Teresa started to come over almost every day to bring Jesus into our hearts and save our souls from hell. We liked her. She was caring, pretty and usually wore a plain dress with a cross and no veil. We often shared our food with her. Though the stores were shut down, in the house we still had lots of different jams, liqueurs, wine, winter vegetables, coffee, tea and bread. I supplied the bread by standing in long lines at the bakery where loaves of bread were handed out to the Christian population.

Jews were pulled out of the line by some men, experts at recognizing their emaciated faces. Nobody touched me. I looked like an Aryan and was always given a loaf of freshly baked bread. I stood in a few lines and accumulated enough bread for us, and some to share with our next door neighbors. Teresa told us about the hard times the nuns had since Vilnius was occupied by the Russians in 1939, when all the convents had been closed.

Usually, we had our instruction about mid-morning, and didn't expect her to show up again until the next day. One afternoon she suddenly appeared. She was very upset, and at first I thought maybe she had been expelled from the convent for spending too much time at our house. But no, she had come over to warn us. Whole blocks of homes on Niemiecka St. close to our house, she said, were being surrounded by Germans and Lithuanians. Jewish people were being taken out in the middle of the night and there were rumors that they were being killed at Ponary or taken to the Lukiszki prison and then executed. She had the Mother Superior's permission to take my brother and me to the convent for the night. My youngest brother, Leo, and I quickly packed a few things in a small bag and followed her to a building about a block away from our house. I slept in a narrow cubicle that was empty except for a single bed and a small table and chair in the corner. The cubicles were separated only by white sheets as the residence was originally a private house and had become a makeshift convent. I didn't see anybody that night.

Early the next morning, Teresa came over to tell us that we had to go back home. We were only invited to stay for the one night when we were at the greatest risk of being rounded up by the Germans. The convent was on the corner of Wielka St. and Sawitcz, about a block from our house. My mother met us at the door with our Lalka behind her. She had spent the night alone in the big, empty house and when I think about how she must have felt, a shudder goes through me. Just a short while before, she had been surrounded by family, husband, friends and security. Now the future was torn away and her life shattered in a million shreds. Sister Teresa continued her visits until the last day, when we were ordered to leave our house. We had learned how to cross ourselves and memorize the basic Catholic prayers, though the well-meaning nun did not succeed in converting us to her faith.

THE GHETTO

A few weeks passed by. We were living in constant dread, but desperately hoped that my father would come home, and the Germans would soon be defeated at the Russian front.

A knock on the door. My mother and I ran to the door. A tall, young, uniformed Lithuanian policeman stood in front of us. Next to him was a civilian man wearing a black leather coat with a swastika on his armband. In a matter-of-fact voice, the policeman said, "You have two hours to assemble in the courtyard and take with you only what you can carry." Just an hour before, my two Polish girlfriends, Janina and Regina, had come over to see if they could help me in any way. My heart sank seeing them walk away from our house. I wished I could join them. For them, I thought, life would go on as before, but the unknown awaited me.

The time to leave our house was nearing, and we didn't know what to take with us, where we'd end up or what to expect next. I never dreamed that this was goodbye to the house, goodbye to the life I had known. A few minutes later our house was invaded by a bunch of Polish people, strangers running from room to room, picking up whatever they wanted, stealing my mother's big black leather purse that she let out of her sight for a second when she turned her head away. In the purse were all of our important documents, pictures and other valuables. We couldn't believe what was happening. I desperately wished that we'd return the next day and my father would be waiting for us. And as usual, he would take care of everything.

Suddenly, it became quiet. The people that robbed us disappeared and two Lithuanian men and a girl about my age walked in the front room, informing us that they were taking over our house and produced some paper of legality. I went to my room to pick something up and one of the men ran after me and tried to grab me by the hand. I kicked him with all my strength. He didn't know that I had brothers and knew how to protect myself. He must have thought that I came with the house – could be taken. He was smiling all the time, thrilled to take over a complete household. I escaped back to the front room and there the girl was already trying on my new blue wool suit with the fur collar and cuffs. I never got to wear it.

This was only the beginning of the next shock and the horrors awaiting us. Now we were walking in the middle of the street with our few belongings. We had to stand in a line and march. It was horrible. There was a mass of people walking, mostly women and children, with Lithuanian policemen directing us. All we saw were people like us, scared, crying, holding small children by the hand or in their arms, carrying a few bundles or pushing little two-wheelers loaded with some household goods. Some people carried suitcases that were soon abandoned as they became heavy with the long walk. We walked and it seemed endless, not knowing where we were being taken.

By this time all of us had heard about the killings at Ponary, but hadn't really believed that things like this could happen in our enlightened age. We walked the whole day, circling the same streets, bewildered, hungry and frightened. It was getting dark and I think the stars must have been crying looking at us. More bundles and suitcases were being abandoned. People were exhausted from marching, mothers carrying crying babies and older people were hardly able to move, and who knows when they had their last meal.

We walked, my mother, brother and I, holding on to each other. I don't think we talked. We had no words and were not ready to say goodbye to each other for the last time. Not ready to die. But it looked like the end was coming and Ponary, the killing ground, might be all that awaited us.

It was after dark on September 6, 1941 when we were directed to enter the ghetto, which was located in an area where some Christians and the poorer Jews lived. Two ghettos separated by Niemiecka St. had already been prepared for the Jewish population. We were directed through a high open archway into Ghetto 2. Lithuanian police armed with rifles, directed us to houses that Jews had occupied before. The homes were all empty and the entire place was devoid of people. They had all been taken away and killed at Ponary to make room for the new arrivals.

We spent the whole night in complete silence sitting in a dark room with a lot of strangers. Early in the morning we heard a ghetto loudspeaker calling all people with skills to assemble in front of the ghetto entrance. We decided to join the work group and were taken to the larger Ghetto 1, with the entrance on Rudnicka St. There we moved in with my Uncle Leon and his family, who lived on Szpitalna St.

About a week after we moved to Ghetto 1, I heard a loudspeaker announcing twenty women were needed to work in the kitchen at the air force base in Porubanek. I volunteered and was accepted. When I was returning from my job that evening, I saw Sister Teresa at the gate. I was able to stop for a moment and talk to her without anyone noticing as the sentries were busy with the groups of people coming back from work

"Where were you? I was looking for you when they made us leave our home. I thought you would come over and help us," I said.

She started crying. "I was thinking about you, but there was nothing I could do. Mother Superior said the orders came from the church officials and not to get involved." Still crying and with her head down, she left. This was the last time I saw her.

I walked into the ghetto feeling sad and abandoned, but with so much else going on around me, I put the encounter in the back of my mind. It was one more disappointment, but I didn't have the luxury of feeling sorry for myself with the chaos going on around me. I had to focus on the present.

THE TRIAL

Every morning, I joined a group of women gathered in front of the ghetto gate to go to work at Porubanek, about six or seven kilometers from Vilnius. We walked out of the gate, formed columns of five and walked on the cobblestones in the middle of the street led by a Jewish man assigned by the Judenrat. The Judenrat was generally composed of leaders of the pre-war Jewish community and acted as a liaison between the Nazis and the Jews. No Jew was allowed to use the sidewalks, which at the time was very humiliating to me. In order to make sure we were recognizable from the rest of the city's population, moreover, a yellow Star of David was ordered to be sewn in the front and back of our garments, one star above the heart and the second on the back.

Mental anguish, fear and stress were gradually taking over and changing our lives. But my youth had the privilege of inner resources. It gave me hope and the strength to fight and try to overcome any misfortune or danger. Walking to work, I heard some people in our column complaining about the German work supervisor named Hans Geisler, who punished the Jewish workers for the smallest transgression. Sometimes he wouldn't even let them have a little midday soup and piece of bread, which could be the only meal for their long working day. Given the opportunity, some people tried to barter their few possessions with the Polish population in exchange for bread or a few potatoes for their families left in the ghetto.

When we came to the base in Porubanek, two women and I were assigned to work in the kitchen. I didn't pay any attention to the German soldier who came in from time to time, checking on our work or giving us instructions. I just tried to concentrate on scrubbing potatoes and working as fast as I could, trying to do my best not to show my ignorance of kitchen work. At the time, we believed that German working papers would shield the bearer from the perils of the ghetto.

I knew one of the women from our high school. Tala, about a year older than me, had been popular in school. She was very pretty with light brown braided hair and blue eyes. The other young woman told us that she was the mother of a small baby. Her widowed mother took care of the child. Her lawyer husband was working in the Jewish community under German directive.

A few times I noticed the German supervisor coming into the kitchen, looking around and asking a few questions connected to our work. I was surprised when Tala told me that whenever Hans came into the kitchen he stopped and watched me, and she noticed the cold, impersonal expression on his face relaxed and changed. I really didn't know if she was just teasing me and trying to put me in a better mood, since I was depressed having left my mother and brother behind in the ghetto. I was worried. Every day people were taken away never to be seen again.

A few weeks went by. One day I was alone in the kitchen finishing the day's work when Hans came in and walked straight over to me. From out of the blue he asked, "Do you have any family in the ghetto?"

"Yes, my mother and brother are there."

"Where did you learn to speak German?" he inquired.

"I took it for four years in high school," I said.

Then to my surprise, he asked, "And where is your father?"

I was afraid to tell him my father was taken away by his people in the middle of the night to Lukiszki prison and killed at Ponary. I didn't know for sure, but in the ghetto we heard rumors that arrested Jews were taken from prison to Ponary and killed. Instead I just said, "I don't know." He gave me a long look, turned away and left. The next day when we were getting ready to return to the ghetto, Hans called me aside and very casually asked, "Is there something I could do to help you?"

The weather was changing. It was getting colder and winter was approaching. Fortunately, we had deposited a big bundle of coats and warm clothes with a Polish neighbor for safe keeping before we had to leave the house for the ghetto.

"Yes," I said to Hans, "I'd like to pick up some things we left at our neighbors." Without his presence, if I had tried to bring a bundle of clothes into the ghetto, it would have been immediately confiscated by the sentry at the ghetto gate, and I could even be jailed or shot on the spot. The law was in their hands.

We left the base together. I walked in front and Hans followed me as though he were taking me back to the ghetto after work. We came to my building. I noticed a man standing near the gate. The minute he saw me, he rushed into the courtyard and immediately returned with a Lithuanian policeman. Luckily, I knew the policeman quite well. Another one might have arrested me. This policeman worked in our neighborhood and I had many conversations with him during the Russian occupation; we were on good terms. The policeman turned to the would-be denouncer and said, "I'll take care of it." Instead, he motioned for me to come into the courtyard. Hans waited at the gate and I ran up the stairs to our neighbors' apartment on the second floor. I knocked on Mr. Wasilewiski's door and his wife opened it. With a surprised look on her face she said, "Thank God you're still alive. Come in. How did you get here?" In a few words I explained, "I don't have time to talk. I'm sorry. I just came to pick up some of the clothes we left." Immediately she ran to the bedroom and came back with the bundle. I thanked her and told her I would try to see her again. I ran downstairs where Hans was waiting for me. He took the bundle, slung it over his back and we walked to the ghetto. I think he would have been in terrible trouble if any Germans were standing guard at the gates, but the Lithuanians didn't dare stop or question a German.

Hans carried the bundle up the stairs to the small apartment we shared with my uncle, his wife, their little girl and four more strangers. Because of the limited space in the room, we all slept on mattresses on the floor left by previous owners who had been taken away in one of the latest selections straight to Ponary – the killing grounds. Hans met my mother, handed her the bundle, said a few words and left. There was dead silence in the room. What was next? Was this a prelude to death?

At work Hans gave me extra food rations to take with me to the ghetto and I shared some with our roommates. The people in the room were suspicious and afraid of a German paying too much attention to me. It was well known that any contact with Germans except at work was forbidden, and punishment was severe, not only to the transgressor but to the whole work force.

45

One late afternoon at work while I was sitting on a small wooden bench scrubbing potatoes, I was surprised to see Hans Geisler walk into the kitchen, as it wasn't time yet to return to the ghetto. He came over and asked me in a lowered voice if there was anything else he could do to help my mother and me. I knew we had Russian gold rubles, American twenty-dollar gold pieces and some jewelry hidden in my grandfather's garden. We were afraid to go there as the neighbors, who had become experts in emptying the houses involuntarily left by Jews, would denounce us.

It's hard to imagine what Hans had in his mind when he volunteered to come with his driver in a closed truck to pick us up in the ghetto. My mother and I hid in the back and we drove out to Lupuwka where my grandparents used to live, not far from Porubanek.

It was starting to get dark when we arrived at the empty house full of shadows. The long hallways that my brothers and I had once gleefully raced through now led Hans and me to a large living room that echoed under our footsteps. The only piece of furniture left in the room was a black leather couch that had many deep slashes and the white stuffing coming out. People had run from house to house and grabbed whatever Jewish property they could. I guess no one thought the couch was worth taking. It stood by the wall on the left side of the entrance like a ghost guarding the last vestiges of a previous life. I was told to stay in the room while my mother and Hans walked into the garden. The driver, a young German soldier, sat in the truck with the lights out. Soon my mother appeared with Hans following her, and I saw that she had a gold watch in her hand that she handed to him. As more digging had to be done, Hans decided to drive back over to the air force base, get a shovel and return to my grandfather's house. The driver disappeared in the darkness and soon came out with a big shovel that he handed to Hans. He drove us to the ghetto where people were coming back from work. Before my mother joined them, she told me where the box containing the gold and jewelry was hidden and described the location and direction measured in steps from the back door of the house. We then drove to my grandfather's house, which was about a fifteen-minute walk from the base, and the driver dropped us off.

I returned to the empty house alone with Hans. It was a starlit night. The darkness engulfed the house and the world around me. It was too late to dig in the garden and long past curfew time. We couldn't drive back to the ghetto. Instead, we decided to wait until early morning to dig again for the buried treasure. We sat on the couch. I sat in one corner and Hans in the other. We didn't talk much. We didn't touch. We were like strangers left in the middle of a stormy sea, waiting for the first light of dawn to come. I can't even imagine now after so much time has passed, what we must have been thinking. How could we possibly expose ourselves to the danger of being together all night? We must have been two fools of a kind. Hans was older than me. He told me he was unhappy in his marriage and planned to get a divorce on his return home to Düsseldorf. Not that it mattered to me, and not because of me. He said he had planned it a long time ago. I guess he must have been in his late twenties, not very tall or handsome.

Hans Geisler had brown hair and blue eyes and I noticed a gold tooth when he smiled. What was going on in his mind at the time I will never understand. All I wanted was some help, a way to escape and rejoin the human race. For that we needed money to buy fake IDs and food, and to pay for a place to hide outside of the ghetto. We were fortunate we had the means, but we needed help to retrieve the buried box from my grandfather's yard.

With all the excitement of the previous day, Hans and I drifted off to sleep at some point, and when we opened our eyes it was already early morning. It would be dangerous to dig in the garden during the day as Polish neighbors would notice and alert the police. We decided to go back to the base and planned to meet in the late afternoon after work and wait for dusk when we'd follow my mother's directions and try again to find the box with the jewelry and gold.

On the way back to the air force base, we noticed some people turn around and look at us. I went straight to the kitchen, saw the scared faces of my co-workers and realized my mistake. The driver must have reported the previous day's breach of protocol to his superiors, and the moment I walked in the kitchen, a soldier came in and told me to follow him.

I followed him to a room in another building where some very stern military men briefly interrogated me. They took my name and address, warned me not to leave the ghetto, and I was dismissed. No more work. I had to go back to the enclosed wired walls of the ghetto with the warning to stay there. I might have escaped by joining a work unit leaving the ghetto. With some luck I would remove my jacket with the Star of David on it, and at the right moment step on the sidewalk and mix in with the population. I had done that before. But this would expose my mother and all the other inhabitants of the building to complete destruction and a horrible death. The Germans would kill everyone who lived in the same building, holding them responsible for one person's transgression.

I wasn't sure what to do next. I told Uncle Leon what happened and asked for his advice. He was extremely alarmed and said, "You need to talk to Jacob Gens immediately in case they arrest you." Jacob Gens was a Jew chosen by the Germans to be the head of the ghetto. I couldn't see Mr. Gens, but another man from the community listened to me for a while, didn't seem to believe a word I was saying and dismissed me with the common Yiddish saying, "*Drey zikh dem eygenem kop*," which translates literally to "spin your own head around," but means – it's not my problem, figure it out yourself. I was all on my own, with the dark cloud of fear hanging over me, but I still had the burning desire to come out of this alive. My mother was scared and depressed, and the rest of the people in our little room avoided me as if I had leprosy.

I don't think it was more than a week later when a car occupied by two Germans wearing brown military uniforms stopped in the middle of the block where I lived. One of them was holding a piece of paper and questioning some passers by as I was leaving the building. I understood they were looking for me.

I went over to the car, saw my name written on the paper and told them it was me they were looking for. I was told to get in the back seat and when we approached the ghetto gate, the car stopped and the German next to the driver told the sentry, "We got her." The car proceeded through familiar streets.

The car stopped at the Hotel Schlackecki (Aristocrat), a place I used to pass by almost every day on my way to school. Now the German flag was hoisted there and a uniformed solider stood at attention in front of the entrance. The door was opened. As I walked through the entrance, the car that brought me sped off. I found myself in a big hall and was told to follow a man in a white overcoat who resembled a doctor into an adjoining room. Another man, tall, also dressed in a white overcoat came in from a side door. I noticed both were older men and didn't look like soldiers. They seemed quite relaxed and looked me over without a word. I forced myself to look calm. I didn't want to show how afraid I really was. They seemed like father figures to me, which for the moment distracted me from the deadly danger I was in.

One of the men asked my name and age and then threw the next question at me in a low, stern voice.

"Did you sleep with Feldfebel Hans Geisler?"

I answered, "No, I did not."

"When was the last time you slept with a man?"

"I have never slept with a man," I answered. The other man repeated the same question. I was burning with insult and shame, my face turning to fire.

"No, I have never slept with a man," I answered again truthfully. I realized they had the means to verify my statement and this calmed me down. They must have been experts on human character and behavior. Their expression during this short time was blank, and I'm convinced they already had the confession of the accused Hans Geisler. With a short nod I was dismissed. I returned to the ghetto where I tried to calm my mother and uncle and wait for what would happen next.

I didn't have to wait long. The next day about noon a Jewish police-man came to the apartment and told me to follow him to the street where a car was parked at the curb. A man from the Gestapo was waiting for me in the car. I was told to take the seat in the back and we drove out of the ghetto without stopping at the gate.

This time the drive took longer, through familiar streets, past our house on Wielka St. until we stopped in front of a tall Gestapo building on Mickiewicza St. I followed the man from the car who took me to the second floor and then into a room with a different scenario. A soldier eating a sandwich sat by a switchboard and a few more uniformed men were in the room. I was left standing at the door until he finished eating. Then, turning toward me, he said, "The trial is tomorrow. I'm going to send you to Lukiszki prison to make sure you'll be here and won't try to escape."

By then it was a definite fact that once someone was jailed at Lukisz-ki, it was a death sentence without reprieve. We had heard that every day the cells were emptied for new arrivals.

I begged him to let me go. I told him, "You can see for yourself how responsible I am. I came every time you wanted me. I promise I'll be here tomorrow."

He must have believed me because he let me go. He also said, "You better tell the whole truth tomorrow because Feldfebel Geisler has al-ready confessed on his German honor."

The next day I appeared at exactly the time I was told. The same man was at the switchboard and a few more military men were sitting next to a closed door. I waited no more than about ten or fifteen minutes before the door was opened and I was called in. The large interior room was full of uniformed men seated in what looked like a theatre, waiting for the curtain to go up. I saw immediately that poor Hans was standing at attention in front of the room with a large Nazi banner on the wall behind him. He looked like a school kid in front of a teachers' assembly, an expressionless figure glued to the floor.

I, too, was called to the front of the room. He didn't look at me. Immediately the questions started coming at me.

"What is your name and age?"

"I'm Rasia Kliot. I'm seventeen."

"Did you spend the night with Feldfebel Hans Geisler?"

"Yes."

"Why didn't you return to the ghetto?"

"It was past curfew time."

"Was he nice to the Jewish people at the base?"

"No."

"Was he nice to you?"

"Yes."

"What did you find in your grandfather's yard?"

"Nothing."

"So why did your mother give him a gold watch?"

I tried to be calm, reserved. My only concern was hope that they wouldn't hear my heart trying to escape my body. "We thought we would find some things in my grandfather's yard."

"No more questions."

I was told to leave and wait in the next room. I thought this was the end of my life, with not even a fleeting chance of survival. Then a uniformed man came out from the room where the trial took place and told me I should go back to the ghetto. I wasn't exactly free, but I was still alive.

I asked him if it was okay for me to move to another street in the ghetto, because this would change my address in case they needed to call me again. I wanted to assure myself that this chapter of my life was over. He said, "We don't care where you live in the ghetto, so long as you stay there and keep working. We don't need you anymore."

I thought at the time that if I'd actually had a sexual relationship with Hans or anyone else, they would have immediately arrested and executed me, as I could have trapped other Germans with my Aryan appearance and their "pure" German blood would have been contaminated.

About a year later, sometime in the fall of 1942, I was hiding outside of the ghetto where my chances of survival were better if luck was with me. I could move from place to place. I had a constant urge to keep moving and if it weren't for my mother and brother left behind in the ghetto, I would have never returned. Outside, I felt I was more in control and could survive by my own wits. I became an expert at entering and leaving the ghetto. I would easily join a work group leaving the ghetto. I always stood at the edge of the walking group, and at the right moment when nobody was watching and we rounded a corner, I'd step on the sidewalk, take off my outer garment with the Star of David sewn on, and slowly walk away. With the Polish acquaintances we had in Vilnius and in the country in Czarny Bor, it was just a matter of time and luck until I found someone we could trust and pay to hide my mother and brother. With good luck we might be able to survive.

Whenever I was hiding outside of the ghetto with Polish friends, I was always afraid of being recognized on the street where I might be denounced by citizens who turned in Jews for their own gain. I would slip into the ghetto to stay for a while, going to work with my mother and brother wherever we were sent. In the ghetto, I felt the walls closing in on me, always threatening, choking and diminishing my chance of escape from the misery I saw around me of dying people, hungry children and abandoned elderly who knew that their days or hours were numbered. Real life as I knew it was gone, and people passed their days in dread and hunger, afraid of being the next in line to be killed. I longed to stay in the ghetto with my people, carry their burden, but I realized I couldn't be of help to anyone, and my death wouldn't prove anything either.

My aim was to leave the ghetto permanently. By now we had heard much about Ponary where mass killings were taking place. Still some doubt lingered in our minds, as nobody came back to tell the truth until a girl I knew from grade school returned from the dead. One day my mother was not at the ghetto gate waiting for me, as she usually was when she expected my return. Terrified and expecting the worst, I ran "home." The door was wide open, a group of people looking like ghosts surrounded the girl, who was crying hysterically, talking incoherently in syllables and waving her hands like a mad woman let out of a mental institution. She had been taken with a group of people returning to the ghetto from work, surrounded by Germans and Lithuanian collaborators on the street, put on a truck and hauled to Ponary to be executed. We heard that the prisoners had to dig their own graves, but she said that this time they just shot at random. She fell. They must have been in a hurry and started to kill the moment the trucks were empty. The call for blood hadn't been fulfilled and the empty trucks went back to the ghetto to fill up with more innocent unarmed victims. At some point during the night, she said she felt cold, woke up and found herself buried beneath dead bodies. She must have fainted and was mistaken for dead. She had blood and dirt all over her and by some miracle clawed her way out of the pile of corpses, found her way back and slipped into the ghetto. She survived, but in September 1943, when the ghetto was being liquidated and the last survivors dispersed to concentration camps, I found out later that shortly before the liberation by the Soviet army, she died of starvation in a concentration camp in Kaiserwald, Latvia.

A few days later, I left the ghetto early in the morning and mixed in with a group of people who were going to work. We started to walk. The street was almost empty. I wondered if Hans was still alive. I had heard from someone that he'd been stripped of his rank and as punishment sent to the Eastern Front.

I slowly moved to the end of the last line, removed my jacket with the yellow star and stepped on the sidewalk, walking away as if I belonged to the free people. I felt very sad about the German soldier who had tried to help me. To me, Hans was a mystery, as I must have been to him. I hope he survived the harsh winter on the Eastern Front, returned home and lived in harmony and peace the rest of his life. But in fact I never knew what happened to him after our brief encounter.

Irene's Secret: My First Fake ID

I became an expert in the art of slipping in and out of the ghetto. I often went to see my childhood friend, Irene, and as always, stayed overnight sleeping in her room. We would talk about the day's events and my situation. One Saturday when I was at her house, I felt that something had changed. It wasn't the same as before. Irene looked particularly upset. It didn't take long to confirm my intuition.

"I promised my parents you would only stay for one night. You have to leave tomorrow morning," she told me. "Our neighbor has been entertaining German soldiers, and we're afraid he'll find out that you're Jewish and denounce us."

"I understand," I said, "I'll leave in the morning."

She thought for a minute and said, "Don't leave too early. Wait until we leave for Mass before you go."

The next morning after I heard the door close behind them, I went into the kitchen, tired and disappointed after a sleepless night, had something to eat and was ready to leave when I noticed my navy blue suit with the opossum collar and cuffs hanging on a hook in the hall. I mentioned to Irene's mother earlier that I would soon need my warm winter clothes. So I put it on, and inside the pocket found my gloves and something wrapped in newspaper. It was Irene's new German ID card and a small piece of paper with the words, "Hope you can use it. Wish you luck. Your friend, Irene. (It's a secret between me and my mother.)"

I couldn't believe my eyes. She was the first person to offer me her ID and risk immediate death or incarceration if discovered by the Germans.

I remembered talking to her about my need for some sort of ID as it was the first step to try to live on the Christian side and not be exposed to the daily hardships of life in the ghetto. However, there was still a problem. The picture on the ID didn't resemble me at all. It had to be changed. I went to our lawyer, Mr. Klemantowiez, who lived in the center of town, not far from my parents' house. He was an older man who visited my parents quite often and liked to have a few shots of whiskey. When he ran out of cash due to a propensity for drinking and occasional gambling, my father would lend him money to tide him over until the next pay day. He was the lawyer who represented my parents when they bought the apartment building on Subocz St. He was considered brilliant and was very well known in Polish circles. I asked him to help me.

Mr. Klemantowiez told me to stay at his house overnight. On Monday we would have photographs taken and then I would leave the rest to him. I came back a few days later and I had a new identity. The ID had my photo and a new name, Irene Krasulska. A passport for life? Not quite. I would have to play the part of Irene Krasulska very well. It was a matter of life and death.

JOZEFOWA: EARLY SPRING 1942

A short time after I got my first ID from Irene, I managed to join a party leaving the ghetto going to work. At the right moment, I took off my jacket with the yellow star sewn on it, folded it up so the star wasn't showing, put it on my arm, mixed in with the general population and continued walking as normally as I could.

I went to see Jozefowa, the janitress in my parents' building at 8 Subocz St. She was an older woman who was devoted and loyal. I could stay there for a couple of days. It was the first safe place I could stop and know I was welcome. I had no specific reason to go there. I just needed to leave the ghetto to feel free and get away from the constant fear of being taken away and killed. I didn't know much about Jozefowa, just that she was a widow. She had one daughter who disappeared during the turmoil when the Russians were running east toward Russia, and the German army was entering the city after the air raids and the short and unsuccessful Polish defense.

She was always friendly, caring and generous. Food was very scarce. Everything was rationed. But the little she had, she shared with me. Once in a while I stayed overnight, slept on a bench by the small wooden table, not wanting to share her bed and disturb her sleep after a hard day's work. Without her daughter being there to help, the whole burden was on her shoulders. Two floors above her lived a Polish couple in their late thirties, friends of Jozefowa's. Both husband and wife worked in a factory for a German company who also employed slave laborers from the ghetto. Bronislav was the man's first name and his wife was called Bronislava, a rural custom.

At work during a short break, a young Jewish woman approached Bronislava and told her about her five-year-old girl who was left in the ghetto with strangers. All her family was liquidated and any day the same fate awaited her. She didn't see any way that she could save herself and her daughter. She begged them to have pity and at least give her little girl a chance to survive. It wasn't an easy task but with some ingenuity, they managed to smuggle the child out of the ghetto and took her to their home. During the day, Jozefowa spent every free minute running up and down the steps watching the poor crying child who wanted her mother. Bronislav and his wife decided it wasn't fair to separate the child from her mother and finally took the mother in as well. Jozefowa told me about the arrangement and that they heard about me and wanted to meet me.

I climbed up the steps and knocked on the door. They let me in and the first thing I noticed was a beautiful little girl, earnest, watchful, detached, standing next to Bronislava. I smiled, but her expression didn't change. Only God knew what was on the little girl's mind. What horrors she experienced. They invited me to their living room where a big picture of Jesus on the cross was the first thing that met my eyes. I asked for the girl's mother and was directed to an adjoining room. I opened the door to a bedroom, looked around but didn't see or hear a living soul. A large armoire covered almost the whole left side of the wall. Two beds stood parallel to each other and one window looked out at the back of a building. Suddenly the bedroom door was pushed back as if by a ghost and a slim, attractive woman came out. I realized then, that when the door was open it covered the space between the wall and the armoire, her hiding place.

I was very impressed with the arrangement. It looked like a safe hiding place. Maybe one of Bronislava's friends could take in my mother and brother. I asked her if it was possible. "I'm sorry, but I don't know anybody I can trust," she said. "It's very dangerous. If the Germans catch us, they'll kill all of us. I didn't even tell my own relatives about this."

My heart sank. "Thank you, Bronislava. I know you'd help me if you could." I still didn't have a place for my mother and brother to hide. I needed to go back to the ghetto for a few days to see them. Then I would have to try again. I was already planning my next step. I was going to visit my father's friend, the lawyer, Mr. Klemantowiez, and ask him for help. Just knowing that people like Bronislava and her husband existed gave me some hope.

A Passport to Life

Mr. Klemantowiez suggested that I go to Orzmiany, a small town about fifty kilometers from Vilnius, where he knew a Jewish woman and a little girl who had been living on a Polish ID for a while and seemed to be doing well. He thought maybe I could stay with them. So I went back to the ghetto, sneaking in with a group of people coming from work, and told my mother that I was going to Orzmiany. There I would try to find a place where we could be together on the Christian side.

It must have been some time in January or February 1942. I remember standing on the road and waiting for a ride. A young Polish girl was also standing on the road and waiting for a ride to a nearby village. After a while a covered truck with two German soldiers sitting in front stopped and we jumped in. The girl must have recognized me and to my horror and surprise started screaming, "A Jewess is here." Luckily, the noise from the motor was loud and the front driver seats were enclosed so they couldn't hear or understand what she was saying as she screamed in Polish, "*Zydowka*!" Jewish woman. To my eternal relief, when the pick-up truck stopped for a minute she jumped out and we continued on our way to Orzmiany.

I had an address Mr. Klemantowiez gave me, but I didn't know the town, and when the German driver asked me where I was going I showed him the address written on the paper. He stopped some people and asked for directions and easily found the place. I went to the apartment, which was located in a short hallway, and rang the doorbell, but nobody answered. I tried the doorbell across the apartment. A young Polish woman opened the door and invited me and the two German soldiers in. After a while the Germans left, and I asked about the people next door and if she knew when they'd be back. In the meantime, an older lady with a girl appeared from another room, and she introduced them as her mother and daughter. I told them a friend of mine suggested Orzmiany was a good place to find work and accommodations, and asked if they knew where I could rent a room. I had a premonition and decided on the spot not to associate with the Jewish woman next door who at the time wasn't home. I told the Polish woman that I didn't really know her neighbors, but my friend had suggested they could help me find lodging.

Luckily the woman told me they had a room off the kitchen and would rent it for a reasonable price. I gladly accepted the offer, though the room didn't have a door, just a curtain separating it from the small entrance hall.

The young woman was a nurse working in a hospital and her mother was taking care of her daughter. The next day I happened to meet the Jewish woman with her daughter as they were exiting the apartment. I was surprised and afraid for them living on the Aryan side pretending to be Polish. To me it was obvious they couldn't disguise themselves very well not only because of their looks, but also the slight Jewish inflection when they spoke Polish. Though the woman was dressed in a nice suit with high heels, she looked especially thin and sickly, with a small, dark-skinned face and big, lost eyes. She told me she was expecting her brother to come from the ghetto and stay with them.

In the meantime, I was looking for work. The nurse told me she knew a doctor who needed a companion for his elderly wife. It was about an hour's walk from my lodging. I found the doctor's big house, which was surrounded by a fence with a long pathway of shrubs leading to the front door. An older, very attractive woman opened the door as if expecting me. She was friendly and seemed very happy to have a helper around the house. She also welcomed the companionship, as her husband was at the hospital working long hours. She showed me a room where I could sleep, but I declined her offer and told her I had my own lodging. She showed me the kitchen and the rest of the house. One room was off-limits. She told me not to go in or open the door. I suspected somebody was hiding there, but I never found out. My work basically consisted of helping her with light housework, making the beds, taking short walks with her in the neighborhood and cleaning up the kitchen after she cooked.

My job wasn't hard and late in the afternoon, I returned to my lodgings. Then one day I ran into the Jewish woman who lived next door to me with her little girl. Her brother had just come from Vilnius to stay with her and told her that a big liquidation had taken place in the ghetto. I was alarmed, as I knew my mother and brother were there. I took a week off and left Orzmiany to go back to Vilnius to look for them. Thank God they were still alive. I was desperate to find a hiding place for them. Through an acquaintance who was married to a Polish man, I found a place for them outside Vilnius for a very short stay, with the hope that soon something more permanent could be found. My mother and brother left the ghetto separately. They attached themselves to a group of people going to work and used the same method as I did of leaving the group at the right moment when no one was watching.

A week later when I returned to Orzmiany, the Polish woman was very agitated. Without waiting for me to take off my coat, she said that the police had just arrested the people next door because they were Jews. I pretended to be very surprised. She looked at me and said, "You don't look Jewish, except for your eyes. Show me your ID."

I said, "Sure," handing her my new passport with the name Irena Krasucka. She put it in her pocket and said the next day she was going to the police station to check and see if it was authentic.

She must have noticed the fear in my eyes, the desperation, and the mirror of my haunted Jewish soul. I went to bed behind the curtain fully dressed, expecting the worst. It was past midnight when I heard some voices and banging on the door. My first thought was that the police were coming for me – the arrested woman must have been tortured and told them that a Jewish girl was living next door. This was my end. I was sweating. My face was on fire. I stood there, fully dressed, waiting to be arrested and executed. The landlady opened the door and I heard two men's voices asking if there was anything the Jews had left behind. They wanted to make sure their looting had been complete. At any moment the curtain would open and she would ask the two policemen to check my ID.

She must have been half-asleep and forgot about my existence. Or perhaps she decided against turning me in. In any case, my life was saved, at least for the moment. They thanked her, and as they were leaving, one of the policemen said in a calm, matter-of-fact voice, "Tomorrow morning the three Jews will be executed for pretending to be Christians." He said this as if it were the most natural thing in the world to kill any Jew who tried to survive the slaughter. I knew I had to act. My time was getting short. Soon it would be daylight.

The only solution was to run for my life back to Vilnius with no documents, food or money. Otherwise, my landlady might keep her word and go to the police as promised and then this would be my end. An electric shock ran through my head – my mother, my brother – who would help them? I needed to stay alive.

Very early, while it was still half-dark, I made my way through the hall and door, and started running outside. It was all white around, with snow covering the road and the trees sticking out like white skeletons grasping for air, or maybe trying to fly straight up to the heavens. I was looking for the highway that lead to Vilnius. I was standing by an abandoned barn for a moment when I heard some cries, then gun shots and silence. I don't know how long I was nailed to the ground. I was freezing; my limbs were slowly abandoning my burning body. I must have fallen half-asleep standing up, my brain taking a rest or bursting out of my skull. The sound of snow falling from a close branch brought me back to reality and action fast. There was light around me. I looked back from where the noises came earlier, saw some dark patches, and slowly, like a shadow moving in twilight, came closer to a scene that I saw in a flash of horror and that has come back to me many times.

Three people – the woman, her brother and her six-year-old daughter, almost naked, their clothes torn to bits – had been shot to death and were lying in a sea of red snow. I heard a scream that sounded almost subhuman, not understanding that it came from me. And, as if chased by the devil, I started to run toward the highway. I heard motorized vehicles coming and was afraid they might be searching for me. I ran off the road. I was getting hungry and knocked at a peasant's door, wanting to ask for a piece of bread. A young boy opened the door, looked at me and screamed, "Mother, a Jew is here."

I had to start running again. I passed by a few villages, walking behind a peasant wagon pulled by a half-dead horse. When a few German trucks sped by scaring the horse, it took off like a bullet hit it, nearly overturning the wagon with the little boy. The woman was holding on to the reins and screaming her head off, hitting the horse with a cord that was tied to a stick.

I kept going. Walking. Running. Moving as fast as I could. It took the whole day to reach the outskirts of Vilnius, and it was starting to get dark. It would soon be curfew until early the next morning.

I knew a woman I'd met at Irene's house who lived with her husband at the edge of the city. Not having much of a choice, as curfew was nearing, I found her and was told I could stay overnight. She said that I could sleep with them, as they had no other bed. At my suggestion that I would rather sleep on the floor and not disturb them, she got annoyed. So I got into their bed. I was tired and went to sleep the moment my head touched the pillow. A hand on my thigh woke me up. I backed off and almost pushed the wife out of bed to the floor. Here I was in the middle between the two of them. The husband tried to continue his advances. I told him to please leave me alone and the wife pretended she was deaf. I was in despair, exhausted from all the happenings of the day. The husband was getting more insistent and I had no choice but to leave.

I grabbed my coat and shoes and fled again, out into the cold, dark winter night. The empty streets looked ghostly. I looked around for patrols that were watching the streets for perpetrators. Anyone caught during curfew was severely punished, and if Jewish, could consider himself dead. I ran toward some homes by a cemetery and tried to find a place to hide for the night. I noticed a cellar door that wasn't locked and went down a few snowy steps, trying the second inner door. It was locked. I fell asleep outside the inner door and woke up at daylight, half-buried in the snow that fell during the night. I didn't feel any cold, but my leg was painful and swollen from the ankle to the upper thigh.

Slowly I walked out of the cellar and found myself facing an old lady. She looked me over and asked me to follow her. I must have looked like a ghost. The house we entered was warm and cozy. She gave me something hot to drink and put me in the warmest bed I ever slept in. I must have been sick a long time. I saw her hover around me – a stranger – who was she? I remember thinking that my grandfather must have sent an angel in the form of an old, white-haired woman to take care of me.

MY SECOND CHANCE

When I had attended the Polish high school from 1940 to 1941, I had a Russian teacher, an older woman, tall and aristocratic with whitish-gray hair, very strict and demanding. After she had given us a grammar midterm around the middle of the school year, she came in with our papers and congratulated me for getting the only perfect grade in our class. Certainly I was very pleased. She then announced that Nina, the most beautiful and popular student, had failed and asked who would like to help her in her studies. I raised my hand and was gladly accepted by both the teacher and Nina.

From then on my friendship with Nina flourished. She came to our house. I met her mother and younger sister Jadwyga, who was dying of tuberculosis. Nina lost her father at an early age and her mother owned a small grocery store. Nina, who was seventeen, was one of the few girls in our class to have a steady boyfriend, who often came and picked her up on his motorcycle. We were all very impressed.

After the episode of losing my first ID and recovering from my illness, I went back to see Nina at her old address. A friendly neighbor gave me the good news of Nina's marriage to a wealthy man and her new address. I rang the bell and a tall man, standing very stiffly and formally, wearing German officer's breeches and high boots let me in. Nina and her mother, Anna, greeted me with big hugs and kisses and invited me to stay for the night. I slept in Anna's room.

"Be careful around my son-in-law," Anna warned me. "He's a terrible anti-Semite and works for the Nazis."

Nina later told me that her new husband owned many businesses that the Germans confiscated from the Jews. And this is how he had become rich.

The next morning, after a restless sleep, not knowing what my next step would be or where I would end up, since I didn't have any documents, I could hardly swallow the sumptuous breakfast of sausage, fresh rolls, butter, cheese, jam and tea put in front of me. After Nina's husband left, we talked for hours. I told them of my predicament and how I lost my ID in Orzmiany. Then Anna, Nina' mother, handed me some papers that she said I might be able to use. It was her daughter Jadwyga's school ID and her birth certificate. Her daughter had died of tuberculosis only a few months before and had been about a year younger than me.

I could hardly believe my eyes. It was like manna from heaven that God gave the children of Israel thousands of years ago during their wandering in the desert after their escape from slavery in Egypt. In no time, my picture was changed and I officially became Jadwyga Szymkowska, born in Vilnius in 1925. The birth certificate and school ID were only the first step in having the necessary valid Lithuanian documents. Now I needed an official identity card.

I knew Rudominy was the government seat located not far from our summer place in Czarny Bor. The police station was quite far from Vilnius. Early in the morning, with the papers I had from Nina's mother, I walked the long distance to Rudominy, full of hope and also the fear of being recognized by the police officer who was in charge of checking and issuing identity cards.

I waited for my turn and a man in a Lithuanian police uniform checked my papers and looked at me. I smiled and thanked God that he couldn't see the storm boiling inside me.

He asked me why I didn't bring my father's ID. I told him that my father died two years ago. He said, "Then bring me your mother's new passport."

I left again immediately, and started to walk back toward Vilnius where I hoped Anna could lend me her passport. Right near the police office, I noticed a couple from the village of Dusienienty, and recognized the farmer and his wife who used to come and sometimes bring us freshly caught fish, or vegetables from their garden. They both looked at me, then turned their heads pretending not to know me.

I walked toward the highway, and was joined by an attractive Polish woman who, coincidentally, was also on her way to Vilnius. She was very friendly and, after small talk, offered me a job. She had a home where German officers were entertained and was looking for the right candidates. She said it was a very easy job with lots of privileges, food and money. I immediately understood it was prostitution. I thanked her, explaining that I couldn't accept because my mother was an invalid, and I had to take care of her and my brother. During the war, people often made fast alliances with strangers, offering them jobs or exchanging tips. The conventional rules that had existed before the war did not apply during the occupation.

After walking about fifteen kilometers to the city, I went straight to Nina's home and told Anna that I couldn't get the new ID I needed without her new passport that the Germans had given to the Christian population. Without hesitation, Anna gave me her passport, and told me, in case I was apprehended and arrested, to tell the police that I had found it on the street. She said she'd wait three days for my return. If I didn't come back she would assume I was arrested, and would then put a notice in the newspaper that she lost her passport, and she'd apply for a new one.

I took the road for Rudominy again, came to the police station, flirted a little with the same policeman from the first visit who recognized me and without any problem received my new ID. I went back to my friend Nina's house, returned her mother's passport and spent the night there.

The next day I went to see my mother and brother, who were hiding at a Polish woman's house. When I got there, the woman was very surprised to see me and said, "Your mother and brother had to leave. My son came from the country to stay with me for a few days and got very upset when he saw them. He told me if we were caught hiding Jews we'd all be killed."

My heart sank. "Where are they?" I asked, imagining the worst.

"They told me they'd go back to the ghetto," she said.

Late in the afternoon I joined a group of people returning to the ghetto. Nobody paid any attention to me. I was back again in the dreaded place, anxious to see my mother and brother. I was overjoyed to find them still alive. We stayed up late into the night, me with my new identity in my pocket, a talisman that gave me some hope of survival. I spent the night in the overcrowded room with my mother, brother, uncle, his wife and child and another young couple, all sleeping on mattresses on the floor in one small room.

LUSIA AND THE TRAP

A few days later I left the ghetto and was again at Jozefowa's place. I couldn't stay there long. Her place was quite small and tenants used to come in and out frequently. She told me about a Jewish girl, Lusia, who was a student at Vilnius University and used to live in the building. She came from a small town close to Kaunas and was now hiding at the house of a Lithuanian professor who had left with his wife on a prolonged vacation. I jumped at the idea of meeting her. Maybe this could also be a place for my mother and brother to stay. I met Lusia at Bronislava's, the neighbor and friend of Jozefowa's, who lived on the floor above her. I couldn't believe that Lusia dared to go out during the day.

She could hardly pass as a Christian. She didn't look Aryan, and her Polish had a Jewish accent that could instantly give her away. She could have easily been recognized by the people-hunters who got paid by the Nazis for delivering Jewish heads.

I asked her if she could show me where she was staying. She agreed, but told me it was too dangerous to go there during the day. We would wait until it got darker outside. I told her I'd follow her. I felt safer not walking together. I wanted to see the apartment for myself so I could get a sense of how safe it was. She left first and I followed her to Mickiewicza St. We entered a nice building, then went up to the second floor and through a small hall with dimmed light to the professor's apartment. It was very quiet. I saw a big room with a grand piano and very little furniture. Lusia's room was off the hall, small, dark and looked like a storage or wardrobe room without a window. We sat on her narrow bed for a while and she told me about her family and how much she missed her parents and siblings who had been killed by the Germans when they'd entered the small town. Her ambition was to become a physician someday. Once in a while, a woman she knew from the university brought her some food. Sometimes she went days without food. She would also visit some people in the building next to Jozefowa's apartment, who gave her something to eat. I spent the night at her place and the next day went back to the ghetto and slipped in with a group of people who were coming back from work.

My mother was worried when I didn't come back the previous evening, as she didn't know what had happened to me. We were aware of the danger of being on the Aryan side. Once apprehended – it was jail and death. But I longed to belong and mix in with the free people. Even to pretend to be one of them for a while. Deep down the fear never left me for a second. I tried as much as possible to keep connections to my old friends, who I knew would never denounce me and would let me spend a night at their homes and find brief respite from the ghetto. I also tried to make new friends like Lusia who could help provide shelter. I was always looking for help, trying to find a place where my mother and brother could hide outside of the ghetto. I was restless and anxious. I was constantly on the move, going from one friend to another. I was afraid if I stayed in one place too long, it might become suspicious and I'd be denounced by curious neighbors.

My new friend, Lusia, was lonely and I told her about my Russian friend, Viera, whom I stayed with quite often. I would gladly introduce her. I felt sorry for her. Maybe she could sometimes visit or stay with Viera.

Viera lived on Ostrobramska St. with her mother, her sister Nadzia and her new husband, Jacek, a Lithuanian policeman. She married him a few months after the German occupation. The building where Viera lived was partially occupied by a police station that had its entrance facing the street instead of the courtyard. The policemen with families resided in apartments inside the courtyard.

I had known Viera and her family for many years. We had met during the summer in the country when we were children. Though she was a few years older, we became friends. After she got married, she moved to Vilnius. We often talked about her life with her husband Jacek. She told me how polite he was and what a gentleman. After having sex, he always kissed her hand and thanked her.

At the time it sounded to me like a fairy tale, and I thought he was a very romantic man. He was about six feet tall with light brown hair parted in the middle, a little mustache and watery green eyes. He was handsome in an unsophisticated peasant way. Unfortunately, Viera gradually discovered that her Jacek was a woman-chaser, party-goer and drunk. Another Lithuanian policeman, a friend of Jacek's, lived across from Viera's apartment with his girlfriend. The girlfriend was selling butter and other food products on the black market. I ordered some butter from her, a prized commodity at the time, to bring to my mother in the ghetto. We were fortunate that we had means to buy food and other necessities. Earlier, when the Russians were occupying the city, we were on a list to be deported to Siberia. At that time, my mother had sewn loose diamonds into the buttons of both of our hand-knit sweaters, the hem of her dress and two 250-gram bars of pure gold into the waistband of my brother's pants. He wore a belt over it at all times. Whenever we needed money, she could always take out a diamond and sell it to a jeweler she knew in the ghetto who gave her Russian gold rubles in exchange. Sometimes I also sold a diamond or a piece of jewelry to a Polish jeweler my family knew outside the ghetto. We were fortunate that we never ran out of money.

Late in the afternoon, I came to pick up the butter at Jacek's friend's house. I rang the bell. Instead of his girlfriend opening the door, a Lithuanian policeman ran out with a gun in his hand, pointing it at my face.

"I was waiting for you to show up. I know you're Jewish and I could shoot you like a stray dog."

I stood there paralyzed thinking my life was over. Then his girlfriend ran out of the house toward him and whispered something in his ear that made him change his mind. He put the gun down and walked back into the apartment with his girlfriend following him. The moment he went inside, she turned around and whispered to me that Viera's husband, Jacek, had gotten drunk the night before at a party at their house and told her boyfriend (the policeman) that I was Jewish. Apparently, he must have decided not to shoot me on the spot as that would reveal he was helping his girlfriend sell butter on the black market.

Still shaking I ran over to Viera's apartment and told her that I almost lost my life because of Jacek. She was surprised and said, "He'd never denounce you. Maybe the two women who came from the ghetto to clean their house saw you last week and said something. Jacek wants to help you. He even found a place in the country for your mother and brother where they can live as Christians."

A few days later I went to Lusia's house. As we had planned, I knocked on the door three times and she opened it. I told her we could meet that Monday evening at our janitress, Jozefowa's house, and then walk over together to Viera's place.

That night it was pitch black outside. The building was in the middle of the block. I walked toward the building, and as I approached it, I took a step to my left, ready to turn through the gate into the courtyard where I would meet Lusia. Suddenly, I saw two red bands on the Lithuanian policemen's navy blue hats illuminated in the small flame of a match. They were standing in the courtyard. While lighting a cigarette they had both momentarily turned their attention and eyes toward each other and didn't notice me. Very slowly and quietly, I continued walking down the sidewalk. I tried to look for Lusia and warn her of the danger. My heart was beating loudly. For quite a while I walked back and forth trying hard to look into the darkness for any oncoming faces. I called out softly, "Lusia, Lusia." But to no avail.

I never saw Lusia again. I could never find out which one of Lusia's acquaintances knew of our rendezvous, wanted us both dead, and informed the police who were waiting to arrest us at our intended meeting.

The trap was closed on my friend and no one ever knew, saw or heard from her again. By a miracle, I had once again escaped a certain death. Maybe it was a sign that I would survive, that somebody above was watching over me. For a while I avoided walking by the building as if it were condemned, but later necessity made me return when I had to stay at Jozefowa's.

I had to keep moving and find a more permanent hiding place for my mother and brother. Life was hanging on a thread in the slowly dwindling ghetto, but I felt that so far luck was with me.

WHAT MY MOTHER TOLD ME HAPPENED IN OSTROWICE, 1942

To my surprise, Jacek did find a place for my mother and brother to stay. My mother told me the story when she came back to the ghetto from Ostrowice, a village about forty kilometers from Vilnius. She said Jacek recommended a man who had been willing to take them to Ostrowice. A price was set for helping them and had to be paid in advance. Jacek assured my mother that he knew the chief of police, a good man who would be willing to help them establish an identity on the Christian side.

The man who gave my mother and brother the ride dropped them off at the police station and, with money in his pocket, happily returned to Vilnius. They went in and asked the policeman at the desk to see the chief of police. They were told he wasn't in his office but would be back the next day. He said he was the chief's assistant and asked them for their IDs. Holding Mother's fake documents in his hand, he turned to my thirteen-year-old brother, Leo, and said, "Where did you come from?"

"From Vilnius."

"What school did you attend?"

"A public school," my brother replied again.

"Do you speak Yiddish?"

"I am Polish," Leo said.

As if the interrogation weren't enough, the policeman added, "You sure forgot your mother tongue," and returned the fake documents. He knew that Jewish people spoke Yiddish, and he must have detected a faint Yiddish accent when Leo spoke Polish to him.

Before leaving, mother asked him if he might know where they could spend the night. He told them that across the street a Polish couple rented out rooms for a short stay.

"Don't forget to come tomorrow morning. The chief of police will be here."

The next morning, Mother was ready to go, but Leo refused to go to the station. He told her about a dream he had the night before. A man wanted to choke him. He could feel the strong, cold hands around his neck. He woke up out of breath in a cold sweat. Mother was never superstitious and went to the police station in any case, by herself. The assistant was at the station and told her the chief was also there and that they'd help her, but only if she brought her son. Again my brother refused to go in spite of my mother's urging. He had a strong premonition of danger. During their argument they heard a light knocking at their door.

A woman asked, "Are you the people from Vilnius?"

My mother answered, "Yes."

The woman told my mother to come outside so she could talk with her in private. She was a Jewish woman from the ghetto who had been cleaning the police station and happened to overhear the police talking about arresting and disposing of the mother and son. Mother came back to the room, told my brother of the danger they were in, and they ran toward the small Ostrowice ghetto behind the police station.

A nice Jewish family took them in and they stayed there overnight. A man from the Judenrat (a representative of the Jewish community) came in around noon the next day and urged them to run away. A truck full of German Gestapo, alerted by the police, had just come to the ghetto looking for the strangers who didn't belong there. Mother and Leo and a few more people started running toward the woods, trying to hide. The Gestapo men saw them and began running after them and shooting. Every time Leo heard a shot, he pulled my mother down in the deep snow.

They noticed the Germans coming closer and closer and no possibility of escaping. They put their hands up and surrendered. They were told to march back to the ghetto. A German soldier in a gray uniform with a rubber whip came over and started blindly hitting them on their heads. They stood there, helpless, exposed to the rage of a brutal beast of unlimited power.

He forced them to stand half-frozen in the snow with his rifle pointed straight at them. Mother thought they would be dead any minute, but not moving and in an appeasing voice not to offend the captor asked, "Please let my son get his coat."

"He won't need a coat anymore," he said.

It was enough for them to understand they were sentenced to death. Mother whispered to Leo to run for his life. She knew both of them couldn't make it, but wanted him to try for life. He could hide between the houses that stood outside the ghetto. But Leo refused to move without his mother. He stood by her and if this was his destiny, he wanted to leave the rotten world together with her.

After a few moments that felt like an eternity, they saw the rest of the Gestapo men coming toward them, devils in human form, expelled even from hell for their crimes against humanity. In a casual manner and tone they told the small group of terrified half-frozen people that their lives were being spared because a hefty ransom was paid by the Jewish community in the Ostrowice ghetto. At the time, Jews in the provinces were put into ghettos but weren't as restricted as in the big cities. They were able to collect money to pay off the Germans on occasion to spare the lives of some Jews.

Mother thought it was a trick and the wild, unpredictable beasts would turn around and gun them all down. As fast as they could, they ran back to the ghetto and thanked the Judenrat for saving their lives. The Judenrat told them to immediately leave the Ostrowice ghetto, as they didn't belong there.

It took them weeks to reach Vilnius. They stopped at isolated peasant homes in the early evening where, pretending to be Polish, my mother addressed them with the common greeting, "*Niech bedze pochwalony Jesus Christ,*" meaning, Let us praise Jesus Christ. The friendly peasants usually invited them in for dinner and put them up for the night. My mother and brother pretended to be poor peddlers and always carried some small notions like needles, thread and buttons to sell. They were often told they could stay a little longer to help out on the farm. Gradually they made their way back to the Vilnius ghetto.

The Polish police and the Gestapo must have worked together and shared the bounty they had extracted from the Jewish community. Unfortunately, the help that Jacek tried to give almost led to my mother's and brother's death. It turned out that Jacek had lied and only pretended to know the chief of police so he could extract some money from my mother to satisfy his drinking habit. Perhaps on some level he wanted to help, but his alcoholism won out.

My New Name, Zoska, and My Father's Shawl

A few days after my mother and brother left for Ostrowice, I slipped out of the ghetto with a group of workers, and decided to go to Czarny Bor, my favorite former summer place, where I could temporarily escape the dangers of the ghetto. The farmers whom my parents had known for years welcomed me with open arms. Every time I could survive one more day away from the ghetto, I felt I had increased my chances of staying alive.

It was a cold, sunny winter day. As always, I carried a small cloth drawstring bag where I kept a little food and my father's shawl. It was navy blue wool with thin, interwoven, light gray stripes, the only belonging of my father's that I managed to hold on to.

I felt more secure in the winter days when I could wrap the shawl around my face and only my eyes were visible. I could see the oncoming people without being afraid that I might be recognized. I have somehow kept the shawl all these years. Once in a while I take it out of the drawer, hold it in my hands and all the happenings of years ago keep flashing before my eyes. I can see my dear father wearing it in the winter, with his gray wool coat lined with fur, coming from the cold to the warm house with our dog, Lalka, barking and jumping all over to greet him. This is a vision my tears can't wash away.

On this occasion, I left Vilnius, went to Porubanek, walked on the side roads of small villages, through a forest where I passed by a cemetery and had a feeling that I was being watched. I didn't see anybody. It was just me and God above. I went into the cemetery and found my mother's friend's grave – Mrs. Wnuk. I crossed myself in case someone was watching. I emerged from the forest, walking toward the road that forked into two branches. Just before turning north toward our summer house, I saw a carriage fast approaching, driven by a farmer with a heavy-set German in a gray uniform as passenger. I knew that Jewish people from the ghetto lived in tents and worked at Bialowaki about five kilometers outside Czarny Bor. Their job was to work in damp peat fields, pulling the peat out and stacking it up to be dried. The Germans hauled it away to be used for heating. Perhaps this German thought I was one of those Jews and was trying to escape.

I heard the German calling, "*Halt. Halt.*" Stop. Stop. The farmer understood if not the words, the meaning, and stopped. The German looked at me and asked, "*Sprichts du Deutsch?*" Do you speak German? I laughed, turned toward the farmer and said, "What the hell is he saying?" He kind of smiled, looked at the German and with a finger pointing at me repeated, "*Zoska, Zoska. Nie Zydowka,*" meaning, not a Jew, but Polish. We both laughed at the joke.

The farmer had made up the name on the spot, realizing the danger I was in. The German must have believed him, because he told the man to continue on his way. I didn't remember ever meeting the Polish farmer who gave me a new name and may have saved my life. I was fortunate there were still a few good people left in the world.

It took me another half hour to get to our neighbor, Mr. Human, whom we trusted. I sometimes stayed at his place. He was a man in his fifties, handsome, a youngish face, salt-and-pepper hair, and a mustache covering his upper lip. He had three grown up children, our former playmates, from his first marriage, and one baby from his present one. At the house, I was greeted by Monica, Mr. Human's young wife, who congratulated me on my marriage.

"What? To who? How come I don't know about it?" I asked.

"Are you serious?" she said.

I thought she was kidding. Marriage was the furthest thing from my mind. My thoughts were with my family and survival.

"A very handsome young man came to our house a few times with his mother to buy or exchange something for food. Mr. Human jokingly said he knows a nice Jewish girl for her son, and they'd make an excellent couple, and he wants to arrange for them to meet and be the best man at the wedding. About two weeks later, his mother showed up again, alone, crying desperately that you had married her son, stolen him from her, leaving her alone. She hadn't seen him for the last two weeks. He didn't show up at work and she wanted to know where she could find me. 'I know he's with her,' she repeated, sobbing." Monica seemed very sorry that her husband's joke was something the poor mother took literally.

I had never met the young man. He could have been murdered. I couldn't stay there much longer as there were rumors that the Germans were trying to trap as many Jews as they could who were hiding or going to the villages in search of food. I returned to the ghetto, partly getting a ride, and partly walking. It was getting harder to enter the ghetto as people were being checked more closely for trying to smuggle in food for their starving families.

After the trial of Hans Geisler, I was afraid of belated repercussions and worried the Germans might come looking for me in the ghetto. Instead of staying at one address, I moved around, staying with different friends and surviving family members. I always kept my Polish identity card with me as Jadwyga, Anna's dead daughter, to use outside of the ghetto. For leaving or returning to the ghetto after work, no documents were necessary.

I went to my Aunt Itel, the last person I stayed with in the ghetto. She was my mother's older sister whose husband, Godin, was arrested by the Bolsheviks as a capitalist and shipped to Siberia. I inquired if she had heard any news from my mother and brother. She was glad to see me and told me to hurry to my Uncle Leon's place, my father's younger brother. She said my mother was there and would tell me what happened to her.

The first words I heard from my mother were, "Thank God you're here." Her eyes held all the fear and pain of her tired soul and spirit. She and my brother had just come back from Ostrowice. It was a hard and dangerous return to the Vilnius ghetto. More and more people were vanishing every day, sent to Ponary, to the mass graves swallowing innocent men, women and children. Terror was intensifying across the ghetto.

THE OPEN WINDOW IN VILNIUS
AND THEN MY LIFE ON THE
FARM WITH JANUCZ

A Polish acquaintance of my father's, Stan Leszczynski, whose apartment I stayed at quite often, told me about a Polish woman who bought a farm from him and was looking for a maid for her city apartment. He knew the family well and trusted the woman enough to tell her I was Jewish. The family consisted of the woman and her husband, their children – a boy and a girl, about five and seven – and the woman's mother, who came to stay with them from Gdynia. Mr. Leszczynski gave me their address. Their apartment was located on the fourth floor in a nice building on Zamkowa St., across from St. Anna's Church. I rang the bell and introduced myself as an acquaintance of the Leszczynski family, who had suggested that they might be looking for a maid. After a few minutes of polite conversation, the woman who had opened the door told me she was a nurse who worked in a hospital. I later found out that she performed abortions at her home.

She looked me over and asked some questions.

"How long have you known Mr. Leszczynski?"

"My father knew him quite well."

"How?"

"He sold a building on Szpitalna St. to Mr. Leszczynski and also lent him money for his daughter's wedding to marry a Polish officer."

At the time a Polish woman had to have a dowry in order to marry a high-ranking military man. I continued answering her questions. "I also met Mr. Leszczynski and his wife at our house a few times."

Mrs. Antosia continued, "And how about your parents?"

"I don't know for sure where my father is, but my mother and little brother are in the ghetto." I answered. She turned around and nodded her head toward a narrow couch near a fireplace in the living room.

"I really need some help with this big apartment. You can sleep here and tomorrow I'll show you what work needs to be done."

"Yes, thank you." I answered, wondering what my duties would be as the whole house looked messy and chaotic.

Early the next morning, Mrs. Antosia's mother, Pani Honora, told me to come in the kitchen and assigned my duties. "You won't cook, but serve, wash the dishes, clean the house and do some other chores."

"That's good. I don't know how to cook."

After a meager breakfast of black bread and tea and half a teaspoon of some kind of homemade jam, Mrs. Antosia walked me down the steps to the cellar located at least one story under the building. She showed me how to carry wood for heating and cooking. I carried a heavy load of firewood strapped to my back with thick ropes, and climbed from the cellar to the fourth floor. There was no stopping. I went up and down with loads of wood. I was exhausted and my whole body ached. Finally, somewhere around noon, they had enough wood for the time being. They showed no compassion and took advantage of my situation. But not having much of a choice, I was thankful to stay out of the ghetto. I still held out hope that any day soon the Germans would be defeated.

Mr. Janusz, the father of the children, turned out to be very young. Standing next to Antosia, his wife, he looked young enough to be her son. He was short, thin, with a small, dark brown mustache and hair parted in the middle. In contrast, Antosia was an attractive, heavy-set woman who seemed to be the boss and acted accordingly by having the first and last say. She told me that her husband didn't know I was Jewish. She didn't have any confidence in him and didn't trust him. She knew her man.

In a moment of confession, she told me about her previous marriage to a man she referred to as a magician, who could conjure up spirits from the other world. And when a spirit became upset during one of his séances, the table would move up, down, and then crash to the floor. After he died, she looked for a man to sire her children before she was too old. Some of her friends mentioned a bureaucrat from the city of Poznan who'd be happy to marry a woman who could support him, and so she found her current husband. Mr. Janusz was a born mediocre civil servant.

After their children were born, she mostly kept him outside the city on a farm not far from Vilnius, which she had bought from Mr. Leszczynski.

I asked her if this is how she got to know Mr. Leszczynski. She hesitated a moment and said, "I don't know if I'll be able to keep the farm."

"But you bought it. It's yours," I volunteered.

"Yes, but the war is going on and we don't know who'll invade the country next."

"What do you think will happen?" I asked politely.

"I'm worried about my children and I hate the Bolsheviks. I want Poland to be free."

"Yes," I said, "I understand your concern." But in my heart this meant a glimmer of hope that the Russian army would come to our rescue before we were all killed by the Germans.

The next Sunday I went back to the ghetto. My mother hadn't heard from me for a few days and was very worried. I told her about the job I found and assured her that I was very careful and had high hopes of finding a place for them to hide on the Aryan side. In reality, my hopes were almost destroyed, after all the failures to find a place so far. But the only thing I could do at the time was give them courage and hope.

In the ghetto I slept on a mattress on the floor with a roomful of strangers. The next day I used my method of leaving the ghetto and returned to my job with the Polish family. It was about midnight when we heard an intense constant ringing at the courtyard gate. Antosia and her mother came in running to the front room where I slept. I was awake and heard the bell, got up and joined them, hoping that the ringing was intended for another apartment. As it was long past curfew and no civilians were allowed on the street, we assumed it had to be the police.

The three of us stood glued to the open window in the cold darkness, listening to footsteps coming nearer the front door. "Tell them we didn't know you're Jewish," Antosia told me. I felt my heart trying to jump out of my body. I tried to appear calm. "Of course you don't know who I am. They won't do anything to you," I said.

In the meantime I felt a strong hand pushing me toward the open window. "Jump! Jump!" Pani Honora, Antosia's mother said. "You will save us all from a catastrophe. They'll kill you either way," she said trembling.

I looked down at the darkness of the concrete courtyard four stories below, waiting for the front door to open. I'd jump to my death rather than be tortured and killed. Antosia looked at me and at her mother and hurried to open the door. A young woman, visibly in pain, and a policeman came in. Antosia said a few words to the woman who followed her into the room that was off-limits to me, where she performed abortions.

Antosia's mother looked at me with eyes ready to kill, and without saying one word, left me still standing by the open window. After the shock of the experience, I slowly came to my senses and thanked God that at the last minute I was saved once again.

The next morning, without much ceremony, Antosia told me she couldn't keep me any longer after the night before. "Wait a minute," she said, "I have an idea. You can go to the farm I bought from Mr. Leszczynski and help my husband out."

"I don't know farm work, but I'll do my best," I answered, trying to put a smile on my face. Antosia gave me the directions and drew a simple map. I had a good idea where it was, between Czarny Bor and Jaszuny, about fifteen or twenty kilometers from Vilnius.

I easily found the farm. The house stood close to the road surrounded by bushes and trees. It was harvest time, with people working in the fields. Whenever I met somebody on the road I would greet them with the traditional Catholic country greeting, "Praised be Jesus Christ." And the response was always, "For ages and ages."

I said the same when I knocked at Mr. Janusz's door. I told him his wife sent me to work on the farm and didn't have time to notify him before I got there. He only went into the city occasionally, as his wife didn't relish his company, and preferred having him stay at the farm.

He recognized me from having met me at his house in Vilnius before. "Oh yes," he said. "I have one goat to take care of, so I guess your job will be to feed her so we'll have enough milk to share." I couldn't understand and asked him, "But what about the fields? I don't have any experience."

"Don't worry. I don't know a thing about farming either. My wife takes care of everything. Even sends me food that I can't get here." I didn't say a word and he continued. "She's glad to get rid of me and keep me away in the country." I thought to myself that she must have a good reason. But this wasn't my business and I didn't make any comments. He showed me a nice, big room next to the kitchen where I would sleep. I noticed another bedroom with a wide bed and a few pieces of furniture that looked almost deserted. In the early evening I went to milk the goat in the small shed by the house.

I thought milking a goat would be very easy. I remembered eons ago seeing the women in the country milking cows and it all seemed simple. All they did was pull the udders and the milk just flew into the pail. But there was much more to this than I thought. The goat moved every time I tried to pull her udders. I followed her with the pitcher in my hand and was glad the shack was so small. I caught her by the head, clamped my legs around her body. I bent down and with one hand held the pitcher and with the other I pulled her small udders. I guess she was as surprised as I. Somehow I got a whole quart of warm milk. I performed the same trick twice a day, proud of my own method, and felt like a real milker.

My thoughts constantly returned to my mother and brother, and I felt guilty for having left them in the ghetto. But if I stayed in the ghetto, it would only be a hindrance, and I'd be unable to look for a hiding place for them on the Christian side.

Janusz was friendly. We ate our meals together and at night each went to his own room. This lasted about two weeks. Then one evening he told me about his feelings for me. "I really like you and I want to sleep with you," he said. I had to think fast. "I can't do it. I'm engaged to be married soon. If my fiancé will find out I'm not a virgin, he'll kill both of us." He wanted to know more about the man I was so afraid of. "He used to be a nice man," I told him. "The war changed him, but I still love him."

"What's he doing now?" he asked.

I had to make it believable. "He joined the Germans and the Lithuanians and is a very dangerous man. And I heard that he killed many people." I liked the idea of scaring him and I said, "He killed two people just before I came here. He has a bad temper and is easy with his gun." It worked. He left me alone for the most part. Sometimes he would grab me and pull me toward him. But I managed to keep his advances in check.

Early on a Saturday morning about a week later I heard a commotion around the house. I jumped out of bed, pulled a dress over my head and ran to the window. The house was encircled with Lithuanian police in their navy blue uniforms and caps with red bands. On the narrow road leading from the highway to the house, a farmer who worked for Antosia had erected some big piles of animal feed to dry for the winter. The heaps looked like tents and were placed along the road from the house to the highway. The police were walking two by two and digging in and out of these huts with the bayonets of their rifles, looking to find Jewish people hiding.

I stood with Janusz in front of the house, thinking that they had come to arrest me. I was terrified. In one moment I turned into a co-matose state – a body without a soul, without a thought. I stood there like a ghost with Janusz beside me; he was smiling as if he were expect-ing company. One policeman with more insignia walked over to us and asked, "Where is the Jewish girl you're hiding? Somebody saw her go to your place."

"I would never hide a Jew," he said. "The only person that came here was a woman two days ago who asked for directions and left," answered Janusz. "I never saw her before or since." Luckily for me, his wife hadn't told him I was Jewish.

In the meantime, another policeman decided to look for himself and ran through the house. I went in and offered him a glass of water. He thanked me. I don't know how long after they left I still had the frozen smile on my face. Janusz looked at me and said, "What are you still smil-ing about?" I was too numb to answer.

"They thought we were husband and wife," Janusz said. A few days went by without any other unexpected intruders, and suddenly Janusz decided again that he wanted to sleep with me. It was still dark outside when I felt my cover moving off my body. Half asleep, I pulled it back. Then I saw Janusz's shadow and heard his voice.

"Don't be afraid. I won't hurt you. I just couldn't fall asleep," he said in a low, soothing voice.

"Mr. Janusz, please go to your bed," I screamed.

"Don't scream," he said. And suddenly like a wild animal he jumped on top of me while I was still lying under the blanket. I knew I had to use all of my wits to stop his undesirable advances. I insisted I had to go to the bathroom.

"I don't believe you," he mumbled.

"I'll wet the bed, you and myself. I'll be back in a moment and we'll talk."

Saying this I worked myself out from under him. I ran out to the outhouse. A dead silence engulfed me with dark clouds covering the sky.

There were no visible stars. No life. Not even a barking dog. What to do? Where to run? Then Janusz's voice. "Come back. I won't touch you." I didn't believe him.

"Please go to your own bed. Don't worry about me," I told him, not wanting to further aggravate the situation.

"Okay. Goodnight," he said.

"Wait a moment, I won't tell any of this to your wife," I said, knowing he'd be happy to hear this as he knew where his bread was coming from. I didn't want to make him my enemy. Parting as friends was the way to go. I took my pillow and blanket and slept under the bed the rest of the night. The bed stood on four legs and there was plenty of space for one person underneath. Rain fell overnight. In the morning the sky cleared up and it promised to be a nice late summer day. I milked the goat, had breakfast, took an extra slice of bread and some cheese and told him I had to go to the city for a few days and would be back soon.

"I'm sorry for yesterday night," he said. I pretended not to hear and turned toward the door. I said, "Good bye, I'll see you soon." I wanted to go back to my mother and the people I loved in the ghetto, and feel my mother's arms around me. But it couldn't be. I didn't have any good news to bring them about a hiding place outside the ghetto. There was still a slim chance that Mr. Leszczynski had found something for them, so I set out for his apartment.

Most of the time I didn't plan where I was going. But the road ahead was straight. I wanted to take the road and try for life. I walked on like a zombie hoping something would show up. I just had to look deeper into the unmarked map and find my way. My head was devoid of any thought. I was a living body with a shut-off mind – a self-imposed mechanism without the burden of thought, of past, of present.

A Room Full of Mattresses:
The Ghetto on Szpitalna St.

Mr. Leszczynski wasn't home. I rang the bell next door where a single woman knew me as Mr. Leszczynski's niece from the country. After a few more rings with no answer, not wanting to wait and get too much attention from the other residents, I left.

It took me a long time to cross the city to my friend Regina's house. Her mother, always friendly, welcomed me to stay with them. I was tired from the long eventful day and soon after dinner went to sleep. Daylight came too early for me, too soon to face a new day of constant fear and the struggle to survive. Regina's mother gave me some food to bring to my mother. I hid it under my jacket, as it was forbidden to bring food into the ghetto. Soon I managed to join a group coming from work and I entered the ghetto. I was afraid of being stopped and caught with the food. I would be beaten up, the food confiscated and if a Christian ID were found on me, I'd be arrested or executed instantly as an example for others.

In the ghetto, I didn't notice any movement of people outside the building on Szpitalna St. It looked spooky. Void of life, but full of ghosts. I went into the building and climbed the stairs to the third floor where my Uncle Leon – my father's younger brother – his wife Manya and Rosalyn, my three-year-old cousin lived. I found my mother sitting on the edge of the bed with a little boy about six or seven sitting next to her, holding her hand and crying, asking for his mother who just an hour ago was arrested with some other people from the apartment next door and taken away. Everybody knew at this time that once a person was gone he or she would never be seen again.

In my uncle's apartment there was also a young couple who moved in just a few days before from the provinces and a few more families I didn't know. The room was packed with eleven people. Walking toward my mother I could hardly find an empty space. The room looked like one huge mattress on an invisible floor. I felt the air loaded with fear and death. Inside or outside of the ghetto was equally dangerous. There was no safe place to hide anywhere. Killings and deportations happened daily. I saw people in the ghetto walking the streets like living ghosts. Children, hungry and abandoned, were crying for the parents they would never see again. Abandoned by God and the world. I was talking to my mother, a few mattresses away, when the couple that was shipped to the ghetto from the provinces started to argue, as their anxiety had brought them to the verge of insanity.

"You're dead! They'll kill you first," the woman screamed.

"No, we'll go together. You're my wife."

"I want something to eat."

"Forget about food, you're going to die anyway."

And so it went on for a while. All I heard was talk about dying, killing, death and who'd go to the gallows first.

"Please be quiet," my mother said, "We have enough trouble without predictions of who lives or dies." We walked out into the courtyard. "It's heartbreaking to have to listen to their fears," my mother said. "It doesn't help the situation and will just make it another sleepless night."

I asked my mother where my little brother was. She told me he went to see a friend, and she was waiting anxiously for him to return. I was ready to run and look for him. A few minutes later he came in agitated, telling us what he saw from his friend's window. The Lithuanians encircled a group of Jewish people with guns in their hands, pushing them toward trucks, hitting people while laughing amongst themselves. I sat next to my mother, desperately thinking to find a way to take them out of the living hell. After a little while a few people that shared the same room came in from work looking tired, thin, exhausted from heavy work. For the majority there was no way out.

I decided to spend some time with my mother and not leave the ghetto for a few days. Mother looked bad. She didn't have enough energy and strength to go out to work. Tears became part of her eyes. The next day I walked over with my mother to see my Aunt Itel, who shared a room with her newly married daughter, Hannah, her husband and my beautiful little cousin, Lila, in addition to four more strangers in the same room.

The next evening as we were getting ready to go to sleep, we heard a lot of people running up and down the stairs and a ghetto policeman's voice screaming, "Everybody assemble in the courtyard." Whoever wasn't going fast enough, he pushed down the stairs. Screams and wailing. Children and mothers separated knowing the end had come.

I was pushed with my brother to join the condemned. The quota had to be filled. I grabbed my brother's hand. In just a split of a second when the capo's attention was diverted, I ran with him back to the room, and caught my mother running to the stairway hysterically calling our names. "Don't go down," I screamed. "We're here."

"I thought I lost you. It all happened so suddenly."

"Calm down. Everything will be fine. We'll find a way," I said, not believing my own words. They were dreams. Not reality.

Just a few days earlier I was told about my Aunt Lisa, my father's younger sister who snuck out of the ghetto carrying her baby daughter, Judith, in her arms. She was on her way to her former Lithuanian neighbor who stored some of her belongings so she could exchange them for food and then return to the ghetto.

While Aunt Lisa was walking to her previous neighbor's house, some young Polish boys ran after her, throwing stones and shouting, "A Jew! A Jew!"

The police quickly came. She was arrested, taken to prison and executed with her baby, Judith. Her husband, a pharmacist, had been killed at Ponary and her sixteen-year-old son sent to a concentration camp where he died. Her other daughter, a girl of about fourteen, tried to survive on the Aryan side as a maid working for a Lithuanian family. The people she worked for at some point recognized that she was Jewish and denounced her to the police. She was arrested and sent to a concentration camp, which she survived. I found out after the war that she had gone to Israel, got married and raised two children. She lives in Tel Aviv and I often speak to her.

I didn't want to stay in the death chamber any longer. I had to get out and find a safe place for my mother and brother to hide. In the morning I joined a group of people who were sent to a place outside the city to transport dirt and stones for road repairs. It was a long day; we were exhausted from hard work, dirty and we had no facilities to clean up. We formed a group and, walking in rows of five or six, returned to the ghetto.

I was walking next to Manya, a friend of my cousin, Hanna, a girl a few years older than me. I told her about my dilemma in trying to find a place for my mother and brother. She said she had a sister, a nurse, who married a Polish doctor who divorced her just recently. This Polish man had custody of their son and found his Jewish ex-wife a hiding place with an older Polish couple, on a quiet side street close to Makowa St. The next day I was at the ghetto gate waiting to meet Manya and walk to work with her. I wanted to find out more about her sister and whether there was a possibility for my mother and brother to hide there.

She gave me the address and said, "It won't hurt to try. Just be careful. Don't look suspicious. Don't look around when you get to the house."

"But I don't know your sister's name. They might not answer the door." I wanted to make sure not to frighten the people. "My sister's name is Zofia. Tell them Manya sends her greetings." She turned her head away from me as a German guard walked by. Talking was not allowed.

MY SISTER'S NAME IS ZOFIA

Late in the afternoon I was at Jozefowa's again, the janitress of the apartment building my parents owned at 8 Subocz St. I stayed there overnight, and the next morning set out to look for the address of the house where Manya's sister was hiding. I found the house next to a little one-horse shed. The shed was separated from the house and front yard by small bushes. After a few gentle knocks at the front door, a man's voice asked, "What do you want?"

"I came to bring greetings from Manya to her sister Zofia. Can I please see her?" I was let in and immediately the door locked behind me. An older lady invited me to a small, well-furnished living room and Zofia came out a few minutes later from a side door. I told her how I'd met her sister and, a little surprised, she said, while looking at me intensely, "Manya must have lots of confidence in you. It's the first time she revealed my new name and residence to a stranger."

I wanted to say something, but decided to wait and hear what she had to say first. "My sister and brother are in the ghetto and, as you know, their lives are hanging on a thread."

"Why don't they come here? Can't they stay with you?" I asked.

"They are scared either way – in the ghetto or here. And they refuse to come because of some idea that they belong with the rest of the Jewish people."

I could hardly believe my ears when I heard that some people wouldn't try to save themselves after all the horrible killings going on daily in the ghetto. I didn't waste any time and got straight to the point. "I'm looking for a place for my mother and brother," I said. She excused herself and went out, leaving me alone in the room. I waited a long time and it occurred to me that perhaps she forgot about me or wanted me to leave before curfew time. Then the old man walked in. Behind him, like a shadow, came his wife, and then Zofia.

"We can't take them in. We're afraid for our own lives," the old man said in a low measured voice shaking his head. "Our house is small. It's very hard for us." I read between the lines and felt a glimmer of hope.

"Please help me. It will just be for a very short time," I said. "I'll soon have a permanent place for them."

The three of them went out again for a few minutes and then came back. "Okay, we'll take them in, but they can't stay long." We agreed on a price that was a lot of money at the time. A few days before, I sold a gold cigarette case my mother had given me. I had taken it to a couple I knew who had a tiny store deep in a courtyard in the last building on the block across from the Bernardine Gardens. I went back to the ghetto to give my mother the good news and directions to the house – which, fortunately, was easy to find.

Two days later my mother and brother snuck out of the ghetto separately, by joining a group of people, and walked to the old couple's house. My mother walked ahead and my brother followed behind her to the door. She paid the couple the agreed-upon amount of money in advance. My mother and brother stayed in the house until darkness fell, then were told by the old man to follow him to the small one-horse stable.

My mother and brother stayed in the attic of the stable day and night. They were half-starved with only a little bread and onions given them to eat each day. They slept on straw underneath a blanket, relieved themselves in the corners and covered it with a little straw. It was not a big problem with the little food they ate. It was getting colder and the nights, longer. Winter was in the air.

After I left them at the old couple's place, I went back to Jozefowa's. A young woman with a little baby in her arms was there, about to leave when I came in. "Don't go, I want you to meet the landlord's daughter," Jozefowa said.

"Okay," she replied, "Let me go upstairs and feed the baby and I'll be right back." Jozefowa told me the woman had just been released from jail.

"But she's not Jewish," I said.

"From what I heard she was accused of being a Communist. She's originally from Kaunas," Jozefowa said.

Soon the Lithuanian woman came back downstairs with her baby. She had a loaf of bread and a small piece of lard. "This is for you."

I was surprised and a little embarrassed, but accepted and said, "Thank you, but please don't deprive yourself."

"Don't worry, I have enough food. Maybe I can help you."

I waited to hear what she had in mind. I was both surprised and curious. My trust in people was becoming questionable, especially in a person I had just met. Jozefowa turned toward me and said, "My dear, you can trust her. She's been a tenant in the building for years and suffered plenty from the Germans."

"I have a married sister in Kaunas. Her husband travels a lot. You can go and stay with her for a while where nobody knows you," she said matter-of-factly.

I liked the idea. She was right. I knew too many people in the city. It was, in a way, to my advantage that I had places to stay, but at the same time, a disadvantage because I was never sure if some informer or collaborator might turn me in to the Germans for their own gain. After moving in and taking over Jewish homes and businesses, they weren't thrilled with the idea that some day they may have to return everything they stole back to the legitimate Jewish owners.

The Lithuanian woman gave me the address and directions to her sister's house and wished me good luck. After spending the night at Jozefowa's house, the next morning I went to the train station and bought a ticket to Kaunas.

KAUNAS AND MY NEW JOB AT THE GERMAN NEWSPAPER

When I write of the horrors I went through, I feel like I'm telling a story about somebody else, as if I'm standing on the sidelines and watching it played out before me.

In all the years since these events occurred, I've mastered putting myself under a cover of complete anesthesia, like major surgery. I am in a trance. The memories are stuck like pages in an empty book. Someone is writing about these events. Deep in my self-conscious I know it is me, but self-preservation and the animal instinct of survival is deeply embedded in me. I try to fill the pages. Maybe someday I will recognize myself.

I don't feel self-pity putting my story down. I try not to feel at all. Maybe I'm just fooling myself. A thought repeats again and again, "Don't run from reality. You can't rid yourself of reality no matter who, where or what you are." I fight to slowly kill my pain and the enemy inside of me. Enough of that. Let me go back to my trip to the city of our deadly enemies – to the enemies who could never imagine a Jewish girl infiltrating their domain.

I easily found the address that the woman at Jozefowa's gave me. I told the Lithuanian woman who opened the door that I came from Vilnius and was a friend of her sister, Mrs. Szaduikis. I asked her if I could spend the night at her home, and she said it would be okay if I stayed there for a couple of days. I slept on a couch in the entrance hall, a dreamless, short night, as I didn't know what to expect from these people who seemed to be lukewarm toward me. They didn't ask many questions about their sister. I told the woman I came to find a job. She suggested I buy a newspaper and look at the ads.

My Lithuanian was very limited, to say the least. But my command of German was very good. Four years of study helped me differentiate my German from Yiddish. I bought a *Kauner Zeitung* and saw an ad asking for a laundress. I found my way to the address by asking in Polish. A heavy, blond, red-faced woman looked me over and dismissed me on the spot saying, "It's a hard job. Not for you. You can't do it. I need strong people. Look for something else."

A few minutes later I was on the street again. I decided to walk back "home." It took me a long time to reach the place. I didn't know the city well and asking for directions too often could be suspicious. That I had to avoid. The first question I was asked by the woman when I got back was, "Did you get work? I hope you don't have to stay here long."

"I tried, but they didn't want me. Tomorrow I'll find something." She was anxious to get rid of me. She didn't find good company in her sister's acquaintances, assuming I also belonged to some Communist organization.

In the morning she gave me a piece of paper with the address of the employment office and directions how to get there. I came to a two-story building with an entrance from the street on the ground floor. There was a big room with compartments toward the wall, and people sitting behind glass windows like cashiers at a train station. As I came in I looked around and turned in the direction of the next window. A middle-aged man carrying an old, brown, small attaché case deliberately crossed my way as if by accident. I can't describe his face, as he wore heavy glasses, a hat and a dark suit. He asked me, "What are you doing here? Looking for work?" In the meantime there was light movement taking place in the room. Nobody was paying attention to us. "Yes. I'm looking for work."

"Do you have a place to stay?"

I was getting suspicious and answered, "Yes. Just a temporary place with relatives."

He turned toward the exit and said, "Come. Follow me." Outside the employment office he told me he had a place for me to stay. I walked for about half an hour – he in front and me following him. I knew he wasn't a Gestapo man or a German collaborator because he would have immediately arrested me if he had any doubts about who I really was. The apartment on the ground floor had a handwritten sign, "Janitress." He rang the bell and a middle-aged woman came to the door and without any greeting shoved us inside. She directed me to the adjoining room and closed the door. I found myself in a small bedroom in a darkened room. I put my ear to the door. I could hardly hear them talking in Lithuanian, a language quite foreign to me. I started to get panicky. What if they were headhunters? Looking around, my only escape was a locked window and unknown streets in a strange city. I heard a door slam. Somebody was coming or leaving. And then the woman opened the door and told me I could stay with her.

Not a word about the man. No explanation. Just acceptance. I shared her bed. The next morning she asked me for my ID and told me she was going to register me at the city hall as a legitimate tenant. I went out to look for employment. I never found out who the stranger was that brought me to the janitress's apartment.

The ad in the German paper said they were looking for a junior clerk with some knowledge of German and an address where to apply. I was interviewed by a German in civilian clothes and told him I was from the province around Vilnius and was staying with relatives. He was very happy to have a Polish woman working for him, as he said the Lithuanians were very lazy. A Polish woman would teach me how to type and until then I would write addresses of subscribers by hand. I screened myself by just listening and limiting my vocabulary to necessities.

The office I was assigned to resembled a regular school room and had about twenty people working in it. I sat next to the Polish woman, who had a typewriter on her desk. In the morning before I left for work I always had some bread and tea. In the evening when I returned to my lodgings, a little food – some bread or potatoes and soup – was always on the table, for which I was thankful. These were my meals for the day. I didn't have food coupons, as they would have been sent to me from my home address, which I didn't dare request, since I certainly couldn't give them my address in the ghetto. I went hungry the whole day. My co-worker, the Polish woman, wasn't helpful and too many questions asked were dangerous. I had to keep a low profile and relaxed appearance. A pleasant but not-too-friendly relationship with others was a way to avoid questions or comments.

I lived with myself. By myself. With the stigma of who I was. A few weeks passed and one day I told my boss I received a letter that my mother wasn't well, and I also had to go back home to get my food coupons as the mail was very slow in coming.

"No problem," he said, "How long will you stay away? You are progressing very well," I was told.

"I'll be back in a couple of days. I really like my job."

He believed me. "I'll give you a letter that you are a government employee and the fare is free to Vilnius, and in Vilnius, go to the office of the *Vilner Zeitung* and they'll give you free return papers." I was very pleased with the offer. The next day, the first thing in the morning, he called me over to his desk and handed me the travel documents. I didn't have to work this day. I went to the train station, waited about an hour for the train and was on my way for the three-hour journey back to Vilnius.

The train wasn't full and I stood in the entrance compartment looking at the passing landscape. Two men were speaking Polish and one mentioned something about the goings-on in the ghetto. One of them must have noticed me standing there and said, loud enough for me to hear, "Even if a Jew were standing next to you, you couldn't recognize him." If it was just part of the conversation or he suspected me, I didn't know. It was enough for my blood to start boiling and imagining the worst scenario: being arrested, leaving the train or being shot in the back by a Lithuanian partisan Jew-killer. When the train stopped, without hurrying or looking back, I tried to blend in with the other passengers leaving the station. It was still early in the day when I turned in the direction of Makowa St., where my mother and brother were hiding at the old couple's house.

They came in from spending the day in the abandoned stable. I can hardly express myself – what the reunion meant to me. The happiness of seeing each other mixed with fear of death and loss. I had to assure the Polish couple that very soon I'd have a new hiding place for them. It wasn't a matter of compensation. They were well paid by my mother, they told me, but they feared being denounced and killed or sent to a concentration camp, which was the same as death. I said goodbye to the couple and promised to come back soon. I wanted to kiss my mother but was afraid to explode in grief and make the parting even more painful. Neither of us knew if we would see each other again. We just nodded to each other when I left, smiled with tears covering our darkened world.

My next stop was my school friend Regina's home. I was welcomed and invited to stay overnight. I told them about my job in Kaunas and how hard it was to get food without a ration card. Early in the afternoon,

Regina and I picked up my other Polish school friend, Janina Nester-owisz, and we walked to Mickiewicza St. to pick up my traveling papers from the *Vilner Zeitung*. Two Polish boys our age recognized me. We knew them from another school where we often attended their parties. They didn't come over, just acknowledged us with a nod. I was glad to leave the premises without being stopped.

I didn't think more about the encounter, and stayed with my friends for a few days. They prepared a box of dried cake bread, a smoked slab of bacon and a few other food items that I paid them for. And then I left for my job in Kaunas.

When I got back to my job, I came in earlier than usual and found just a few people in the office. The Polish woman whom I worked with was there. She tip-toed over to me and asked me, "Which one is your boyfriend?" I was surprised, as it seemed to be a very odd question.

"I don't have a boyfriend."

"You don't have to confess. They're both handsome boys and came from Vilnius looking for you. They told me they're working at the same newspaper company, the *Vilner Zeitung*.

Suppressing my fear, but alert to the imminent danger, I asked her, "What else did they say?"

"Oh, I see a romance boiling," she smiled with satisfaction. "They said they'll be back soon." Saying this, she went over to her desk. I wasn't satisfied with her answer. Maybe there was something else she wasn't telling me. The Gestapo may have been alerted and any minute I could be arrested – a Jew working for a German newspaper.

I went over to her and said, "Boys will be boys. They're good friends I've known for a long time. I just forgot something at home and I'll be back in no time," I slowly walked out of the room, the floor burning under my feet and my fear urging me to run, run away from the iron net before the murderess could catch me. On the street I felt a little better and walked toward my "home," stopping at a newsstand pretending to read the latest news, and at the same time glancing behind me to see if I was being followed. It was clear; there was nobody behind me. People were walking by in different directions, no one paying attention to me. My thoughts ran through me like fire. Why did the boys from Vilnius come all the way to Kaunas to see me? What did they want? Money? Or was it blackmail, lust or to denounce me to my employer, a German national?

I couldn't imagine a friendly visit from two people I didn't personally know. I felt like a small insect that could be crushed in the blink of an eye, like a speck of dust, the smallest wind could blow me into oblivion.

I picked up my belongings, said goodbye to the good Lithuanian woman. No questions asked. She just looked at me sadly and said, "God be with you, my child."

I kissed her and left. I still had the necessary documents that allowed me to travel to and from Kaunas, given to me by the German department head in Vilnius after I told him that my mother was very sick and I might have to return soon. In the afternoon I arrived back in Vilnius again. People were hurrying to their homes, families, friends, lives. I had to think hard and decide where to go and what to do.

A group of Jewish people walking toward the ghetto in the middle of the road accompanied by a group commander pulled my heart toward them. For a moment I wanted to join them, but reason erased my emotion and sentiment. I wouldn't be able to survive and help my brother and mother. I had to be "free" to look and find an escape from the fiery storm that engulfed the lives of my loved ones behind the walls of the ghetto. I decided to rest for a while and looked for a place to calm my nerves and clear my mind.

I walked to Ostra Brama, a Catholic chapel built centuries ago. It was built on top of an archway, and inside, on a recessed balcony, masses were held hourly during the morning and evening. I found a place to sit, crossed myself, put my head down pretending to pray. I didn't have the comfort for more than a short while, as a woman with a little girl took a place next to me. The woman casually asked me if Father Alexander would be giving Mass today. I shook my head affirmatively. I didn't trust the look she gave me. I crossed myself and walked away. Evening was approaching and I had to decide where to go for the night before curfew.

I went to Mr. Leszczynski, where I always felt welcome. I told him about my flight from Kaunas and the two boys from Vilnius who came looking for me. Concern showed on his face.

"You were very wise to run away. Who knows what their intentions were. Terrible crimes are being committed daily. People are abandoning the law of God, turning into savages. Their selfishness and greed is rampant. It's spreading like a plague."

"I see it. I feel it," I said sadly.

"It will change. Don't worry too much. One of these days humanity will prevail again."

"Yes, Mr. Leszczynski," I said. "I hope it won't be too late for us."

"I'll see what we can do to help you. You know your family is dear to me. The way it's going, the war will soon come to an end, and your father, my good friend, will come back home. Tomorrow we're going to the country. I want you to come with us," he said. I was happy to hear the invitation, but my mother and brother were on my mind.

"What about my mother and brother. Can they come too?" I asked, hoping for the desired answer.

"Not at this time," he said. "I have friends staying at the house. My daughter and her in-laws are there. It's a busy place now. Maybe I can arrange for something later."

"I understand," I said. I knew he would take us to his estate in the country if he could. I spent the night at Mr. Leszczynski's house. The next day I went to see my mother and brother, who still were temporarily staying with the older Polish couple. I rang the bell. Nobody answered. I walked around the house and saw a curtain slightly move. I rang again and knocked lightly on the window. I knew my mother and brother should be there. A door opened and a hand abruptly pulled me into the house. Immediately the door was shut.

"Your mother and brother had to leave. It was getting cold and we let them sleep in the house." And in a low voice as if some ghost were listening, the old woman said, "Yesterday a neighbor with her little boy came to visit and the child's ball rolled behind the curtain where they were hiding. The boy ran to get the ball, screamed, "There!" pointing his finger at the curtain. I don't know if he saw them, but the people next door are Jew-haters. Thank God the child was too young to say anything. We were afraid, so we asked them to leave."

I thanked the woman for her kindness and walked out without looking back.

WINTER 1942

After my mother and brother had to leave the Polish couple's house, we stayed in the ghetto for a while. Early on a Monday morning we went to the ghetto gate and when the assigned Jewish leader called out that he needed a certain amount of people for work, a group was formed. My mother and brother joined the group and left the ghetto. It was dangerous to leave the assembly outside the ghetto, but after a while we became experts at the deadly game. Though my mother had brown hair and brown eyes, she could easily mix in with the Christian population. Nobody paid any attention to my little brother who had his hat half pulled down over his face. Children that could work often accompanied their parents. As agreed before, we met at the lawyer's house, Mr. Klemantowiez. He gave them some handwritten Polish documents without any photos or government seal, signed by a village priest to verify that they were born in the village and that he knew them. Mr. Klemantowiez told them the papers had very little value, but were better than nothing and it was the best he could do.

It was close to the end of winter 1942. He told us he had good news. He found a place for my mother and brother in the country, and I would have to wait a little longer as he had something in mind for me as well. A nephew of Mr. and Mr. Klemantowiez who lived in the country would arrange for a farmer to come and take my mother and brother to his nephew's home close to Kozysc. The price was set and the money paid in advance. We still had some money, jewelry and gold left. We managed to gradually sell it and buy some time.

Two days later, my mother and brother were on their way. At the house there happened to be another Jewish family who ignored them and pretended to be Christian. Pretending to be a believable Christian was very difficult. The slightest gesture or a word spoken with a Jewish inflection could easily give a person away. They spent the night there and the next day Mr. Klemantowiez's nephew told them he knew a widow who lived alone and he'd introduce them as his relatives from the city. The woman was glad to have company and get paid.

The new place consisted of a kitchen with a dirt floor and one room where they all slept. My brother was always afraid that he might speak Yiddish in his sleep and betray himself. He often woke up shaken and scared at what the woman might do if she discovered that they were Jewish.

On Sunday morning they all went to church, Mother covered with a shawl hiding half her face and my brother with his boy's cap pulled down to his nose. Nobody paid attention to them and the cold and frost didn't encourage the peasants to stand outside and socialize. The widow was pleased with the arrangement and many times thanked God for sending them to her to alleviate her loneliness. On a snowy, cold day I walked from the farmer's house where I was staying (also arranged by Mr. Klemantowiez) through a forest to the highway. I had directions and looked for the house Mr. Klemantowiez's nephew had described where my mother and brother were now staying. A boy was skiing on a big field covered with snow. He noticed me and when he came closer, I saw his skis were two pieces of flat wood tied to his shoes with string.

It was my little brother, Leo, or Lebele, as we called him using the diminutive. Together we went to the house. My mother didn't look well. She could hardly move, her legs were swollen, covered with open sores. She was afraid to take the chance of seeing a doctor, be recognized as a Jew and denounced. We embraced, holding back our emotions, both aware that this short time belonged to us. I stayed there and left before darkness fell.

Our future was bleak and could be eliminated in the blink of an eye. I left the house feeling depressed and helpless. It was getting dark, the wind was blowing, snow pouring from heaven, and the thought of the nice, warm place at the farmer's where I was staying was pulling me ahead.

A month went by peacefully with very few visitors at the widow's place where my mother and brother were staying. One morning they heard guns firing close by. A neighbor came over and asked Olek (my brother Leo's Polish name according to his fake papers) if he'd heard the shots and said, "The police just killed a Jew. It must have been your father."

"Uncle, you know I'm not a Jew," my brother replied, crossing himself and trying hard to smile.

"They caught the Jew and were bringing him back to the ghetto where he belongs," the man said. "He wanted to escape," he added, "but guess what? They shot the Jew before they brought him to the police station so they don't have to share his belongings with the others. They just got rid of him."

As if this was not enough good news, the Pole asked my brother, "How do you know how to cross yourself? You're a Jew."

My brother said, "Uncle, you must be kidding. I'm Polish just like you." But he knew they would have to leave the place immediately. They didn't know where I was at the time, and couldn't go from village to village looking for me. There was no way for them to get in touch with me. My brother Leo told me what happened to them next. When the widow came in, my mother told her they were going to leave for a few days to sell some socks, needles and thread in order to get money, and they'd be back soon. Carrying their few belongings, they walked to Mr. Klemantowiez's nephew's house, told him what happened and the reason they had to leave. He recommended a village close to Eiszyski, about twenty kilometers away, where they might be able to live as Poles. He found a peasant with a horse and sled who was willing to take them. It was bitter cold. They traveled through forests and roads hardly visible, covered in deep snow. About halfway to their destination the peasant stopped, jumped out of his seat and screamed at them to get off the sled. He wouldn't take them any farther, and threw their bundles in the snow. Scared, cold, not knowing where they were, they followed the road. When they emerged from the forest they saw a small village about a kilometer away.

They walked over the snowed-in fields as fast as they could, freezing, dressed in too light attire for the extreme cold. The afternoon turned dark and gloomy, the snow clung to the pines. A few times they heard a sound like a gunshot. They thought the farmer alerted the police. They ran off the road, hiding behind trees and leaving deep marks in the snow, a giveaway for the hunters. After a while they realized the sound came from branches cracking under the heavy load of fallen snow.

At the first house they saw, they knocked at the door and an old woman asked them to come in. They told her they were peddlers from Vilnius where hunger was dominant and were selling a few things in exchange for food. Leo ran over to the fireplace, pulled off his worn-out gloves to warm his frozen hands, but the pain was unbearable. The woman ran out and brought a bowl with snow and made him put his hands in it and rub them together. The peasants knew this would bring back the circulation. The pain slowly subsided. They stayed overnight, slept on the floor near the fireplace, were given some food and left the next day.

The wanderings on the road continued for about three to four weeks. They went from village to village and home to home. Nobody suspected they were Jews. There was a shortage of food in Vilnius, and city dwellers often went to the villages in order to barter small items for food. Along the way they sold a few things. During their wanderings they came to a village where a wedding was in progress. As strangers from the city they were invited to come in and join the party. By this time most of the peasants were drunk and singing. A harmonica was playing, and a few couples danced in the corner of the big room. The rest of the room was taken up by a long table loaded with food. In the early morning hours most of the guests were asleep with their heads on the table supported by their arms or sprawled out on the floor. Mother and Leo found a corner in the room with an old, heavy, home-woven blanket thrown on the floor. Tired and disregarding the noise, they fell asleep. The next day, after a plentiful breakfast, the guests started to leave in horse-drawn sleds with bells ringing, covered with fur – warm, happy and on their way to their own homes.

They stayed a few days longer, helping in the house and my brother doing some chores with the owner's two sons who were about his age. Some boys from the village came over to play and one of them looked at my brother and said, "You Jew, what are you doing here? You should be dead." The rest of the boys burst out laughing. The leader didn't give up easily and said. "Let's pull off his pants. I know he's a Jew."

My brother tried to act cool. "I'm not a Jew, but I think you are." He ran toward the house, hearing the boy shouting "Jew, Jew," until he closed the door behind him. He told mother what happened and they waited for a short while so as not to look suspicious and left. They walked and ran, not knowing what to expect. They saw some homes scattered around across a narrow frozen river. Taking a chance, they crossed it, not sure if the ice was solid. They knocked at a farmer's home and told the same story about being peddlers from Vilnius.

My brother looked out the window and from a distance noticed a group of uniformed men coming toward the house. Afraid that someone had denounced them, they ran out of the house and the men started chasing them. They came to a river, frozen at the sides and flowing in the middle. This was the end. They knew they couldn't make it across and would be swallowed by the icy current. They stopped, resigned, without hope, awaiting their execution.

About five or six men reached them, looked at my mother and asked her in Polish, "Why were you running away from us?"

Mother said, "We're Polish and thought you were Lithuanian police looking for black marketers. We're just poor people from the city looking for work and food."

The men wore army uniforms and were government employees. They said, "We were only following you because you were running away." They apologized and left.

My mother and brother decided to go back to the Vilnius ghetto. They took a different route, trying to avoid the previous villages. They walked through forests, fields, and one-horse roads to reach the ghetto. An escape from fire to flame.

MY LIFE SOLD FOR A LITER OF MILK

Mr. Klemantowiez told me about a wealthy farmer who came to the city every week exchanging or selling food to his liking. He knew about the farmer, Mr. Anton, from Mr. Waronki, the janitor in his building. Mr. Anton's farm was close to Podbrody, and he became a businessman exchanging or selling farm products for exorbitant prices in the city. A few weeks before, he had hauled away a piano received in exchange for a small piglet. When Mr. Anton came to town, he spent the night at Mr. Waronki's apartment. He shared with him his homemade whiskey that he never forgot to bring from the farm, and after a few drinks, Mr. Anton talked about his personal life, his successful business and his good luck of marrying a wealthy widow much his senior who had a huge dowry. He and his wife adopted a little seven-year-old girl who was very lonely. They were looking for a companion to spend time with her and help with schoolwork, as the adults were busy taking care of the large farm. This was the position that Mr. Klemantowiez had in mind for me. He introduced me to the farmer as his relative, and I would leave with the farmer the next morning to be his daughter's companion.

We arrived at a nicely furnished farmer's home. Mr. Anton was a pleasant older man, tall, heavy, with eyes like an owl and a smile with a mouth full of gold teeth. His wife, an older, heavy-set woman, didn't expect my arrival so soon, but was civil and made me feel welcome. The little girl, Fela, stood next to her. I was pleased with the new setup. The farmer's wife showed me the house and opened up a big armoire packed with beautiful treasures they accumulated for their daughter's future. Fela

101

was very sweet, and I spent a pleasant evening, looked at her schoolbooks and read her a few short stories. I also met Marta, an older girl (to me at the time) in her twenties who worked on the farm and helped around the house, but didn't have enough spare time to take care of Fela too. Marta had her own small room at the side of the house with a separate entrance.

The house was a few kilometers away from a village and a few farmers' homes were scattered around. The big armoire and an extended redbrick oven separated the neat living room from a long, narrow bedroom, with beds arranged in a row by the wall and covered with expensive damask coverlets. The man slept in one bed and the woman and little girl in the other.

Next to their beds stood a crib enclosed all around by wooden planks. This was assigned for me. I slept all curled up, couldn't stretch my limbs, but was happy to be there. I remember trying to stretch my legs on the frame, extended in the air. The food was very good and plentiful. In the morning we usually had a breakfast of buckwheat pancakes with sour cream or smoked bacon. All the meals were well prepared by the woman, with Marta's help. Pork meat was plentiful, bread and butter were served with every meal, and I could stuff myself to my liking.

I became friendly with Marta. She confided in me she was the farmer's daughter from a previous liaison, and her fat stepmother never accepted her. Marta wanted nothing to do with the adopted little girl. She had a nice-looking boyfriend from the village and planned to get married in the near future. Every morning a young schoolteacher from the next village would come to the farmer with a pitcher for fresh milk. Besides her, once in a while some neighbor would show up for a short visit. The teacher saw me in the morning sitting at the table and reading with the little girl. She never exchanged any words with me, but looked at me with certain contempt. I heard the farmer telling his wife to stop giving the teacher free milk. "If she wants milk, let her pay." The next time she left with an empty pitcher.

One early morning about three days later, Mr. Anton was getting ready to go to Vilnius on business. I suddenly felt the urge to go with him and started to dress quickly. I was restless and constantly going from one place to another, as though if I kept moving I'd have a chance to outrun death. Something was telling me to leave, pushing me to go away. Mr. Anton tried to talk me out of it, but I just couldn't change my decision.

It was an intuition. A higher power watched over me and made me act without hesitation, reason or purpose.

When we came to Vilnius, Mr. Anton, as usual, spent the night at the janitor's apartment. I told him I wouldn't be leaving with him the next day, but would stay with my parents and return with him the following week when he came to Vilnius again.

The atmosphere was heavy with danger in the city. The Germans were finding new methods of apprehending Polish people who didn't have the proper documentation, arresting them and transporting them to the Reich for slave or forced labor. If they caught a Jewish person, it was a death sentence. Rumors were circulating that young Polish girls were being kidnapped. They were used as prostitutes for the German soldiers, or for blood plasma for returning Germans from the Russian front. I even saw Germans standing in line outside a building that had been shut off on Subocz St. waiting to see prostitutes who had been forced into service.

Later in the day I went to see my high-school friend Nina and her mother, Anna, who had given me the documents to get my ID. They were two exceptional people who risked their lives by helping others. It was a rare occurrence during those stormy days. The next day I used my old method to get into the ghetto. My mother and brother weren't there. I later found out they were still wandering from village to village as Polish city people looking for work or selling small items in exchange for food. In the ghetto, I stayed with my father's youngest brother, Leon. My little cousin, Rosylin, about three years old, was constantly around me, clinging to me from the moment she saw me, following me, not letting me out of her sight. I tried to ignore her, not kiss her or feel her little arms around my neck. I was afraid to lose her and miss her for the rest of my life, if I survived.

A Russian acquaintance of my uncle's wanted to take Rosylin and adopt her, but my Aunt Mania couldn't part with her only child, and said that whatever happened she wouldn't give up her little girl. Unfortunately, my aunt's whole family was eventually discovered hiding in a cellar by Lithuanian collaborators with the Germans, and killed a few days before the Russian army re-entered Vilnius in 1944. My uncle was shipped out before the liquidation of the ghetto in September 1943 to a concentration camp in Estonia. After the liberation of the camp, he came back to Vilnius where he learned he was the only survivor left of a once-large family.

A week later, as agreed upon before, I met Mr. Anton and was ready to return with him to the country, when he told me the "news." A few hours after we had left for Vilnius, about six policemen had burst into the house to catch the Jewish girl they were keeping. His wife told them that a Polish friend's daughter from Vilnius was staying with them for a while and she had gone back home. She invited them all in. She put a few bottles of vodka and plenty of food on the table, and after a few drinks they became friendly and seemed to forget about their original mission. Once the vodka took effect, they told her that the teacher to whom they stopped supplying free milk had denounced them a few days before for hiding a Jewish girl. They would have come to the house sooner, but couldn't because they were waiting for the chief of police to return from a business trip to another village. Because of a few days delay, my life wasn't traded for a pitcher of milk.

Though he never said it, Mr. Anton must have known I was Jewish. In my haste and sudden decision to leave his farm, I had forgotten my gold bracelet, chain with a cross, and a gold ring with a ruby. He didn't return the gold cross with the chain and said he was giving it to his daughter to keep as a souvenir. He was honest enough to bring the other two items and leave them at Mr. Klemantowiez's apartment for me.

WALTZING WITH THE ENEMY

After the encounter with the honest farmer, Mr. Anton, I decided to stay at my Polish high-school friend Regina's house for a few days. There weren't many people on the street and a light rain was falling. Regina, a Polish girl, lived with her mother and younger sister close to the train station. Regina's father was the president of a worker's union during the Russian occupation and was arrested by the Germans as a leading Communist. His whereabouts were unknown. The family was left without any means and tried to make a living on the black market selling whiskey to German air force personnel in exchange for cigarettes and food. The air force base was walking distance from their home, and they often entertained Germans by having parties in the evening.

Walking to Regina's house, I sensed somebody following me, but I didn't want to turn around. I was already in the courtyard and quickened my step. When I got to the door, the person who was following me stepped ahead of me and flung it open. I turned my head and saw a German pilot from the nearby base. A party was already in full swing. I couldn't turn around and walk away as it might seem suspicious. It had become second nature for me to never act in any way that might draw the slightest bit of attention to myself.

"Please come in, *Fraulein*," he said and gently took my arm as if we were coming in together. Regina's mother looked surprised, embraced me and asked in Polish, "What's going on? Where did you find him?"

"At your door. I want to get rid of him," I whispered in her ear as we embraced.

She opened the half-closed door to the living room where five or six couples danced to loud music coming from a gramophone. It was a popular Polish song. It began, *mala kobietka czy wiesz, ze lusterko klami czytez*. "Little woman, do you know that your mirror also lies to you?" When the song stopped, Regina said, "Let's put on a waltz." She put another record on the gramophone, a Johann Strauss waltz. The German, smiling happily and without much ceremony, took my hand and directed me to the dance floor. We began to dance.

I was waltzing with the enemy. I saw my other Polish school friend, Janina, dancing with a handsome German officer and conversing in her perfect German. She greeted me with a nod and I heard her telling her partner that I was a good friend of hers. The German officer was eager to start some kind of conversation with me.

"*Fraulein, sprechen Sie Deutsch?*" he asked. Miss, do you speak German?

"*Nicht vestehn.*" I don't understand, I said in deliberately broken German, shaking my head. I couldn't wait for the dance to end. I liked the familiar melody and for one second imagined myself dancing at my birthday party with the brother of my best girlfriend, Misha.

The music stopped, I grabbed my forehead, put my head down feigning pain and turned toward the door. He stepped in my way, asking me to stay just a little longer. I pretended not to understand and left the room. Like a dog on a leash he was right behind me and in front of Regina's mother who explained to him in her broken German that I'd come back as soon as my bad headache was over. He hesitated. Looking a little sad, he touched my hair, and without another word left the room. In other circumstances, in a normal world, I would have been flattered by a handsome man paying attention to me, finding him very attractive. At seventeen, romance could have been part of my life and he could have been a friend or a lover.

Regina's mother told me to go to the bedroom, lock the door and she would knock three times when the party was over. I must have been exhausted and fell asleep immediately. My last thought before closing my eyes was a wish that the night would never end. The morning would bring a new day to struggle through and try to stay alive.

In my heart I questioned if the German air force pilot had known who I was would he have shot me on the spot, arrested me or maybe let me go? I know from Regina that he came over to their house a few times later, asking for the blond Fraulein, Hedwig (my name at the time) who disappeared from the scene, running for life and survival. He was one German, an enemy, most likely a member of the Nazi party and loyal to the so-called Fuhrer. Or perhaps he belonged to the minority – a soldier forced into battle, hating every minute of it and not willing to give his life for a cause he may have despised. I will never know.

THE FARMHAND

I didn't stay at Regina's as long as I would have liked to. They had parties too often with many Germans from the nearby base coming and going. I was worried about my mother and brother, as I hadn't seen them for quite a while. The next day, late in the afternoon, I managed to get into the ghetto, went straight to my uncle's apartment and there they were. They had just come back a few days ago after a long, dangerous wandering for weeks from one village to the next. I was happy to see them, but afraid to stay in the ghetto. My fear and rootless streak wouldn't confine me for long.

We were luckier than most, as we could still afford to buy food and pay our way if necessary. Without money I don't think we could have survived. We hadn't run out of jewelry, and my mother still had a few gold American twenty-dollar coins and some gold Russian rubles left.

In the couch at our home, underneath the cushions, was a small built-in box where we had kept some jewelry and gold coins. Before we left our house, my mother took out a few gold bracelets, a gold cigarette box, gold powder compact and some other jewelry that she stuffed into the inside pockets of her coat and mine.

My desire to keep moving intensified. I had to do something, find a way out of the quicksand pulling us in with its deadly power. One early morning I managed to get out of the ghetto and went straight across the green bridge to Mr. Leszczynski. He wasn't at home, but his son Stach, short for Stanislaw, told me his father would be back soon. He went out for some provisions and was getting ready to go to their estate in the country. Mr. Leszczynski was a good businessman with many connections.

Without any time constriction, he gave me the keys and told me I could stay at his apartment in the small, pleasant room where I had spent some time in the last few months. I did a little cooking and went out twice a week to buy milk from a farmer who came into town. I was bundled up in a big, blue shawl tied around from my head to the back of my waist and my navy wool coat from my school days, without the insignia.

One day, I went out carrying an enamel jug with a wire handle to buy milk from the farmer who was staying at the janitor's house across the street from Mr. Leszczynski's building. The janitor and his wife occupied a basement apartment, the interior neat and warm. A big built-in oven stood in the front room constructed of shiny brown tile. An old woman with a heavy black wrap covering most of her body was carrying a small can in a shaking, gloved hand. She came to buy milk and walked in behind me with her bare fingers like icicles sticking out of worn-out gloves.

The bench at the side of the oven was taken up entirely by a man in a heavy, unbuttoned fur coat, showing a peasant's garb, wearing shiny, tall leather boots, looking out of place in the small, overheated room. He became the big businessman bringing food stuff from Lithuania, exchanging and selling it for exorbitant profit. For a few seconds I stood by the oven feeling the heat penetrating my limbs. I paid for the milk and was ready to leave when I heard the farmer asking the janitress if she happened to know of somebody who was looking for farm work. His help was quitting and he badly needed a replacement. I turned so fast that a few drops of milk found their way onto my coat. Little pearls of hope.

"I'm looking for work," I said. "I can cook and do any work necessary on the farm."

At that moment I somehow believed I could handle any chore, do anything just to get away from the city where someone could recognize and denounce me. He asked me a few more questions about my family, was satisfied with my story. To assure himself that he found the right farmhand he asked, "Did you grow up on a farm?"

"Oh yes," I said, "in Czarny Bor," as I couldn't at the moment think of a nicer place in the country than where we spent the summers before the German invasion. This closed the deal.

He was so generous that he even promised to pay me several kilograms of grain every year. I agreed and was hired for the year as an experienced farmhand. There was plenty of talk on his part about milking cows, feeding pigs, cooking and general work. I agreed to everything. I didn't ask where the farm was. He mentioned a place in Lithuania that I had never heard of before in my life, but it sounded good. The farther away, the better. He was leaving later in the afternoon and I told him I could go with him.

When I came back, Mr. Leszczynski was home, and I told him about my encounter with the farmer and my new job. He didn't say much, just, "I hope you know what you're doing. It might be a good idea. You can always come back here."

I thanked him and left immediately to visit Jozefowa, our janitress. I told her about my new-found job and asked her to inform my mother whenever she next saw her so she wouldn't be worried about me. It was cloudy and dark. It looked as if the snow would come down any minute on the cursed earth.

I was back on time. The farmer was loading his sled. It was fully packed and I wondered where on earth I would sit. Would the horse be able to pull such a load? Somehow I managed to find a place in the back of the sled on a hard piece of furniture, which I later discovered was a beautiful baroque table he had exchanged for a kilogram of lard. We traveled through small towns, forests, narrow roads covered with snow. I was getting cold, hungry and scared. I tried not to think. I just wanted to go to the end of the earth and completely disappear. Miracles happened before. Why not now when I was in desperate need?

I must have fallen asleep. I heard somebody calling a name. For a split-second I forgot my present identity. Slowly I crawled out from under the table. Some lights twinkled in the windows of the houses strewn around. A small house with a dim light in the window was all I could see when we turned toward a short, snowed-in road and stopped in front of a low entrance. I could hardly stand on my feet, numb from the cold, and prolonged lying in one position. His wife, a woman with a hunchback, opened the door, and I found myself in a darkened room lit by a kerosene lamp, a stove at the side by an open door and a dirt floor. It wasn't much of an introduction.

"This is the new farmhand," he said, and disappeared into the other room. In the meantime his wife put a loaf of black bread and a bowl of milk on the table.

I was too tired to eat. All I wanted was to stretch out and go to sleep. I was directed to a bed where a girl was fast asleep and didn't move when I took my place next to her. The bed was warm and I fell asleep immediately, but something crawling over me woke me up. I grabbed it with my hand and it felt like a worm. I threw it on the floor. The night turned into a silent war with the huge bed bugs trying out the fresh blood that happened to be mine. It was dark when the girl almost pushed me out of bed, jumped out as if electrocuted and told me to follow her. She showed me how to light the oven and prepare breakfast. I watched her. It looked very simple. A few splinters of wood formed a triangle, then a match, and the fire started. Again some more wood. A pot with water and cereal was soon cooking on a metal three-footed stand.

In the meantime, like little terra cotta figures, people started emerging from the bedroom. A small boy, then two more, and at the end, a little girl, the parents following behind them. It looked like a happy family, all sleeping in the same room and now having breakfast together!

After breakfast the girl showed me how to break the ice that covered a water hole in the ground, lower the big pail, fill it up to the brim, and bring it up. I could hardly walk on the ice. It was slippery and the girl insisted the pail had to be full, not to waste time, so we could fill up the wooden barrel in the kitchen for daily use. I was afraid to slip and fall into the ice hole. When the girl wasn't watching I tried to distance myself from the hole, lying flat on my stomach and stretching my arm to pull out some ice-cold water. The girl noticed my new method, didn't raise her voice, and said, "What the hell are you doing here? You're lucky I'm leaving."

Everything went well as long as she was there. The pigs were fed. The cows milked. And the horses taken care of. A couple days later she left, and I had to take over. I tried, but nothing worked. The fire didn't start. By blowing the small flame to engulf the wood, the flame died. The farmer's wife helped me make breakfast, but the rest of the work was left to me. I was afraid to feed the pigs. They ran toward me and I turned around and ran out. The farmer's wife was a kind, sad and suffering woman. She could hardly walk. Her body was curled up and twisted. She tried to help me when her husband wasn't around. He was harsh and cruel toward her.

The third day during breakfast she said something in Lithuanian I didn't understand. He ran over to her, grabbed both her hands and pushed her against the wall, hitting her back and head. She didn't say a word and slowly walked out of the room. The children just sat like statues. Not a word was said. He slammed the door and left. I also noticed when the older boy started to say something when the farmer was

111

around, the mother gave him a look and a sign with her hand to shut his mouth. The atmosphere was heavy. Everyone was afraid of him. He looked at me with contempt, as he was very disappointed with his choice of the cheap worker who couldn't light a fire or milk the cows. I tried to milk. I pulled, pushed, squeezed. I talked to the cow. No milk came out of the heavy, thick udders. The only little creatures that didn't mind me were the chickens. All I did was feed them grain and they happily enjoyed the feast.

I understood that the farmer wouldn't keep me. I wasn't the girl who could do all the work expected of me. On the fourth day during breakfast he got furious at me; the cereal was overcooked and a little burned. He threw the enamel bowl with the cereal on the floor. It made the biggest mess and when I ran over to clean it up, he started to scream at me like a wild beast, "You Polish whore with a hole in your stomach. Today I'm taking you back to Vilnius." I was devastated and afraid he might kill me on the spot. A thought came back to me. If only he knew. I wouldn't be here today, as I was later told that he was a partisan who killed many Jewish people in the small town nearby called Gedroiczy.

About one hour later he had finished packing the sled with products he was taking to the market in Vilnius. He was ready to go. He ran in the house, "Come, you good-for-nothing Polish shit." I started to cry and begged him to let me stay, promising to be a much better worker in the future and told him how much I had improved in the last few days. He didn't want to hear it. His decision was final. I had to leave.

The whole time, his wife just stood there, not uttering a word. Then she came over and talked to him in a low voice. A few times I thought he was ready to jump out of his skin. I heard her say, "Let her stay till tomorrow."

"If I find Jadzka (diminutive of Jadwyga) here when I come back I'll kill her and teach you a lesson for interfering." I'm sure she knew what he meant. After he left, she told me to take my little bundle and we'd walk over to a large farm about three kilometers away that belonged to a couple with a daughter about my age who might need a maid. It was a sunny, frosty day. All around, a blinding white covered the fields with fresh, soft snow.

We came to a low house about a hundred feet from the road. We walked through a wide, short hall with a primitive door. On the right side of the hall, a door led to the kitchen where the Januszkewicz family happened to be. I was standing by the side of the entrance and the farmer's wife talked to them in a mixture of Polish and Lithuanian. Mr. Januszkewicz asked me, "Why did you come all the way here from Vilnius? Don't they have enough work there?"

"They have enough work, but they don't have enough food."

"What about your parents?" He asked.

"They're staying with some relatives in the country where they're having a very hard time getting by. They're glad to have one less mouth to feed. I'll be happy to work just for food and help you around the farm." Again a family conference and the daughter turned toward me and said, "What is your name?"

"My name is Jadwyga."

"You can stay with us," the farmer's wife and the lady of the house, Antonina, said. "We'll find work for you. My daughter, the Miss, will show you around."

Her name was Genia. I had to address her as *panienka*, "Miss." Even if I had to call her Your Highness, it would have been fine with me. She was about my age, a pretty, slim girl dressed in a brown school uniform. I followed her down the hill to the water well, let down a pail attached by an iron chain, filled up a pail of water, carried it to the kitchen and poured the water into a big round wooden barrel. A few more trips and the barrel was full.

My next chore was feeding the chickens that were kept in the room on the right side of the entrance hall across the kitchen. The smell there was terrible and, like the one in the kitchen, the floor was uneven and made out of dirt. In the corner of the room stood a tall, narrow metal oven of a type that I had never seen in the city, where potatoes for the animals were cooked. Miss Genia handed me a big wooden stick with four blades attached at the end to mash the already-boiled potatoes that were then put into a wooden barrel next to the oven. It was hard work and she helped me finish the huge pile. Then she told me to go to the horse stable with her, and gave me a pail to fill up with horse dung. Next, I had to bring the pail to the chicken coop, pour boiling water over the dung, add some of the mashed potatoes, and mix it all up as feed for the pigs. This magic formula was supposed to help speed the pigs' growth. Before being taken to the market, the formula was changed and they were fed grain to fatten them up.

It was getting closer to evening. I was hungry and wondering where I was going to sleep the night. I didn't see any bed in the kitchen. A wall divided the kitchen halfway and an old wooden chest stood by the wall with some old, scattered clothes. Opposite, an oven as may be found in a bakery took up almost half the narrow space. The kitchen had two small, low windows facing north, and one facing east. A long, wooden table with a bench in front took up the whole width of the kitchen. One nice, comfortable chair caught my eye and next to it, a short, red, painted bench that didn't seem to belong in the cold, neglected kitchen.

Antonina told me I would sleep on the wooden chest behind the wall. In the meantime, Genia was getting ready to prepare supper and asked me to watch her so I could learn how to do it in the future. It was simpler than I thought. Mix semi-dark flour with water to form cereal-like crumbs, boil the water, add the cereal, then whiten it with milk and add a little salt. The hot soup was filling. At the end of the day, I was exhausted and fell asleep immediately on the chest behind the kitchen wall in my clothes.

The cold woke me up. I was shaking. The windows were frozen and the wind blew in snow through the loose, old wooden frame. It was still dark. I tried to fall asleep again. I was afraid I'd get sick and die in a strange place.

Somebody called, "Jadzka, it's time to get up and feed the pigs." I covered my head with my old wool scarf. I already had my navy blue coat on. I slept with it and hardly ever took it off during the cold winter days, as there were only a few rags to use as a blanket on the chest where I slept. I was wearing my old high leather boots that were falling apart and had seen better days.

It was a very cold morning. I filled up two pails with pig food that I'd prepared the evening before, added some hot water and was going down the hill to the shed when I slipped and the whole warm, dirty mixture spilled all over me. Very little of the pig food was saved at the bottom of the pail. As fast as I could, I ran to the pig shed, smelly and wet, cleaned myself up as much as I possibly could with some dry straw and gave the pigs whatever leftover food there was. The pigs were still hungry and soon squealing for more food. Mr. Januszkewicz bolted into the kitchen and asked me why I didn't feed the pigs, as they knew when their feeding time was supposed to be. I was afraid to tell him what happened and just said, "I don't know. I forgot."

About noon Antonina showed up in the kitchen and was served by her daughter who, after putting the food on the table, rushed out like a hurricane and slammed the door behind her. I didn't understand what happened, but very soon found out that it was an unhappy, dysfunctional family. Everybody for himself and no love lost between them.

Antonina was a very attractive woman. Dark, shoulder-length hair, blue eyes, light skin with dark, well-shaped eyebrows and long lashes. The daughter, Genia, was taller than her mother and didn't resemble her at all. She looked more like her father who was over six feet tall, a real peasant-turned-landlord, with reddish skin and large, hard features. He shaved his head. People were afraid of him. Later, though, he turned out to be a good human being.

There was a constant war between the three of them. It helped me in a way. He screamed at me if I didn't do my chores his way, but Antonina's contradicting him protected me. She called him, "You stupid ox. She's not your maid. She works for me." I stood there listening to what was going on with my mouth shut.

"Go help the woman milk the cows," he barked. There were about thirty cows in a huge stable. Four women were already milking. One of them showed me which cow had to be milked next and gave me a big pail to put under the cow's udders. This I did. But with my milking, there was no success. A young peasant woman noticed and showed me another young cow with smaller udders, and said it should be much easier for me to milk. A thin stream of milk hit the empty pail. I surprised myself. But then I heard a voice behind me.

I turned around and there stood Mr. Januszkewicz screaming at me, "What the hell are you doing? Playing around? Get out of here."

I ran back to the kitchen. Antonina was there sitting in the comfortable chair and I saw a few dirty dishes left on the table. I wanted to wash them and put them away, but she said, "No, this is the Miss's job. Come sit down on the small bench." I did as she said, expecting the worst, to be dismissed and sent away.

"Go catch a young rooster," she said. "The knife is in the drawer, and make me a good lunch." She got up and showed me where the cutlery was kept that was for her use only. It took quite a bit of skill to catch the poor rooster, but this was just the beginning of my experience as a slaughterer. I held the poor, scrawny bird with one hand and with the other, tried to reach the throat, as it was constantly flapping its wings and wanting to escape. I cut in a little. The rooster started bleeding. I got scared and the rooster escaped from my hands. I ran into the kitchen crying hysterically. Somebody caught the half-dead rooster, cleaned it up and I had the

115

honor of cooking it. I asked the Mrs. how she'd like it cooked, as I could prepare it in many different ways. In reality, I had no idea how to cook it. Together we cooked, she instructing me and I doing the work. It was a success. She was very pleased and didn't share the food with either her husband or daughter. She told me to save the leftovers for her for later.

The kitchen was separated from the main house by about a hundred feet. It was a beautiful, big building where the family slept, each in their own bedroom. A big apple-and-pear orchard surrounded the house and a pagoda stood amidst the trees. I changed Antonina's bed linen and was told that from now on it was my duty. Their daughter would take care of her own and her father's bedroom. I didn't have to milk the cows anymore. And Mr. Januszkewicz told me to go to the barn and watch the women milking the cows so that they wouldn't steal any milk for their own use, but pour it all into huge metal containers that stood by the door. The women then deposited the containers in a cellar about three feet underground, close to the barn. My job was to lock it up after them. The next day the milk was picked up by a driver from the co-op.

Early every morning I went to the cellar with a ladle and a half-liter sized container to skim off the cream that had accumulated on the milk during the night. Sweet cream and a couple of raw, fresh eggs were Antonina's daily late breakfast. Alone in the cellar I enjoyed the sweet cream to my liking. I also ate raw eggs whenever I had the opportunity.

As Antonina's personal maid, I had to wash her laundry. Then she would send me to prepare the iron. I had to go to the well to rinse the iron, then to the barn to take some straw and yellow sand and rub it inside and out. Then I had to rinse it again by putting it into a tin pail and lowering it into the well. It didn't make any sense to me, but I did all this without question or comment.

A few days later she told me to accompany her for a walk. The snow was starting to melt. It was a nice, cool day. A woman walking on the road saw us, came over, stood by the trees and talked with Antonina for a while. The moment the woman left, Antonina said to me in a very soft, pleasant voice, "Dear Jadwyga, go bring a pail of water and the big drinking cup. I will wait here."

It was quite a walk to the water well and I came back carrying a full pail of water. She said, "My dear child. Fill the cup up with water and rinse the trees. The woman could be sick and she touched it with her hand." I went back and forth at least five or six times and poured cups of water on the trunks of the old trees. A lot of the things she asked me to do seemed crazy, but who was I to question my benefactor?

Back in the kitchen I helped Genia clean up the oven, bring in flour from the next building, sweep the floor and scrub the kitchen table. Once every two weeks we had to go out in the fields, gather clean snow, melt it in enamel pots on the stove, heat it and fill up the wooden bathtub for Antonina to take a bath.

Genia was furious at her mother as we had to go to the far-off fields time and time again. She screamed at her mother, "You're crazy. A mother like this should be burned alive." All she would answer was, "My child, it isn't nice to talk like this to your mother." And the daughter would add, "The devil take you. All you care about is yourself."

Something was really wrong with all of them. Antonina was selfish, conceited, always talking in a moderate voice with the expression on her face unchanged, telling her husband what a brute he was, calling him a drunkard and stupid peasant. When he raised his voice she ran outside to the kitchen window, walked back and forth and poured out insults at him loud enough for all to hear. He looked at her and called her, "You rotten good-for-nothing."

In the meantime, I learned how to prepare and make cottage cheese. I warmed up soured milk on the stove, then poured it into linen bags, tied them with strings and hung them up to deep dry on nails in the wall behind the kitchen. The whole place was swarming with flies. Many times I woke up in the morning finding a dead fly in my mouth. After a while the flies didn't bother me much, but the lice drove me crazy. I learned to live with them and their eggs – the future generation of lice.

I had no way of washing myself. I lived and slept in the same clothes. Mrs. Antonina trusted me with the small key where she kept sugar just for her own use. At night when all of them left the kitchen, I shut off the lantern and started my nightly feast. I untied one bag of cheese after another taking a little from each so it wouldn't be noticeable. I put it in a cup, unlocked the box with the sugar and poured handfuls into the cheese. I mixed it up and ate as much as I could hold. I'm sure at the same time I consumed a lot of flies, as the kitchen was swarming with them and they were attracted to the white cheese. In the back of my mind, I thought if I was going to be killed at least it wouldn't be on an empty stomach. The fear of hunger at the time overshadowed even the fear of death. Anything edible was my pacifier. It calmed my fear of being killed hungry.

While at the farm, I was living in constant fear and worry about my mother and brother. A feeling of guilt afflicted me for leaving them alone. I never had enough sleep, as Antonina used to sit in the kitchen for hours on end, telling me stories from World War I, how beautiful she was and how many admirers she had back then.

Mr. Januszkewicz saw it. He didn't like that she kept me for long hours at night as I had to get up early in the morning. He cursed at her. "You will burn in hell for not letting the help go to sleep."

I was called Crazy Jadzka and Mr. Januszkewicz said, "Even the sun cries looking at you." I had acquired yet another name. They called me crazy because out of frustration and anxiety, I talked about nonsense and sometimes laughed without reason. I helped myself to food whenever I could, sometimes stuffing myself too much, but other days living mostly on what I could salvage for myself. I never knew what the next day would bring.

One late evening, I went to sleep as usual on the wooden chest, behind the wall oven that was never lit, covering myself with old rags, sleeping in my clothes full of lice. Mr. Januszkewicz would often ride off to town in the evening and show up in the kitchen at different times early in the morning. One night, exhausted after a long day, a noise woke me up. Mr. Januszkewicz was in the kitchen. I was surprised, as he'd never come to the kitchen before at night. He went behind the wall where I was sleeping. Smelling of alcohol, he fell on me.

I pretended not to know his intentions. I started laughing and screaming at the same time saying, "Sir, please get off me. Go away." I pushed him away with all my strength.

"The cholera take you, you poor idiot," he said, slammed the door and left. The next morning he was himself again, as if nothing had taken place the night before. It never happened again. I had heard rumors that he fathered the child of a former servant, who quit after many years of service, and went to live with her family in a close-by village.

It was early spring. Snow lay around in patches exposing the black earth underneath. It was cold and wet and rained constantly. I was walking barefoot with my feet ice cold and swollen. My old boots had fallen apart and I had no way of replacing them. One early morning Mr. and

Mrs. Januszkewicz decided to go to Ukmerge, where the German authority had their headquarters. In conversation with them I once mentioned that I possessed some knowledge of German from high school. They asked me to come with them and try to persuade the Germans to cut down the amount of grain they had to deliver to them. They wanted me to also include that they were patriots and their ancestors were originally from Germany.

For this occasion, Genia lent me a pair of shoes that were much too small for my swollen feet. I could hardly push my feet in and walked liked a geisha. We arrived at the German office and Mr. and Mrs. Januszkewicz pushed me ahead of them to talk to the officer. I only uttered a few words in German using a heavy Polish accent. I was afraid of causing the smallest suspicion. The German in charge looked at my swollen feet and started asking me some questions.

"Where did you learn German?"

"*Wenig, wenig, nicht gut, Deutsche soldat gut Freund.*" Little, little, not good, German soldier good friend.

My deliberately poor German worked. He turned away and didn't pay any more attention to us. My being there hadn't accomplished anything, but Mr. and Mrs. Januszkewicz thought that the few German words I uttered would further their cause. The whole time we were there, I was terrified that my badly fitting shoes would be cause for suspicion, as the Lithuanians lived quite comfortably and could always exchange some food with a city dweller for shoes, clothes or even a piano.

After returning to the farm, Mr. Januszkewicz said that he was getting ready to go to Vilnius on some business. I told him, "I have to go back to buy some shoes and see my family."

It was late in the afternoon when we arrived in the city. Mr. Januszkewicz stopped for the night at the house of some people he knew and I ran barefoot to Mr. Klemantowiez to inquire about my mother. The janitor told me Klemantowiez had moved in with his aunt on Wielka Pogulanka St. and gave me the address. Again, I ran in the semi-darkness hopping like a little girl on the edge of the sidewalk. I was afraid of being noticed, as nobody walked barefoot in the chilly weather. I was lucky.

I rang the bell at the right door just a few minutes before the entrance gates were locked for the night. Mr. Klemantowiez opened the door and there were my mother and brother. We just looked at each other and burst into hysterical tears, happy to be alive and coming together even for the shortest time. Mother told me she came in the morning after an "action," a deportation or killing of people rounded up in the ghetto. We stayed there overnight.

The next morning we returned to the ghetto separately. It is hard to describe the mood and depression of the people who were temporarily left alive until the next massacre. Most people in the ghetto, unlike my mother or me, didn't have any chance of survival outside, especially if they didn't have any Polish acquaintances willing to help them. Even if they had, there was a very slight chance for survival.

Mother went with me to a building in the heart of the ghetto on Rudnicka St. We climbed the stairs and came to a long apartment that looked like a poor, overcrowded clinic with mattresses on the floor that formed a narrow passage we could hardly cross. People like shadows without life or future stood around or sat on the bedding. It was horrible to see what had been done to them in such a short span of time.

Mother bought me a brown coat and a pair of shoes from a woman she knew before the ghetto and I was no longer barefoot. Late in the afternoon I said goodbye to my mother and brother. We embraced with no tears, no kisses, trying not to add to our sadness of parting. I was on my way to the house where Mr. Januszkewicz was staying. As I was walking toward the green bridge, I noticed a Lithuanian policeman randomly stopping some people and checking ID papers. It was too late for me to turn back, as I would immediately arouse suspicion and probably be arrested. I continued walking across the bridge, hoping I wouldn't be stopped. At the far end of the bridge two policemen stood at both sides and this time my luck ran out. I tried to act very calm, pretending to take it all in stride.

"Where do you live?" A tall, uniformed Lithuanian policeman asked me.

"On the farm in Dusinienty," I answered, smiling.

"Show me your passport," he said. Without hesitation and in a normal and relaxed manner, I handed him my passport.

"How long are you staying in the city?" He asked, looking straight into my eyes.

"Just a few days."

Still observing me, he said, "Come with me." It sounded like a death sentence. But I said, "Sure, gladly," without showing any sign of fear or hesitation. After a few very scary seconds, he said, "You can go," and gave me back the passport. I walked away, my heart pounding, aware that if they had checked my passport they would easily find out that the person whose ID I was carrying had died.

I returned to Becoupe with new shoes and coat, but the fear never left me for a second. Not long after my return, I happened to be in the kitchen when Antonina, looking very nervous, came over to me and said, "The Polish woman from Vilnius who came in this morning to buy some food told one of the farm workers (who lived in a little house, semi-attached to the back of the kitchen) that a Jewish girl is hiding at the farm."

Mr. Januszkewicz came in, heard about this and asked me if it was true. I categorically denied it, but knew I had to run away from the farm. It wasn't an easy escape, as the way to Vilnius was long and I had to go through the small town Gedroiczy. If word had spread around, the police might already be looking for me. They'd arrest me, which would mean certain death.

I grabbed my talisman, the little bundle with my father's shawl that I always carried with me, and told them, "I'm going home. I don't want any problems for me or for you."

About halfway to the main road, Antonina caught up with me and said, "Tell me Jadzka, is it true? Are you Jewish?"

"No." I said. Even under torture, I would have never admitted the truth. It would have meant giving up hope.

"If you are Jewish we'll help you. Just tell me the truth and come back with me to the kitchen." Not seeing much of a way out, figuring I would probably be apprehended on the road and killed anyway, I told her, "Yes, I'm Jewish."

"Come with me and we'll help you."

I could hardly believe my ears. She sent her daughter for a farmhand to ready the horse and carriage, and took me to the nearby police station in Gedroiczy to sign me up as her cousin's daughter. In no time I became a legitimate resident under the name of my ID, Jadwyga Pinkovskaite. I changed the 'SZ' spelling on the Polish version of my last name to 'P' for the Lithuanian version. On my newest false identity, I was now Lithuanian. It was better than being Polish, as the Lithuanians were well known for cooperating with the Germans and had more privileges than the Polish. There was no more mention of a Jewish girl hiding at the Januszkewicz farm.

One day a young woman with a teenage daughter showed up. On her latest visit to Vilnius, Antonina had hired her as a cook. I was glad to be relieved of trying to prepare the usual meal and happy to see my replacement in the kitchen. The new cook tried to prepare some dishes for the family, but her cooking wasn't satisfactory and she didn't last more than a week. Mr. Januszkewicz had to arrange with one of his farmhands to transport her back to the city. I decided to join them and check on my mother and brother.

GRADUAL LIQUIDATION OF THE GHETTO

It was late in the afternoon when I came to the city with the farmhand where we deposited the cook and her daughter. He was ready to return to Becoupe. I told him I was staying with my parents for a few days and to tell Mr. Januszkewicz I'd be back soon.

I wanted to join a work group returning to the ghetto, but it was too late. I went to Mr. Leszczynski's house. A neighbor whom I'd met before thought I was a relative, told me the family had left for their country estate and gave me the keys to their house. I stayed there overnight, and early the next morning, I went to see my mother and brother at work at the same location where we had all worked together before. When the German guard wasn't watching, I walked by casually as though I were Polish, looking to sell or buy something from the Jewish workers. My mother noticed me and I quickly told her I just came from the farm and would be staying a couple of days.

"Be very careful," she whispered. "I heard rumors that the ghetto is going to be liquidated any day now." We couldn't talk any longer, as the German was calling the people to work at a different railroad track.

"I'll see you tomorrow," I said, and left.

Before noon on the following day, I went to see my mother and brother. They weren't at their usual place at the railroad, but a friend, Mrs. Sheine, told me they had been sent to do some work in a different location and would be back soon. I was afraid to stay and wait for them and instead wrote a short note to my mother: "Dear Mother, tomorrow I am going away and I don't know when I will see you again. R." I gave it to Mrs. Sheine and left. After I walked away about half a block, I realized the note I wrote didn't make any sense considering I didn't plan on going anywhere and was going to return and see them the next day. I hastily returned to take the note back from Mrs. Sheine, but she was gone. The place seemed deserted.

The German patrols with Lithuanian collaborators were closing up parts of city blocks at different times and locations. Documents were checked. The smallest suspicion, even the slightest expression of fear, put the document holder in danger of being arrested, interrogated and, if a Jew, then killed.

I almost fell into their bloody hands on my way back to the Leszc-zynski residence. I noticed a few uniformed Germans following a man in civilian dress. They walked quickly past me and suddenly more police-men came out of nowhere and encircled a bunch of civilians, trapping them in the middle. By sheer luck, I managed to evade the trap by a few steps. It is possible my behavior and false documents wouldn't have aroused suspicion, but no one ever knew. At the time, some young men and women tried to flee the ghetto through the sewers to the Aryan side and, if lucky in their escape, then joined the partisans in the forest. They knew their days were numbered. Many were caught, immediately taken to Ponary or prison and killed.

Early the next day I went over to the place where my mother and brother had been working, but there were no Jewish people there. Instead, some small groups of Polish men and women were standing around and gesturing toward the direction of where the Jews had been working. I stood in the back of the crowd listening to their chatter. That morning when the Jewish people came from the ghetto to work, they were en-circled by Lithuanian and German soldiers, forced into big closed trucks, and taken to Ponary, the killing ground.

I noticed a tall Polish woman walking next to a Lithuanian police-man pointing out someone hiding under an open terrace. I recognized Mrs. Sheine. The poor soul had tried to escape the murderers. I walked away, semi-conscious, my head on fire and believing I had lost my moth-er and brother. I had nobody left in the world. My life and hope were slipping away. It was late summer 1943, and the remaining ghetto popu-lation was being swept away with a fiery broom of death to immediate liquidation or concentration camps.

I went back to Mr. Leszczynski's house. Desperate and helpless, I cried myself to sleep. My will to survive was diminishing with every day and sleepless night. I did not leave the room for days. I had no reason to go out. My whole world had collapsed around me.

I don't know how long I lay there semi-conscious. I heard a door open and close and felt someone touching me and telling me to wake up. Mrs. Leszczynski and her daughter, Marila, told me later they thought I had fainted or committed suicide. With a broken heart and spirit I told them what happened. They were moved by my misfortune and tried to give me some hope and courage.

"The war is going badly for the Germans," they said. "Your family might survive wherever they are and you could soon be reunited."

It gave me a glimmer of hope. With encouragement from my dear friends, I decided to go out and look for my mother and brother.

First I went to my friend Viera. She told me they came to their house, stayed a few days and left. Then I went to another Polish acquaintance, Zawucki. He hadn't seen them. They weren't at the couple's home who had sheltered them once before either, or my friend Nina's home, where they'd spent a night but were afraid to stay longer because of her Nazi husband.

It was getting late. Curfew was at 7:00 PM. I had to hurry on, one more place to look: Jozefowa, the janitress. If they weren't there, I had lost them. I was at the end of the line.

With a shaking hand I knocked at the door. It was my last try.

"Oh thank God, she's alive," Jozefowa opened the door and grabbed me in her arms as if she'd seen a ghost and was trying to assure herself I was real. There were my mother and brother, crying, talking, telling me of their dilemma and their fear that I had been caught and killed since I hadn't shown up for so many days.

My mother took out the little note that I'd left with Mrs. Sheine. I read it over and over again and couldn't believe my eyes. What I'd written didn't make any sense. It was my own handwriting, but dictated by some higher power. My mother had understood the note to be a warning that I knew something bad was going to happen the next day.

After finishing work they put their shovels in the shack and hid behind it, waiting until the rest of the people, accompanied by the German guards, left. Each walked on the opposite side of the street, close to the building, Mother pretending to gather grass into her apron to feed the rabbits, which was very common at the time. Nobody paid any attention to my little brother with his hat pulled down over his face, or my mother, who looked like an average sunburned working woman. They slipped away and went to the safety of Jozefowa's house, but they couldn't stay there permanently.

Having survived so far was a combination of luck, coincidence and fate. On a cloudy Saturday I was on my way to Becoupe to try and find a place where my mother and brother could stay. By then I could travel the road with my eyes closed. A farmer giving a Lithuanian policeman a ride brought me halfway there. The Lithuanian invited the farmer and me into his house to have something to drink. Soon the farmer was leaving and I tried to follow, but the policeman stood in my way and wouldn't let me out. He pulled me back into the room. He tried to push me on the sofa, jumped on top of me, and wanted to rape me. I started to scream and cry, cross myself repeatedly and pray loudly to the Holy Mother and Jesus Christ to save me. Somehow by good luck he let go of me and I ran out of the house.

I started walking in the direction of the farm. It was getting dark and I was afraid to walk on the highway. I was also terrified of walking through the fields and forests at night. If a police patrol car noticed a girl walking alone on the highway, it would be cause for suspicion and the police would probably stop and question her. So I walked for a little while along a narrow dirt road parallel to the highway. I passed a small village and turned in the direction of the Januszkewicz farm. Along the way, I stepped into a puddle of water and my only pair of shoes became soaking wet. I took them off and continued walking barefoot. I saw a light in a house and to make sure I was going the right way, I knocked on the door and asked where Becoupe was. I followed the directions, went over a wooden bridge and, after walking through fields and a small forest in the dark, I reached the Januszkewicz's house.

The dog didn't bark when I came into the yard. I tried the kitchen door, but it was locked for the night. I went to the building where the family slept and knocked on the window. Mr. Januszkewicz opened the window and told me where to find the kitchen key.

My Mother and Brother at the Farm in Becoupe

The next morning, Mr. Januszkewicz told me the news he'd heard the night before at his drinking companion's place. The war was nearing an end. The Germans were retreating from the Eastern Front, but at the command of Hitler, had to fight until the end. It was music to my ears, but right then the present was burning under my feet. I put both my plate and my hope on the table.

"Please help me bring my mother and brother to your place. We'll be forever thankful to you, and I promise we'll do anything we can to repay you for your generosity and help."

I also promised him an apartment of his choice in our building in Vilnius on Subocz St. He knew the building, as he had some friends living there and was very impressed with the offer. The decision was not taken lightly by them. Not a word was mentioned the whole day. It's hard to describe the anguish and hope playing games in my tired and desperate mind.

On a dark, rainy Sunday morning, the good news came like a gift from heaven. In the presence of his wife and daughter, Mr. Januszkewicz told me that my mother and brother could come and work as hired help on the farm. A few hours later, I was on my way to Vilnius, first walking, then getting a ride, and reached the city late in the afternoon.

My mother and brother were not at Jozefowa's. She said that the evening before, a policeman had come to her apartment looking for Jewish people because someone in the building had denounced her. My mother bribed the policeman with a few gold coins begging him not to arrest them. As he was leaving he said, "Get out of here. Don't stay here any longer. If I come back without arresting you both, the sergeant might send someone else. Not everyone is like me." As a rule, once you fell in the hands of a Lithuanian policeman, you were as good as dead.

I remember Mrs. Antosia, the woman who sent me to work on her husband's farm, telling me about a Jewish woman who gave all the money and jewelry she possessed to a Lithuanian policeman who promised to let her go free. Instead, he killed her. His wife complained and accused the dead woman of not letting him sleep peacefully since then. Jozefowa told me that after the policeman left, my mother and brother went straight to my friend Viera, whose husband, Jacek, was the Lithuanian policeman. I found my mother and brother at Viera's. The news I was bringing them from Lithuania was encouraging. If we could manage to survive a little longer, we might make it.

On a lucky Thursday my mother and brother left Vilnius and according to our plan, walked on the highway toward Gedroiczy on their way to Mr. Januszkewicz's farm. I told them to look out for a brown and white horse with two people sitting in a nice carriage, the mark of a wealthy farm owner. A carriage drove past them. In the front seat, holding the reins, was a worker who lived and worked with his family on their farm. In the back seat were Mr. and Mrs. Januszkewicz themselves.

Mother gestured for the carriage to stop, but the driver continued without paying attention to the woman and child who looked like poor city folk. My mother and brother were in terrible danger of not having any place to go. It struck them like a death verdict, as the possibility of survival was almost nil. The documents they had were primitive, handwritten, forged birth certificates from a church. They didn't have the recent, valid passports given by the authorities to the general Christian population. After about two or three hundred meters, the carriage stopped and the woman waved her hand for them to come.

Mr. Januszkewicz asked them where they were going and wanted to see their IDs. They showed him the fake papers and said they were going to Savelis, a village where there was a market every Thursday. He told them to jump into the wagon, as he was going their way. Mother said she was a widow; the Russians had killed her husband, and it was hard to get food in the city. The plan worked out to the last step. It was important for Mr. and Mrs. Januszkewicz to have a witness for the meeting in case there might be any suspicion later that the new farmhands were Jewish. They needed to pretend my mother and brother were just strangers they'd met on the road. The Lithuanians and Germans applied the greatest punishment to anyone found helping or harboring Jews, and sometimes killed both them and the Jews.

When my mother and brother arrived in Becoupe, Mr. Januszkewicz suggested they could help around the house and then go to the market on Thursday. They accepted the offer. They stayed another week, then Olek (my brother Leo's Polish name according to the false documents), who was twelve years old, was put to work with three other adult workers who lived on the farm with their families. They were sent to the forest to cut wood for the winter.

It was very hard work for my mother and brother. The days were long and food was very scarce. Luckily when the Januszkewicz family left at night for their big, comfortable residence, in the darkness my mother would fry some eggs that she had hidden during the day in the chicken coop. She had saved some leftover bread from the family's evening meal and cooked the eggs on the still-hot coal left in the kitchen. This was their great feast and meal of the day.

During this time, I was going back and forth to Vilnius. I had been the lady's maid on the farm, but now that my mother and brother were there, it was too dangerous for the three of us to be together. I left them and went back to Vilnius. I stayed with my Polish friend, Marysia, whom I had met at Nina's. After a week I returned to Becoupe. I was concerned about my mother. She looked tired and very thin. She was working from dawn to dusk. We didn't talk much. We kept our emotions to ourselves. My heart ached to have to leave them again, but I figured it would be best in the long run not to stay together.

After spending a few days with my mother and brother on the farm, one morning a German soldier driving a truck stopped there on his way to the city. I took the opportunity, gestured for him to give me a lift, and asked him in Polish for a ride to Vilnius.

Januszkewicz's daughter saw me getting into the truck and started screaming, "Where the hell are you going? Come back. It's time to feed the pigs."

I said, "To Vilnius. Please tell my mother and your parents I'll be back soon." The German was in a hurry to be on his way and it all happened so suddenly, I didn't have time to tell my mother I was leaving and would be back as soon as possible. I never imagined it would be years before I saw her again.

I went to my friend Viera's house, disregarding the sentry who knew me and stood at the entrance to the courtyard. A young woman I had met once before by the name of Helen was visiting. Viera's mother was busy preparing a big party for her husband and his Lithuanian policeman friends. They didn't tell me directly, but I knew I couldn't stay there. Helen knew my predicament and said I could spend the night at her place. We went to her small, neat apartment on Wielka Stefanska St. After a short conversation, she said she'd be leaving and would come back the next morning, adding that I could help myself to the food in the pantry. I spent a sleepless night, as I didn't know her well and thought that the door might open any minute and death would come next. The abundance in her kitchen of delicacies I hadn't seen for ages surprised me. She came back the next morning, asked how I slept and if I'd had breakfast.

I said, "I was waiting for you," and thanked her for letting me stay overnight. "I want to talk to you," she said. I wasn't inquisitive, thinking it was just a way of being told by one more person that I had to keep moving.

"I didn't know you or your family," said Helen, "but from what Viera told me, I want to help you in any way I can." I didn't make any comment, curious as to what would come next. "I spent the night at my boyfriend's place," she said. "He's an Austrian from Wiener Neustadt and works at the Arbeitsamt. It's an employment agency where people are either recruited by force or volunteer to work for the German ammunition factories or wherever they are sent."

I knew that young, unemployed Poles were occasionally apprehended on the street, but to go to work in Germany or Austria was news to me. Helen gave me the Arbeitsamt address. She told me about the bad situation in Vilnius that was getting worse by the day with Germans and Lithuanians patrolling the streets and checking IDs. She also said that some of the young Polish girls found without IDs or working papers were arrested and forced to work as prostitutes for the German soldiers. The ones who contracted venereal disease were killed. She knew this from a reliable source.

ON THE TRAIN FROM VILNIUS TO VIENNA

Helen suggested I spend the weekend with her. She told me to wait there until Monday, when her boyfriend would be back at work. I followed her advice and went to see him at the Arbeitsamt, employment office, where I signed up as a volunteer to work for Germany. I told him I wanted to go to Vienna to join my sister who had been working there for the last two years. Helen suggested I ask to go to Vienna, as it was a safe place and hadn't been bombed by the Allies. Her boyfriend checked my ID, gave me some traveling papers and told me the transport was leaving the next day from the train station, and I'd be on the list. No questions asked. I thanked him. During our short conversation in German, I had made sure to sound like I had a Polish accent. It was a big relief to leave the premises.

The next day I walked to the station accompanied by Helen, who was holding my small suitcase and made it just a few minutes before the train started moving at 9:00 AM. Afraid to be recognized by my travel companions and denounced, I took a seat as far away as I could from a Polish woman about my age who was crying hysterically. She had been forced on the train and wanted to get off and go home.

Once the train started moving, I saw German soldiers at the exits locking the doors. I sat very calmly. What was happening around me seemed unreal. I knew I was leaving my beloved city where I had spent the best and worst days of my life. Slowly the city disappeared from the horizon. I felt relieved and sad at the same time. I was moving to a new destination where nobody knew me. I felt sorry that I never asked Helen for her family name, so if I survived I could look her up and thank her.

* * *

The first stop on the way was Bialystok. We were transported to a big building that may have once been a school. Our group consisted of about fifteen to twenty mostly young people. A Polish-speaking cook with a white apron around his full belly served food in a huge cafeteria. I noticed him being extremely friendly toward me. We were staying there overnight and commencing our travel the next day. Unexpectedly, the smiling, overweight Buddha came over and tried to persuade me to stay in Bialystok, and after a few preliminary sentences told me he would take the best care of me. This was the last thing on my mind. He confided in me that the war would soon be over and our beloved Poland, once free again, would need all of our people.

"My sister in Vienna is waiting for me. I have to continue my trip," I told him. "But I hope to be back when Mother Poland will gather us all in her holy arms," I said, speaking in the same kind of formal patriotic language the Poles used. It appealed to him that here was another Polish patriot, and he told me he regretted I couldn't stay.

It was in the afternoon when the train stopped in Vienna. Standing on the platform with my suitcase in hand and not knowing what to do or where to go, I found a woman at the counter in the train station and told her I was a volunteer worker. She gave me the address and directions to the camp for foreign workers. I came to a very tall building where I found myself in a big office with a man sitting behind the desk. After looking at my Lithuanian passport he told me that it would be better to sign in as a Lithuanian than as a Pole, but I had to pay him something. I didn't have any money, I told him, but I'd give him a scarf that came with the coat my mother bought for me.

He sent me to a camp where many foreigners from all over Europe were housed until they were sent to different branches of industry as blue-collar workers. There wasn't any intermingling between us and the Austrians. We were the workers and they, the masters.

One day I was called to the office and an Austrian man, wearing a national costume that looked strange to me at the time, took me and two other foreigners to a factory. All we had to do was follow him. It was a long ride on the tram, the Strassenbahn. A woman dressed in a dark uniform was checking tickets and calling out the street names to an accompanying bell. It was the first time in my life that I had taken an electric tram with a female driver.

VIENNA 1944—45

The factory I was assigned to work at on March 8, 1944, was in Ottakring, a blue-collar district where parts of airplanes were manufactured by H. Schuster & Co. on Odoakorgasse 28. I sat on a high bench with a big, electric metal machine in front of me and two large wooden boxes on each side. A huge metal drill about five inches thick was moving at a tremendous speed cleaning and smoothing out the inside of big screws. I had to take a big, oily screw, from a box on my right side, put it under the huge metal drill that was moving rapidly and then deposit it into another wooden box on my left side.

As it was my first day on the job, I turned my head too close to the machine and my long hair was pulled rapidly into the turning drill. Luckily, I quickly turned off the three-way switch in the right direction, just by instinct, and slowly the machine stopped.

A big chunk of my hair mixed with blood was twisted around the metal. I don't know if I screamed but suddenly it became dead quiet and all work in the big hall stopped. Some people ran toward me, helped me down the bench and called for the "master." I was taken to a room where a woman in a white uniform cleaned me up, put something on my scalp that burned like fire, sent me back to the barracks and told me to stay there.

A few days later, a woman came from the factory and informed me they didn't want me to work there anymore. She told me to go to a factory close by where wooden soles and heels were manufactured. In the meantime, the little food I had in my locker and some clothes were stolen

from me. Someone had removed my locker key from the pocket of my gray uniform while I was asleep during the night. There was nobody to complain to or accuse, as there were forty strange women in one large room.

On May 15, 1944, I started my new job at Alfred Haas and moved to a new quarter on Degengasse 14. It was a four-story building and the lager was on the ground floor with the only toilet outside in the hall. I was given a bed and two blankets. I shared a room with about seven women from different European countries that were occupied by Germany.

Near the wall on the left side was a kitchen-like cabinet divided into small compartments where we kept our few dishes and food. A closet for our clothes was on the opposite wall, divided into small compartments, each with a key. My bed was close to the right side of the entrance and next to it, along the wall, was Maria's bed. Maria was a Greek woman, a seamstress. She had a French boyfriend who often stayed overnight with her in our big room. She got pregnant, had a baby girl, and after the liberation, went with him to France.

Erica, a girl from Yugoslavia whose real name was Hasna Ibrahimowicz, was a Muslim from Croatia who was sleeping with a young, blond Austrian boy, Gustav Homular, who was rejected by the German military for health reasons. And there was Paulette, a French woman, short, lean, charming, who got pregnant every year and went to France to leave her child with her mother and then came back to her latest lover. Barbara, another Croatian, never had any male visitors in the lager, but used to disappear for the night and show up at work the next morning. Another woman, Janette, from France, had her bed across the room on the opposite wall from me. She was older, hard looking, with narrow shoulders and a big behind. I never saw her in anything but her gray uniform. Her lover was a good-looking, young French man who often stayed overnight with her. Their encounters always ended with a fight the next morning with her crying and him slamming the door on his way out, disturbing us all. The same evening he was back again. He spoke very little German, and her friend Paulette told us that Janette's lover had a family in France and would never marry her.

Our beds had a webbed metal base and a straw mattress and at night, "love" with all the boyfriends was in full swing. The room sounded like a working beehive with the beds moving and noises coming from every corner. It often awoke me and I'd forget where I was. The women

were mostly from lower – or working-class families from all over Europe who were forced, or volunteered, to work for the Germans. Women from better families had ways of coping with the times, and did not volunteer to work for the Germans.

The work at my new job wasn't as demanding as the previous jobs. I sorted and packaged wooden soles and heels, and one of the male workers carried the heavy packages to a storage room. At the end of the day I was always tired and hungry. I received a few shillings and some food stamps at the end of the week. Food was very scarce for us foreigners, and my food stamps were often withheld by my boss due to my frequent absences from work. I became sick with stomach problems, and it got so bad that help had to be called and the *Masterin* would come to the camp and give me some pain pills. The women at the camp thought I might die as I lay on the floor in a fetal position twisting in pain. The so-called *stammgericht*, food without stamps, may have to a degree saved my life. Usually it was some potatoes cooked in a stew with sour pickles. The *blodwurst*, blood sausage, a delicacy at the time, was also available once in a while.

One day I met Mira, a Polish girl, who came from Rudniki, a small place close to Vilnius. She refused to work and moved in with a middle-aged Polish man, Tadeusz, who was caught in Warsaw dealing on the black market. Thanks to good business connections he was sent to Austria instead of jail. In Vienna, he had a profitable job and continued in his old trade – buying and selling food stamps and other illegal business. At the beginning of their relationship he told Mira that he was married, had a child and after the war would be returning to his family in Warsaw. It was a temporary arrangement for him and a way for Mira to avoid working.

One day Mira came over to the camp and told me the good news. "Guess what? There's a boy here from Vilnius who came to work and is staying at the men's camp."

"How nice," I said, noncommittally. "Now there will be three of us from the same city."

My heart jumped. This was all I needed. He might know and recognize me. I couldn't wait for him to show up, to get the suspense and my worries over with. Sooner or later I'd have to face him. A tall, young, blond boy came over the same evening after work, and was happy to meet one of his own kind – another Pole from the same city. We had nothing in common and nothing to talk about.

Once in a while Mira asked me to stay with her when Tadeusz went out of town for business. There was always plenty of food in the house, which was unusual at the time, and I looked forward to being there. On a Sunday morning in early spring 1944, I was walking on Thalia St. with two Greek girls I knew from the first camp, who were employed by the Schuster Company. One of them, Marika, with light brown, wavy hair, spoke Russian she'd learned from her grandmother who came from Russia. Her friend Vasilika, was the opposite of her, dark skinned and dark eyed. I didn't know if they were related and I asked myself why two young girls would come to a strange country, as they both didn't speak a word of German.

But no questions were asked and no answers were expected. They spoke Greek, a strange language that sounded to me like one long sentence.

Suddenly a young man going in the opposite direction stopped and said something to the girls and then turning toward me, asked, *"Fraulein, sind Sie Wienerin?"* Are you from Vienna?

"No, I'm from Lithuania, I said.

"My name is Christos," he said and extended his hand.

He seemed to be very confident, was well dressed, and wore a brown suit with a matching shirt and tie. I found him quite attractive in a strange way, with his black, shiny hair, large, dark, dreamy eyes and a small mustache. He asked me if I would like to meet him across the street in the coffee house in about half an hour.

I shook my head, "No, I'm busy."

Marika almost screamed at me in Russian. Her exact words were, "You fool. Go with him. He's very nice."

When I came to the coffee house he was playing billiards with some other men. He immediately stopped and directed me to a nearby table. We talked a little about our jobs and where we came from. All very impersonal and light. I was impressed with his knowledge of German (at the time I didn't know he had a Viennese girlfriend) and outgoing personality. We agreed to meet again the coming Sunday at the same place.

Once in a while, a few young men who worked with me in the factory and lived in the camp across the street from the company used to come over to our camp. An Italian by the name of Anthony came to the women's camp once in a while to see Emilia Bonatti, the woman I described before, who spoke many languages and who I thought might be Jewish. A few times he asked me to go out with him as did other men from different nationalities. I wasn't interested in any romantic encounter and sex was out of the question. In the first camp, I had enough of hearing the women call each other *putana*, whore in Yugoslavian. And I saw the men come in, stay for a while, then escape as fast as they could as if blown away by the wind.

At the first camp I became friendly with a girl from Yugoslavia by the name of Danica. One day after work I went over to visit her. She was out and an older woman, an acquaintance of hers, told me the terrible things going on in the camp. Danica was shamelessly engaging in sex in the hall or any available corner with different men who lived in the barracks that belonged to the factory. I confronted her when she came in disheveled and red-faced. She was totally surprised to see me and find out that I knew what was going on.

A girl from the back of the room screamed, "Putana, get out, a line is forming. The boys are waiting to fuck you."

Without a word she ran out of the room. She got pregnant, had a daughter and didn't know who the father was. I saw her again after the Russians entered Vienna in April 1945, sitting at the window with a little bundle in her arms. Most of the women left the camp, but unfortunately she had no place to go. I felt bad for her, but I couldn't help with food or in any other way. At the time, the only rations we were receiving from the Russians were dried peas with worms. It had to be soaked overnight in water, and afterward, the peas opened up and the dead worms would float to the top. We skimmed off the worms, put some fresh water in the pot, and made a meal out of it. After a while some smelly oil was also rationed.

As if this weren't enough of a good thing, it was proclaimed that all foreign workers had to register with the Russian commandant and would be repatriated to their country of origin. Soon rumors started going around that trains loaded with *fremdarbeiter*, guest workers from different countries – no matter why they came or from where – were being shipped straight to labor camps in Siberia. The Russian theory was that if you survived the war you must be a spy or a German collaborator.

In the meantime, my friendship with Christos had begun to blossom into romance. It was a new chapter in my life. He seemed to always be in a good mood and full of hope for better days to come. Every day, we met after work in a small coffee shop on the corner of Talier and Enenkel Strasse in the Ottakring district where there were many factories that employed foreign workers. As I drank my *ersatz* imitation chicory coffee and watched Christos play billiards, I started to let my guard down. I felt I could trust him and told him about my real identity. He said, "It doesn't matter to me, there's only one God for all of us." He wanted nothing more than to protect and take care of me. We fell in love. One night we went to the room he was renting from an Austrian widow, Mrs. Paul. He asked, "Will you be my wife?" I said, "Yes." This was my first romance and great love. He was the first man I slept with.

I met Christos, or Chris as I later called him, every day and my life started to change for the better. I had somebody who cared for me and loved me. The only documents I had in my possession at the time were my Catholic ID papers given to me at the police station in Rudominy. We went to the nearby Catholic Church of the Holy Spirit and got married. We had a very simple ceremony and afterward were invited by an Austrian couple for a light lunch of pancakes.

A New Window of Freedom
Opens Up in Vienna

Just before the Russians entered Vienna in April 1945, food stores and warehouses of every kind were plundered by the local population and by the starving foreign workers hoarded together from all of Europe who had almost no other means of acquiring food.

Later, the Russian army confiscated not only food, but also machinery and shipped whole factories to Russia. We had to use our wits to survive and not die of hunger, as Vienna had one of the highest mortality rates right after WWII. One day, one of my husband's Greek friends told him he often traveled to Hungary – a rich agricultural country where there was plenty of food to barter for items brought from Vienna – and asked my husband to join him on the next trip. The first time they traveled together, they sat on the roof of the train, as the interior was reserved for Russian military. It was very dangerous, and Chris soon figured out a better way of going there.

In order for Chris to ride inside the train, he needed some kind of authorization showing that he participated with the Russian military in the liberation of Vienna. He asked me to write down in Russian, on a piece of plain paper, that he had participated in the liberation and should therefore be given special consideration from the occupying Russian forces. I signed the letter with a name I made up – General Vasilenko. With this in hand, he went to the Austrian government office and asked them to translate the paper into German, then stamp and date it. With this newly authorized paper in hand, he was able to take the train to Budapest, Hungary.

A neighbor who owned a general store gave him some kitchen towels and a few pairs of women's stockings to exchange for food. He also bartered an inexpensive bead necklace that someone had given me for a small piece of ham. He often traveled to Sapron, a small town on the border of Austria and Hungary, and became acquainted with farmers who were pleased to barter and who gave him smoked ham and cheese – items which, at the time in Vienna, were priceless and could be found only on the black market. We sold some of the food and used the profit to buy more expensive items like women's and men's underwear, stockings and costume jewelry, which was very desired by the women in Hungary. Chris made many trips, sometimes by himself and sometimes with his Greek friend. We had plenty of food and even managed to save some money.

After a few months, Vienna, as well as the rest of Austria, was divided into four zones by the occupying forces – American, British, French and Russian.

As it happened, we were living in the American zone, and because of this our lives greatly improved. We started receiving parcels of food and clothes from the Joint Distribution Committee (a Jewish relief organization) in the building of the Kultusgemeinde (Vienna Jewish Community, at 18 Gruzenbergstrasse). We moved from the lager to a room with an Austrian family at Halbgasse 8.

Through friends I met at the Jewish Survivors Association, my husband got a job with the American military, working in the headquarters as an assistant to Major Oscar Lifshutz, an American rabbi. He was an intelligent, well-educated person with a big heart, who tried to help whomever he could. He invited us to move into his spacious apartment on Zieglergasse. This apartment had been confiscated by the American military when a highly ranked Nazi fled the country with his family. Shortly after, headed by Major Lifshutz, the Americans created a club for the Jewish officers of all the occupying forces. It was on Ringstrasse, close to the American Military Headquarters. Jewish military personnel from the four occupying forces met there every weekend to get to know each other and socialize. Major Lifshutz assigned Chris as his representative for civil affairs and paid him a small salary with American military script. One of Chris's job responsibilities was to also oversee the distribution of items to the Holocaust survivors.

One Saturday night I received an urgent call from Chris. He was at the club and told me to come immediately. There I met a high-ranking

Jewish officer from the Red Army, whom Chris had told of my dilemma in trying to find my mother and brother. He said he would try to help me find them. I had to write a letter and he'd send it through the military post, but I was told not to put a return address on the envelope because it was strictly forbidden to send private citizens' letters through the military post. The regular mail system was still not re-established.

The letter was addressed to Jozefowa, the janitress of my parents' building. I had no other address to contact my mother, and I hoped that she and my brother survived and had returned to Vilnius to try to find me. I hardly believed that the letter would reach Jozefowa, or that the older woman would even still be alive. I wrote, "Mother, I am in Vienna." Miraculously, the letter reached Jozefowa and got to my mother. My mother and brother had survived posing as Christian farm help at the Januszkewicz farm. After Germany was defeated, and the Russians took over Vilnius again, they returned to the city, where there were no friends or relatives left alive. They decided to join a transport of Holocaust survivors going to Israel by way of Salzburg, Austria.

The transport stopped for a short time in Salzburg, waiting for more people to join the group. By total coincidence, a man in the transport, Mr. Jegerman, who was originally from Vienna, was going there first to find out if any of his relatives had survived the war before he rejoined the transport group in Salzburg to continue on to Israel. My mother showed him the letter she had received from Vienna, gave him a description of me and asked him to try to find me. The man went to the Holocaust Survivor's Association in Vienna. By description only, and by sheer luck, he found me, as I was there quite often helping out with distribution of parcels of food and clothing from the United States to the Jewish Holocaust survivors. When he told me my mother and brother were alive, I was overjoyed. I felt like they had returned from the dead.

Immediately, with great cunning and bribing of the officials, Chris made travel documents that allowed my mother and brother to cross the Russian zone from Salzburg to Vienna. Using his connections with the American military, he obtained special permission for himself to travel to Salzburg, where he found my mother and brother in the transport camp. There he gave them the necessary documents to travel to Vienna. Without proper documentation, a person trying to cross the Russian zone could easily be arrested by the Russians, accused of being spies or smugglers and anything of value would be confiscated and the person thrown in jail.

Along with the travel documents, he gave them the address and directions to our apartment in Vienna. Chris returned first and two days later, my mother and brother arrived by train at the Westbahnhoff Station in Vienna, where we were waiting for them. The reunion with my mother and brother was tears and kisses. I could hardly believe they were alive and standing in front of me. For a while they stayed with us at Major Lifshutz's apartment, where Chris and I were now living, until they rented a room nearby at an Austrian widow's house, a Mrs. Dolezal, who prided herself on being the spouse of a German nobleman.

When my mother first met Chris in Salzburg, she told me she liked him even though at first she found him a little unusual. He was temperamental and overly confident. As time passed, she got used to him and accepted him as a family member. I don't think she cared much that he wasn't Jewish. If she did, she never said anything to me. We were aware that in a different time – a different world in Vilnius that was now gone – it would have been unimaginable for me to marry outside of the Jewish faith. But now, here in Vienna, with the traumas I had gone through still fresh in my mind, I did my best not to look backward. I was focused on daily life and tried to better myself, adapting to the new circumstances I was thrown into. I was deeply in love with Chris and naively believed there was nothing our love couldn't conquer.

My brother, Leo, attended *Machinenbau* (machine construction) Engineering School at night in Vienna, but had to give it up, as he had difficulties with the German language and a limited educational background. A Jewish organization, ORT, an acronym for the Organization for Rehabilitation through Training, was founded in 1880 in Russia to provide work skills for Jewish men and women. The organization helped Jewish refugees in Vienna, and it sent Leo to a workshop for leather goods to learn a trade.

None of us intended to stay in Austria permanently. We knew we could never return to Vilnius, which for us was now a cemetery. We couldn't stay in Austria as it reminded us of the Holocaust. Hitler was from Austria. When my mother and brother came to Vienna, their goal was for all of us to move to Israel. The plan was for Chris and me to go first, and then soon after have my mother and Leo join us. But it didn't work out that way.

A Short Visit to the Young State of Israel and a New Start in Montreal

In 1948, after Israel was declared a state by the United Nations, I talked Chris into going to see my older brother, Benjamin, who had left for Israel in 1939. Chris wasn't thrilled with the idea of going to Israel. After many discussions, we found a compromise and agreed to stay for a while and see if we liked it there. His first choice would have been to go back to Greece, but the country was in the midst of a civil war that lasted from 1944 to 1949. The Communists were aided by Stalin's Russia to try and take over the country. If we had gone to Greece, Chris would have immediately been conscripted into the army as he was a trained soldier and had already served military duty before.

Benjamin was now living in Ir-Ganim with his family. My mother had located him through her oldest sister, Freida, who had left Vilnius as a teenager years before the war and moved to Johannesburg to marry her second cousin. From the time Benjamin arrived in Israel, he was in touch with Freida.

We had no problem getting visas for Israel. Chris used his Greek passport and I got all my necessary traveling papers through the Israeli legislation in Vienna. Shortly after, we were on our way. We took the train from Vienna to Trieste, where we boarded a boat for Israel. We went to Ir-Ganim, a small settlement ironically given the name of "garden city," as it was a barren piece of land between Haifa and Kwar-Atta. The houses were built by the Israeli government for war veterans. I was introduced to Benjamin's lovely wife, Inez, who he met in Tripoli, Libya during his service in the British army. He filled us in on what happened to him since I last saw him at the train station in Vilnius. After a long, dangerous voyage, he arrived in Palestine and all the Jewish people on the boat were immediately arrested by the British for illegal entry. He was jailed for a few months and after his release, voluntarily joined the British Army. After basic training, he was sent to Egypt at the border of Libya, under the command of the British General Wavell. Then his battalion was shipped to Greece, and when the Germans occupied the country, my brother and the other soldiers ran to Milos, then to Crete, where a boat picked them up and brought them to Alexandria, Egypt. From there he was stationed in Tripoli, and after getting married, moved to Israel.

At the time, Israel was a country saturated with poor European survivors of the Holocaust, with a shortage of jobs and accommodation. Food was scarce and expensive. Luckily, we had made enough money in Vienna while working for the Americans and were better off than a lot of other people. We were in constant touch with my mother and brother in Vienna. In our letters, we told them of the hardships they'd encounter. We advised them not to come because we had decided to return to Vienna. In addition, Chris looked into getting a job, but found it very difficult because he wasn't Jewish. The Jewish newcomers were given priority.

During our absence from Vienna, my mother and brother received visas to immigrate to Montreal, Canada. They had decided to take our advice and move to Canada instead of Israel. This time they'd go first and Chris and I planned to follow them as soon as we could. Though it wasn't easy, we managed to return to Vienna, stayed for a few months in a camp for stateless refugees in Hallain, close to Salzburg, and soon after, received immigration papers for Canada.

It took over two and a half stormy weeks on the sea to arrive in Halifax, Canada from Bremenhafen, Germany. We had a terrible voyage on the Anna Salem boat, which had been built for the American military and intended for only one Atlantic crossing during WWII. I was seasick the moment the boat started moving and thought I'd never make it to dry land. I spent the rest of the trip in a narrow berth in an overcrowded room with many other women. One of the things that kept me going was thinking of Mahatma Gandhi and his decision to fast for three weeks. It gave me hope that I might survive the voyage.

A Jew in Public

In 1951 we arrived in Halifax at Pier 21. There was a Canadian National Ticket Office nearby and a walkway connected the pier to the train station. We continued on by train to Montreal. At that time, it wasn't very difficult for young, stateless Europeans to immigrate to Canada. But it was a bittersweet arrival. In the back of my mind, I knew that only four years earlier, in 1947, the first orphaned Jewish children had arrived in Canada after the war. Before and during wwii, Canada almost totally refused any Jewish immigrants, but we were now the lucky ones. We were welcomed with open arms, and the Canadian government paid for our trip. In exchange, people were given the option of signing up for a year or two to work on farms or as domestic help. We chose domestic help. The Canadian Labor Division arranged our employment and sent us to the McCall's family mansion. Our plan was to study English and French in Montreal, assimilate quickly and scramble up the immigrant ladder of success.

I became very depressed. After all my losses and suffering during the war, I had now emerged as a servant in this new country of my choice. But I had to comply with our obligation to the government. I was the cook and Chris – or his nickname, Taki (short for Christaki, a common Greek name that is a derivative of Christos) – was the butler. If it weren't for me, Chris wouldn't have lasted a day. He bitterly disliked serving other people. On one occasion the McCall's son-in-law, David, came to visit for the weekend and asked Chris to carry his suitcase up to the room. "Take it yourself," he said. "I don't work for you." He was used to giving orders, not taking them. He came from a line of brave military heroes and was proud of his glory days as a soldier in the hills of Albania during WWII.

Chris spoke German – our common language – and the little French he had learned in high school. I spoke fluent German, Russian, Polish, Hebrew and Yiddish, and had a good knowledge of Latin. That I was once one of the best in my Latin class at the Epstein Gymnasium and could conjugate verb declensions and translate Virgil didn't count for much in the Canadian job market.

Our employers were Alan and Dolly McCall. Alan McCall was the president of the steel company, Drummond McCall, from 1955 to 1965. He also founded the Boys and Girls Clubs of Canada, which became a national institution.

The McCalls were modest and thoughtful, treating us with respect, not as servants but as employees. Occasionally, they gave us tickets to the theatre, and lent us their country house at Lake Manitou South for our vacations, complete with their gardener and housekeeper. We stayed with them for two years. During that time, they never inquired directly about my background or religion, assuming perhaps that I was from Vienna since Chris and I spoke German and had come directly from Austria.

One day, Mrs. McCall came into the kitchen to show me how to make Yorkshire pudding. I had been using an English cookbook she gave me and often had to translate recipes into German with the help of a German-English dictionary. She always complimented me on my cooking, even when a meal didn't turn out quite right. On this particular day I was struggling with the unfamiliar recipe and feeling sorry for myself; I broke down in tears. Part of my frustration was from trying to prepare the meal, but the real reason was the accumulated unhappiness of working as a servant.

Mrs. McCall asked me, "Is something the matter?"

"No, everything is fine," I answered, not wanting to talk about my feelings.

"Don't worry about making the Yorkshire pudding," she offered, "We'll have something else tonight."

A part of me wanted to open up and talk to this kind, understanding woman and tell her how I really felt, but my habit of concealing my real feelings and identity took over.

"You know," she continued, "We have a lot of similarities, but I was just lucky."

Her kindness impressed me. I knew Mrs. McCall had not come from a wealthy family, but had been Mr. McCall's secretary before they got married. She meant well, but she didn't know that we had very few similarities and came from entirely different backgrounds.

What had been half-conscious in my mind until then suddenly crystallized. I realized there was no point in ever telling anybody that I was Jewish. I never knew what their reaction would be. In addition, I convinced myself, they could never understand what I'd gone through unless they'd experienced it themselves. For the rest of the world I would continue to play my role as I did during the war. From this moment on, I decided that no matter where or what the situation or who I was with, I would conceal my Jewish identity and past. I made a conscious decision to not socialize with immigrant Jews in Montreal outside of my immediate family, but would instead immerse myself in my husband's Christian world.

At the end of the second year of working for the McCalls, I became pregnant. Chris and I were overjoyed and started to make plans for this important event. Our commitment to work as domestics would soon be over, and we were eager to start an independent life. We had saved some money, as everything was provided for us in abundance. In our spare time, we took English classes provided by the government for new immigrants. Chris knew some English from having worked with the American military in Vienna, and could communicate in French. We were ready to embark on our own. We were ambitious and put the chapter of working as domestics as far behind us as we could. I wanted my child to have all the advantages in life that I could give her.

The McCalls told us we could stay at their home for a few months after our baby was born. It was a huge three-story house where we had lived comfortably in a separate wing on the first floor. We had planned to start a family earlier, but the circumstances weren't right until we moved to Canada. When Helen was born, I was in heaven. We chose the name Helen because I wanted to give her a Christian name, and it was also the name of her deceased Greek Orthodox grandmother. On the birth certificate, in the blank for religious affiliation, I didn't hesitate for a second and wrote down Greek Orthodox. I felt a huge sense of relief and accomplishment. I had given her the right start in life. I didn't want her to be

Jewish and face the prejudice I'd gone through. I felt that anti-Semitism would always exist, and I wanted to shield her from any obstacles and the persecution that she might face as a Jew.

Soon the day came to leave the McCalls' house. Mrs. McCall gave us a big photograph of the family in a brown, leather frame. She hugged us and said, "Don't forget to stay in touch and if you ever need anything, let us know." In a way I was sad to leave them and the security they represented, but it was time to move on. We had already found an apartment on Park Ave., where many immigrants from Europe lived. In no time, Chris got a job at The Bank of Nova Scotia, where he was trained to work in the foreign currency department. I stayed home and took care of my young daughter, throwing myself into being a mother and wife. My mother often took care of Helen, and on occasion we'd go over to my brother Leo's house on Friday night for supper. My brother and his Orthodox wife observed the Sabbath. To the outside world, I put on the face of a Christian, but at my brother Leo's home, I was still the Jewish girl from Vilnius.

FACED WITH MY OWN CONTRADICTIONS

W hen I left Montreal for Phoenix in 1960, I felt like I was living on the other side of the planet. I was far away – both geographically and emotionally – from my family in Montreal. At the time, I believed we were making the right choice in starting a new life on a clean slate.

So far removed from my relatives, I could almost deny to myself that I was Jewish. Publicly, I took on the persona of a nice Greek wife, a church-goer, who was preoccupied with raising her daughter and making sure all the right Greek dishes were prepared for family dinners. With my blond hair and green eyes, not speaking Greek, I didn't fit in with the stereotype of the Greek wife. But I was determined to try. I felt like I was playing a new role, but after a while it almost became a natural part of me. I could run away from being Jewish. It was a way to try to heal myself. I was shell-shocked, suffering from post-traumatic stress, and not ever wanting to be reminded of the fear and dread of imminent sudden death again. I wanted to turn a corner in my life and raise my daughter as a Christian too.

Even though I liked the idea of moving to Phoenix, Arizona, I never imagined we would live there for years. In the back of my mind, I felt we could always return to Montreal. But that never happened.

My husband first went to Phoenix to visit his uncle, who had been living there for many years. He was coming from the cold winter in Montreal and in Arizona the sun was shining. There was no snow and no need for heavy winter clothes. It was love at first sight. He returned to Montreal filled with enthusiasm about the small desert town, and soon we were on our way. Chris found a part-time job at a liquor store owned by his uncle's Greek friend. He worked there for a few months until we settled down and got more acquainted with the new surroundings. He wanted to find a new job. He had experience from Vienna, where he had trained reading plans and making precision parts for Messerschmitt airplanes at the Viener Farwerkbau in the 19th *Bezirk* or district. With this background, it wasn't difficult for him to find a job at Standard Computer Company. The man who interviewed him was an engineer by the name of Darwin Golben from Germany. It was a stroke of luck for Chris, as they conversed in German and he was hired on the spot. The company was very successful in building early computers. Chris worked there until he was later hired at General Electric, which sold its computer division to Honeywell. We moved from Phoenix to the nearby suburb of Glendale, Arizona to be near Honeywell, which was located on the Black Canyon Freeway about a fifteen-minute drive from our newly built home in Glendale.

My first impression when we came to Phoenix, with our baby daughter, was of a small place in the middle of nowhere with unpaved streets, very few pedestrians and almost no public transportation. The heat was unbearable. I was hoping it was just a heat wave that wouldn't last more than a few days before it cooled off. But despite the intense heat that I never grew accustomed to, we stayed on. After a while we replaced the swamp cooler with an air conditioner.

Whenever we went to Montreal to visit my mother, brothers and, by now, their extended families, I couldn't help but think I would have been one of them if I had stayed there. They were deeply rooted in the Jewish community. Helen was surprised when she spoke to her cousin Iona, a year younger than she, and found out that Iona never had a friend who wasn't Jewish. At the time, the suburb of Cote St. Luc was almost entirely Jewish.

I realized we lived in a completely different world in Arizona. I was glad we were assimilated into the large, non-denominational middle class, and, more importantly, that my daughter didn't belong to any particular ethnic – that is, Jewish – community.

To our advantage, when Chris and I met, our different religions weren't a consideration. I was too young, too inexperienced to ever imagine that marrying someone from a different culture and class would inevitably lead to problems. What eventually bothered me the most was

Chris's insistence on sticking to the old-world Greek mentality that the man is the unquestioned leader in the family who makes all the decisions. In my parents' home, I had often overheard my father and mother talking over important matters together.

With the wisdom of hindsight, I think it might have been better if I had insisted we move back to Montreal. I missed my mother, my brothers Leo and Benjamin and our other relatives, but at the same time, I felt safer in Arizona. I was still afraid of the anti-Semitism that exists in the world – and exists to this day. My fear that something could happen again never left me, even though I knew it wasn't rational. It was in my blood. Maybe, I joked to myself, if I could have a total blood transfusion it might help. I wanted Helen to grow up in a more secure world, not a Jewish ghetto in Montreal. By enrolling her in a Catholic grade school, even though I wasn't conscious of it at the time, it was a way of providing her with a Christian identity if the need ever arose. Without my fake IDs as a Christian, I would never have made it through the Holocaust. I equated Christianity with survival.

It never occurred to me I'd be depriving my daughter of growing up with the feeling of having an extended family around and bonds that can last a lifetime. I thought I was offering her more choices, not fewer. I didn't want her to be rooted in a Jewish community that could entrap her and leave her vulnerable to discrimination. I didn't think it would lead her to years of questioning and searching for her own identity. I always hoped that someday she'd find her own way and choose what would make her happy. I left it at that. I made an instinctual choice; I didn't analyze the situation.

MANHATTAN: 2009

Since I wrote the last paragraph of my book, my life has changed dramatically with the sudden death of my husband. Overnight I became a widow with a broken heart and spirit. I felt as if the ground I was standing on suddenly collapsed. For the first time in decades, I had to face who I was as an independent person. It all came so unexpectedly. I never imagined he'd die before me. We had shared our thoughts, our ideas, went through good and bad times together, and chose our own way of life. We had more than our share of differences, but together we did what we wanted, went where we wanted to, and lived in Arizona where we weren't constrained by his family or mine.

After I had made my decision so long ago in Mrs. McCall's kitchen to never present myself publicly as Jewish, I hid for years in my husband's world. I was so used to pretending to be a Christian during the war, that it was easy to continue the charade. Then, it became too late. I trapped myself into continuing to live a lie, as though I were still living during the Holocaust. Unfortunately, as my daughter was growing up, I encouraged her to hide both her identity and mine. I thought it would be best for her, but now I realize I should have told her to be proud of who she is.

Luckily, she found her own way. "We shouldn't be ashamed of being Jewish," she tells me, "It's nothing to hide." By writing my life story, I have reclaimed the past and taken it out of hiding. I have taken myself out of hiding too.

Now I spend most of my time in New York. I don't find the transition difficult, since I often visited New York over the years. Recently my daughter suggested I walk over to a nearby synagogue to meet some people, and said, "Just see what it's like. If you don't like it, you don't have to go back." Though I hadn't been to a synagogue since I was a child, I decided to give it a try. I was curious to see how it would feel going back to my roots, long abandoned, but never forgotten. I didn't know how I'd feel in a Jewish environment again after all the years.

On Friday evening, I walked toward the synagogue, past Trader Joe's on 14th St. where I like to shop. I walked up the steps to the synagogue known as "Town and Village." It felt strange not knowing anyone and I almost turned back. Or was it fear at seeing myself go to the synagogue, the place I had been estranged from for so many years. I said to myself, *You've come this far, just go in*. Rabbi Sebert was standing at the entrance greeting people as they walked in. We talked for a while before the service and he invited me to join him later so he could introduce me to other members of the congregation.

A teenage girl sat next to me during the service and seemed to know all the prayers and songs by heart. I felt like an intruder holding the prayer book, trying to keep up with the rest of the congregation, but with little success. It seemed like a dream embedded in a fleeting memory that brought me back to a lost past. I felt I didn't belong there. A stranger among my own people. I was glad when the service was over, and I left the premises without going to see the rabbi. For some unexplained reason, tears covered my face. I didn't feel like talking and thought there wasn't much I could say or share with the young, friendly rabbi.

In the meantime, my friend Vera told me about YIVO, The Institute for Jewish Research. Founded in 1925 in Vilnius as the Yiddish Scientific Institute, the research center is dedicated to the history and culture of Ashkenazi Jewry and the Yiddish language. The main office has been in New York since 1940. Now YIVO is known all over the world as the most important resource center and the largest collection in the world for East European Jewish Studies, Yiddish language and literature. The acronym YIVO comes from the original initials in Yiddish.

YIVO is located on 16th St. in New York, just a fifteen-minute walk from my apartment. I went over there, talked to a few people and met Ella Levine, the Director of Development and External Affairs, who was very friendly and welcoming. She showed me around and then introduced me to the Acquisitions Archivist, Leo Greenbaum, who told me about the work volunteers perform and said the United States army helped salvage the Vilnius archives and library in 1954. I was very impressed and thought this would be a nice place for me to work. I decided to volunteer and asked if I could contribute in any way.

Now I work in the archives a few days a week. Most of the collection stems from pre-war materials. It is accumulated from people who have donated correspondence, manuscripts, photos, art work, rare books, diaries and all kinds of other materials. I sit in a large, long room with shelves full of books lining the walls and people working on different tasks at desks and computers. I sort through Yiddish documents and summarize them. The next step will be to arrange and catalogue the collection. The volunteers who work there come from different countries and sometimes it feels like an international Jewish club. Some volunteers take the documents out of old paper folders and put them in acid-free folders, and the most fragile papers are put in Mylar sleeves.

It's a good feeling to find a place where I belong. I don't have to hide being Jewish. At YIVO, I'm with my own people again. I met a few people from Vilnius, though I didn't know them when I lived there. Sometimes I go out to nearby restaurants for lunch with the other volunteers. We talk about politics, current topics or ballet and opera performances in the city. No one here dwells on the past very much, perhaps because we're all immersed in it while we work in the archives.

I sometimes think that I'm looking at my own future. One day, I will donate to the YIVO archives the documents that helped me survive the Holocaust, family photographs that were saved by relatives who left Europe before the war and this memoir. I know where my memories will be housed; they will live on.

Now in this memoir, I'm proud to be reunited with the name I was born with. I thought I would never use it again. For the first time since I took on the role of my false Christian identity papers so many years ago, I am free to be Rasia Kliot.

PART TWO
HELEN'S STORY

FIRST THINGS FIRST

I was born with a silver spoon in my mouth, but it didn't belong to me. It belonged to the McCalls, the people my parents worked for as domestics in Montreal. My mother was a cook and my father was a butler. When I was born, for good measure, on my birth certificate my mother wrote down Greek Orthodox in the section for religious affiliation. Even in the womb, she willed me to be Christian, and gave me a name and religious identity that ensured I'd be immune from anti-Semitism. I was brought home from Royal Victoria Hospital to a grand, three-story, ivy-covered house with an even grander English garden. My big, sunlit nursery was on the top floor of the residence at 3246 Cedar Ave. in Westmount.

Westmount is an affluent community on a small mountain in the middle of Montreal called Mount Royal, where people build homes in a hodgepodge of styles – gothic, tudor, arts and crafts and other less identifiable hybrids suited for the infamously cold Canadian winters. Originally, Westmount was an enclave of wealthy British Canadians and the richest community in Canada. The Jewish Bronfman family, owners of the former Seagram company, once the largest distiller of alcoholic beverages in the world, and the British Molson family, owners of Canada's largest beer brewery, have homes there.

Westmount is also where Leonard Cohen is from. He was my literary and musical hero for many years. I was always proud that like Leonard Cohen, I too was a Jew from Westmount. Like mine, his grandfather was also from Vilnius. In fact, my Uncle Leo's mother-in-law, Regina

Nissenbaum, was Leonard Cohen's mother's seamstress. The Montreal Jewish community is a very small town in that way. At one point Leonard's mother gave her seamstress a tablecloth Leonard used when he lived on the Greek island of Hydra. In my mind, the tablecloth was like a sacred relic. Through the chain of passing it around, one day it strangely enough ended up on my aunt's dining room table. Perhaps Leonard's mother and mine crossed paths on a sidewalk in the hush of the expansive green Westmount Park or King George Park. Maybe I even played in the same playgrounds that he did when he was a boy.

One day I asked my mother if she ever felt like looking up the McCalls when we visited relatives in Montreal. "Wouldn't it be interesting to see them after all these years?"

She looked surprised and gave me an answer I didn't expect. "I never thought about it." Then she added, "I don't even know if Mrs. McCall is still alive."

"But if she is, wouldn't you want to see her?"

"For what?"

It occurred to me that I was trying to idealize my mother's life as a cook. Until that moment, I wasn't aware that I was superimposing a pleasant fantasy of my own on the harsh realities of her past. The thought of my mother suffering made me feel helpless and depressed. Instead, I devised a convenient way to both spare her from indignities and myself from sadness. I had imagined she was delighted to be a servant.

In my mind, I envision a warm reunion with Mrs. McCall. In the scenario, she embraces my mother while I smilingly look on. Then we all move to the living room where we have tea together in front of the fieldstone fireplace I saw in a photograph. A servant delivers the gleaming silver teapot on a large silver tray. And this is where my fantasy comes to a dead end – it dawns on me that my mother wouldn't be upstairs in the living room, but in the kitchen preparing small triangles of crustless cucumber and watercress sandwiches. Then it suddenly occurs to me that I'd be downstairs in the servants' quarters too. This is not at all what I had in mind. No wonder my mother didn't want to re-visit this part of her past.

One year Mrs. McCall gave my mother a silver and blue enamel swordfish brooch for a Christmas present. When I was a girl, I always admired the brooch even though the silver had tarnished, and somehow in storage the swordfish's nose became crooked and the safety catch had broken. A few years ago, I suggested we could have it repaired. My mother and I took the little swordfish to a shop in the Diamond District on 47th St. Now it's as good as new. It feels like a secret emblem of my mother's past — of our past — since she rarely talks about her days as a cook. Whenever I see the brooch, I picture Mrs. McCall in her gray flannel skirt and blue cashmere cardigan handing the beautifully wrapped present to my mother under a towering Christmas tree near a mantle hung with needlepoint stockings.

Recently, my mother gave me a small rose-gold Doxa watch my parents bought in Vienna, not long after they got married on October 16, 1948. To me it's a magical piece of jewelry. When I hold the watch or the swordfish brooch, they're like talismans — like tiny time machines — that allow me thought trajectories to the past. I close my eyes and feel immersed in my mother's world, immersed in her past experiences. It's a paradox: I can so clearly picture the incidents she's told me about, yet another part of me can barely imagine the person she was before she became my mother. It's hard for me to fathom she was once a young woman growing up in a country I never saw, speaking languages I don't understand, and was almost killed simply for being Jewish.

Whenever I wind the Doxa watch, I'm amazed it runs so well. After all these years, it still keeps perfect time.

WELCOME TO PHOENIX

When I was four years old, my parents left Montreal, and like the pioneers, moved west and more or less, started over. The presenting reason for the move was my father's interest in being closer to his uncle, and he also vehemently disliked the harsh Montreal winters. My father's uncle was from "back east" and had come to Phoenix for health reasons. He used to work on the railroad in Detroit and contracted tuberculosis. In those days, the arid climate of Phoenix was thought to be the answer to breathing problems and a health haven for anyone with tuberculosis, arthritis or bronchitis. In reality Phoenix has never really been a particularly healthy place to live, a fact that natives know and attest to. The dust, crabgrass and olive trees, as well as other allergens, make Phoenix fourth in the nation for its asthma rate.

As long as I can remember though, my mother always hated the Arizona heat and complained about it. Phoenix is usually the hottest place in the country, and even though people always say it's a "dry" heat, the average 110 degree summers are still scorching. It's too hot to spend any time outdoors, unless you're lounging on a covered patio next to the swimming pool where you can take a dip and cool off.

In the 50s, moving to Phoenix was the best solution for my parents. And the real reason we left Montreal – one that didn't surface until I was older – was that my father didn't feel comfortable living so close to the Jewish relatives. He knew he'd never be fully accepted by Esther, my grandmother, and Leo and Benjamin, my mother's brothers, no matter how friendly they were to him. At that time, Jewish newcomers to

Canada lived in their own immigrant ghettos after arriving from Europe. My father didn't like being the odd man out in the small Jewish community, and got tired of always being called "the Greek." The outsider. In Phoenix, he wouldn't have that problem.

Phoenix was a small Western town in those days. Now it has an estimated population of more than 1.6 million and is ranked in the top five fastest growing cities, and also happens to have the distinction of the highest divorce rate and bankruptcy statistics. The February 2010 issue of *Phoenix Magazine* says the city has the fastest growing unemployment rate in the United States.

When I was a child, my parents often took me to visit my father's uncle, whom we called Uncle Papu, in his rooming house in downtown Phoenix. To me he was a kindly old man with white hair and a white stubble of beard. He had never married. He had large stones paper-weighting newspapers and odds and ends around his room, so that the fan wouldn't blow them away. This was in the days of swamp coolers, before air conditioners. I instinctively felt that there was something sad about his life. My mother had often said what a kind person he was, what a good heart he had – a mensch. Uncle Papu died when I was five. After that, the closest relatives we had were in Montreal, which was a long way off – and so was being Jewish.

Once in a while in the early years before first grade, my mother would put me in a stroller and walk a few blocks on a dirt road to 16th St., where she could catch the bus. We took the bus to go "downtown" to Washington St. Even downtown, the population was sparse and the city's main shopping hub felt like a half-deserted dusty cowboy town. At the time, F. W. Woolworth Co., one of the original American five-and-dime stores housed in an iconic art deco building, was a hot spot of local activity. My mother and I sat at the counter where she ordered coffee with cream for herself and milk and a chocolate-covered doughnut with rainbow sprinkles for me.

I was living a normal life as an average child with parents who took on traditional roles. My father worked. My mother stayed home and took care of me and I basked in her undivided attention. Before I entered first grade, she had taught me the capital cities of Europe, a fact she was always proud of. I still didn't know how to read or write, and only knew a few words of English, which would soon become a cause of great anguish to me in the first grade. I attended grade school at Loma Linda Elementary School at 2002 E. Clarendon St. The school consisted mainly of two long rows of buildings facing each other across a narrow ribbon of patchy, dried-up grass. The rooms were cooled by water coolers that were perched on top of flat Arizona-style roofs, and the buildings were painted a pale green that matched the delicate trunks of the Palo Verde trees in the yard. After a few months, I could still hardly read English, couldn't speak fluently and was struggling to keep up with my classmates. Mrs. Ganzie, my first grade teacher, tutored me in the "Dick and Jane" reading series until I started catching up with the other students and English became less alien.

When I was in third grade, my mother gave me a small, Indian, turquoise and silver-toned necklace. She smiled and proudly said, "I skipped lunch for a few days to buy this for you." At the time, she was attending English classes at the local high school. I felt a pang of anguish when I heard of this sacrifice. The necklace was given to me as a gift of love, but I could never put it on without being reminded of my mother's sacrifice. I think that's when I made the association between the two – love and sacrifice were linked in my mind for a very long time.

Whenever I see the necklace, I remember the stories my mother told me about her hunger during the war, even though when she talked about the Holocaust it was in a detached way, like she was recounting the plot of a TV show she had just watched.

Even today it still pains me to look at the necklace. It's emblematic of the burden of my mother's love. It's a burden I've always carried, and one that for years affected my ability to experience love or intimacy without the fear of losing myself in the too-great sacrifice it demanded.

In Our House We Were
Still Living in Europe

Until I was in the third grade, we lived in a house centrally located in Phoenix at 1920 E. Osborn Rd. It was about a half-hour drive from touristy Scottsdale, which "snowbirds" (the begrudgingly admiring name we gave to winter visitors from the east) were besotted with. Paradise Valley could have been in another galaxy as far as I knew. It was the area adjoining Scottsdale where large Frank Lloyd Wright-inspired homes (as well as a couple of originals) dotted the mountains – magnificent multi-leveled houses with huge expanses of flat roofs and windows, half-cantilevered from the mountains and half-hidden behind reconfigured desert landscaping.

My childhood was unremarkable, and in retrospect I would say it was dull. Though the inner workings of our life were different, old-world, European at home, to all outward appearances, my parents were taking on the trappings of a comfortable American lifestyle. I didn't know I was Jewish. I didn't know what immigrants were, even though we were the only immigrants in our middle-class neighborhood. I just knew we were a little different because none of our neighbors had a foreign accent.

My mother had her own ideas about how I should be raised. She wanted me to have the same cultural privileges she had as a girl in Vilnius. She wanted me to learn to play the piano, speak French and take ballet classes. She often talked about how as a girl she had struggled through piano and violin lessons until the music instructor finally told her parents she was tone-deaf. "Still, I love to listen to the violin," she'd say. "It speaks to me."

When I was six, my mother decided it was time for me to start taking piano lessons, and my parents bought a Baldwin upright piano. Every Saturday afternoon, my piano teacher came to the house. She was a Native American woman, a former concert pianist, who taught music at the Phoenix Indian High School, a federal boarding school for Native Americans on nearby Indian School Rd. I continued weekly lessons with her every Saturday until I was seventeen.

While I was growing up, my mother did the best she could to make a home for us in the desert. She attended school, taking a typing class and English classes at Phoenix College, hoping to improve her accent and grammar. Her favorite pastime was reading. She also liked to browse through cookbooks and regularly cooked Greek specialties like *spanakopita*, spinach pie with feta cheese, and *mousaka*, a layered dish of ground beef and fried eggplant. Once a week, my father attended a Greek AHEPA meeting. AHEPA is the acronym for The American Hellenic Educational Progressive Association, the largest Greek American organization in the United States.

Not unlike other middle-class families in our neighborhood, we sometimes took car trips. On summer weekends when the heat was more unbearable than usual, and the swamp cooler struggled to keep the temperature at a habitable coolness, my mother suggested we get in our new Rambler and drive to Prescott, a town ninety miles northwest of Phoenix. "Prescott reminds me a little of the forest in Czarny Bor," she said. "I used to pick blueberries and mushrooms there when I was a girl."

"What if you picked a poison mushroom?" I asked. Fairy tales always came to mind when my mother talked about her childhood. I pictured her as a blonde princess strolling through a magic forest.

"That would never happen. We knew every mushroom and which ones were poisonous."

"How could you tell?" I wondered out loud.

"The peasants taught us when we children. We followed them in the forest when they picked mushrooms."

From a cultural point of view, we weren't assimilated. In our house, we were still living in Europe. My mother and father spoke a mishmash of German and Yiddish, with some English thrown in. The Yiddish language is a mixture of Old German, Hebrew and Aramaic, and as my father knew German, it was quite easy for him to understand Yiddish and pick it up.

Eastern Europe and Greece were the air we breathed. My mother spoke to me in German-Yiddish while she prepared potato *latkes* or *blintzes* on the kitchen stove. My father played Greek records on the stereo. We were living in a European bubble, even though Americana was in full throttle around us. We had no visitors from Europe. It was too expensive and far away. It wasn't until 1961 that Julia Child probably did more than anyone to introduce international cuisine to the American housewife and change the perception of Europe from a war-torn country to a place with glamorous people and elegant food – all it took was a bottle of Chanel No. 5 and a French cookbook for a housewife to feel sophisticated and worldy. My mother didn't like perfumes or any cosmetics except for lipstick, and there was always a jar of viscous, delicately orange-scented Elizabeth Arden face cream on her dresser. "Cosmetics ruin the skin," she'd often say. "The less you put on your face, the better."

My mother managed to create a sense of ease and abundance at home that replicated her own childhood. For birthday parties, she bought me beautiful chiffon and lace dresses to wear. She baked chocolate multi-layered cakes and decorated them with a metal pastry tube from which borders of icing and pink flower buds with celadon green leaves magically emerged. The big, yellow kitchen was filled with the aroma of sugar cookies, honey cakes, sponge cakes and other sweets that my mother liked to bake. The kitchen windows opened on a vast backyard where I played on a swing set and slide. A row of tall oleanders with hot pink and white flowers circled the perimeter of the yard blocking out the chain link fence behind it. A space between the oleanders was left unplanted, just big enough to unlatch the back gate and step into the alley to walk along my regular path to school.

Our house was small, about nine hundred square feet or eighty-four square meters, but I felt we lived in a palace. My parents were in the midst of striving for the American dream, but in my child's mind, we already had everything.

GREEK ORTHODOX FATHER, JEWISH MOTHER, CATHOLIC DAUGHTER

I still didn't know my mother was Jewish. She didn't observe any Jewish rituals or holidays. Nor was religion ever discussed in our house. My father hung a reproduction of a Greek Byzantine diptych of Jesus and the Virgin Mary in the bedroom hallway. I assumed it was for the benefit of guests who got a tour of the house when they came to visit.

Every Sunday we went to the Greek Orthodox church. We always came in late and attended the last forty-five minutes of the service. For me it was a social event devoid of any spiritual impact. It was just something to do on Sunday mornings, not much different from our excursions to one of the largest shopping malls in the country, Metro Center, which often took place after church, on Sunday afternoons. Shopping was by far the more enjoyable of the two.

At the Greek Orthodox church, I found the service pointless and tedious. The only diversion was the assault on the senses – the rich sound of the choir's singing, the sunlit glints of ormolu on paintings and statues and the frankincense incense clouding the air as it wafted out of a medieval-looking, pierced, brass container attached to a short chain, which the priest swung at what appeared to be arbitrary moments. The names Jesus, the Holy Spirit, the Virgin Mary and some of the saints were becoming more familiar to me by virtue of weekly repetition. But the service, performed primarily in Greek, was a big mystery. I didn't speak Greek. I suppose my father assumed I'd pick things up along the way and learn to be Greek Orthodox. But it never happened.

My mother treated our Sunday excursions without any reverence and only liked the priest's sermon. I didn't know she wasn't a Christian. For my mother, the church services were an occasion to get dressed up, socialize and put on jewelry that for the rest of the week was stashed away behind the floor-to-ceiling, pine-green dining room drapes that matched the color of the shag carpet. After the service, there was a social hour in a lackluster room with folding chairs and tables reserved for the congregation's get-togethers. The adults were served coffee and traditional Greek *kourambiethes* cookies on paper plates while the children drank watery red punch in polystyrene cups.

I was eight years old when my parents moved to a newly built tract home on Morten Ave. in Glendale, a suburb of Phoenix, to be closer to my father's new job at Honeywell. Glendale is a suburb on the west side of Phoenix and was founded as an important agricultural Mecca in the desert. The pre-historic Hohokam Indians had built an extensive series of canals in the area that were later excavated by early settlers. The Arizona Canal and Roosevelt Dam provided a stable supply of water that irrigated crops primarily of cotton, lettuce and melons. Then, as now, Glendale had a sizeable Mexican population. At night huge parks that stretched as far as the eye could see were lit up, giving the neighborhood a benign and wholesome feeling. Boys played baseball and football late into the evening and people hit tennis balls on free outdoor courts. However, until the Superbowl took place in Glendale in 2008, most people had never heard of this suburb of Phoenix.

Though the desert light is a source of inspiration to artists and sun-worshipers, I always found the relentless sun harsh and eerily bleak. I think Georgia O'Keeffe captured the feeling of the desert perfectly in her painting of a steer head cow skull bleached by the sun. Leonard Cohen once made a remark about the sunlight on the Greek island of Hydra where he had a small home. He said, "There's something in the light that's honest and philosophical." The desert sun in Arizona is honest too, but in a sterile way, like a beaming light on an operating table.

There were no Jewish landmarks, no Jewish touchstones as I was growing up. My parents didn't have Jewish friends. I didn't know I shared only part of my mother's life – the tip of the iceberg, the part exposed to public view. She kept her Jewish self hidden, even from me. At home our lives were steeped in Eastern European culture and *yidishkayt*, but the word "Jewish" wasn't in the vocabulary.

* * *

Going to the Greek Orthodox church on Sunday was bad enough. But I had no idea what lay in store for me next when my mother decided I should leave public school and attend a private Catholic parochial school, Our Lady of Perpetual Help. The change of schools coincided with my parents' move from Phoenix to Glendale when I was halfway through third grade. My mother had chosen to enroll me at OLPH in the same matter-of-fact way she made all of her decisions – that is, quickly, with intuition, and not much analysis. My mother wasn't from a Jewish anxiety-ridden tradition like a stereotyped stock character in a Woody Allen film. There was no looking back in the rear view mirror once a decision was made. When I recently asked her how she chose the school, she said, "Because a friend recommended it and I thought a private school would give you a better education than a public school." As an afterthought she added, "I thought it might be good for you to learn about being Catholic." Of course, she didn't mention what an important role religious instruction had played in helping her adopt mannerisms and learn prayers so that she could convincingly present herself as a Polish Catholic.

My parents didn't visit OLPH to look in on the classes, meet the teachers and tour the grounds the way parents so often do today. I doubt they even knew I'd be going to an institution where Catholic Mass was performed in Latin every day.

On the first day of school, my mother drove me to OLPH. She parked the car next to a small administrative office that adjoined the school room building, where a smiling nun awaited us with a friendly greeting. After a brief conversation, my mother turned to me and said, "I'll pick you up later, after school today. I'm sure you'll have a nice time here," and left. I had never seen a nun before. I was now alone with a woman wearing a strange headdress and unusual-looking clothes. The medieval-looking outfits were modified to suit the hot weather, and the nuns were swathed in pale gray gabardine-looking fabric that reached their ankles. They wore highly starched white cotton wimples that covered their foreheads and the sides of their faces. On their heads were long, gray veils that trailed behind them reaching just below the waist. A crucifix was on a long cord around each of their necks and on their left hands, a gold wedding band that symbolized their marriage to Jesus. (I later wondered how so many women could be married to Jesus at the same time, not to mention the sexual implications of the arrangement.) They wore flat, black, leather shoes with thick, utilitarian rubber soles, hopelessly out of fashion then, but the kind of comfortable walking shoes one sees all over today.

Mass was about to begin. Together the nun and I walked the short distance to a large auditorium that had been converted into a church. She led me to the pews where the third-grade class sat. Mass was a required daily ritual, and grades one through eight filed into the church auditorium every morning before school started. This time the priest wasn't speaking Greek, the language I associated with church, but Latin, one I'd never heard before. After what seemed like an eternity, out of nowhere the students started standing up and slowly filing toward the altar at the front of the church. It was time for the Rite of Communion. My heart racing, I followed along. We solemnly walked toward the priest, who was attended by altar boys on each side wearing white smocks with an eyelet pattern over their school uniforms. The altar boys held large gold platters, like flat saucers, underneath the students' chins while the priest dropped the host, a thin white wafer embossed with a cross, on the tip of their tongue and said, "The body of Christ" in Latin. This was different from the Greek Orthodox church. There the priest held a big basket of torn bits of bread and handed one piece each to the members of the congregation who then made their way down the center aisle and exited the church.

I self-consciously extended my tongue in this bizarre new ritual. Unfortunately, the host got stuck far back on the roof of my mouth. In vain, I tried to discretely dislodge it with my tongue. Starting to gag in my nervousness and with the host now stuck far back in my throat, I fought back nausea and tears. By the end of the first day, I had worked myself into a frenzied state of anxiety. When my mother came to pick me up, I burst into tears, telling her I hated the school and never wanted to go there again. She drove me back the next morning.

At the end of the first week of school, another unnerving ritual took place and sealed my fate as a claustrophobe forever. Every Friday, the third-grade class was required to go to confession. I didn't know what confession meant, but I followed the others to the penitentiary (the area where confessionals are) and soon it was my turn to open the door to the small closet-looking space and step inside where something was supposed to happen. "What do I do?" I asked one of the students next to me. She responded, "Say 'forgive me Father for I have sinned. It has been a week since my last confession, and I accuse myself of the following sins.'" I pulled open the door of the dimly lit confessional booth divided into two halves by a grill where a brown, plastic, padded kneeler awaited me. The priest's face was mysteriously shielded.

He asked me if I had sinned and I answered honestly, "I'm not sure." Father Maynihan must have guessed I was the new student and took a few minutes to explain the ritual of confession to me. While I was trying to figure out my sins, the priest kindly interjected, "Say one Our Father and four Hail Marys," and I was free to go. I didn't know the prayers, but had already made the connection that if I said the right thing I'd be forgiven. Sins, I later learned, came in two categories: mortal, the bigger ones that were like felonies, and venial, the smaller ones, that were like misdemeanors. I was starting to feel panicky in the darkened, small wooden chamber and in vain, looked for a doorknob to turn so I could get out of the confessional booth. Unable to find the doorknob, since there wasn't one, I pushed and pushed until the swinging door finally gave way and ejected me from the coffin-like embrace of darkness.

Mass took on huge proportions in my small world. With the adaptability that childhood provides, within the year I went through a steep learning curve and became accustomed to the once-strange rituals of the Mass, like genuflecting, making the sign of the cross, and accepting the body and blood of Christ at Communion.

It wasn't long before I became devoutly religious. I fervently repeated the rosary and prayed on my knees. I had an enormous hunger for belief. Spiritually, I had been an empty shell, but now for the first time, I developed a capacity for "otherness," something outside of the narrow confines of my life. I found religion. I prayed to Jesus through the Virgin Mary – as the nuns instructed us not to petition him directly. I learned about the lives of the saints and apostles, and collected holy cards with vivid depictions of saints in primary-colored robes and embossed gold halos.

Catholicism filled my spirit and imagination. I don't think I was so different from other children. Recently, I heard the child psychiatrist, Robert Coles, interviewed on the National Public Radio station and he said, "There is no doubt that a lot of the religious side of childhood is a merger of the natural curiosity and interest that children have in the world with the natural interest and curiosity that religion has about the world, because that's what religion is."

I hid my new-found religious passion from my parents. Though my mother, as always, took great interest in the minutia of my life and asked many questions about schoolwork, teachers, friends and daily events, she never inquired about religion class. I was relieved since I always felt extremely self-conscious talking about religion and was embarrassed to be seen praying in public. Prayer felt like a private act that would be diluted if it were shared. I would have preferred to be a hermit in a cave, but settled for being alone in my room with the door locked, where, on my knees, I devoutly recited the rosary, my fingers following the corresponding small beads for the Hail Marys and the larger ones for the Our Fathers.

Much to my dismay, my mother began insisting I should be baptized as a Catholic. Though I was becoming more religious each day, I didn't feel the need to go to such an extreme. I found the whole idea distasteful, as I knew this ritual was usually performed on infants. Father Cornelius Maynihan baptized me when I was nine years old. With my parents standing behind me, he performed the sacrament in front of a small basin that looked like a marble drinking fountain. I was sprinkled with holy water and my soul was now guaranteed its chance in heaven. I wasn't happy about the baptism and felt like I had been marked in an irrevocable way. But I didn't have a choice.

My mother had succeeded for the time in burying her past and my potential Jewish future. Her motivations were still unspoken, still unknown to me. Sending me to a Catholic school was based on a visceral emotional need, not a rational one. If I was Christian, in her mind, I was now "safe" from being a Jew. It completed the picture and allowed her to live an entirely non-Jewish existence. Though the Holocaust was over, she chose to appear as a Christian to everyone except our relatives in Montreal. My father didn't want anyone to know she was Jewish either.

Like a boat speeding through water, my mother's focus was on steering ahead, not what was left behind in the wake. Now she had achieved her goal. I was a Catholic and safe from an anti-Semitic world. Like most of my mother's decisions, once she made up her mind, she was on to her next idea. She often says, "Think, take your time, and once you make a decision just stick to it." I had a tendency to do the opposite. I was a waffler, not a dualist. There were always too many shades of gray in between my blacks and whites, and I would endlessly ponder whether or not I had made a right choice, hesitating to take action. I was afraid that if I came to a fork in the road and turned one way instead of another, my action would lead like a domino effect to tip over the other dominoes with no turning back, like the sentiment in a poem by Robert Frost: "Knowing how way leads on to way/ I doubted that I should ever come back." Decision making left me with dread. I didn't see making choices as expansive or life affirming, but reductive. I wondered if reflection is a luxury that my parents, like most immigrants, didn't allow themselves. They left their country behind and immersed themselves in a new life. They didn't sit around – they *did* things. They reinvented themselves in a new country, and in that sense, reinvented my life too. If I had stayed behind in the Montreal Jewish community with my parents, I would have been raised as a Jew, not a Catholic.

Until the middle of the third grade, I had gone to school at Loma Linda Public Grade School where there were no Mexican children in my classes. But here at OLPH, there were many Mexicans, or Chicanos, as we called them without prejudice or politically correct concerns at the time. They were outsiders like me, and I felt comfortable around them. They spoke Spanish at home. Like my parents, their parents also sounded different and didn't speak English with the broadcast accent common to everyone else around us. The Chicanos had their own culture and weren't considered poopular by the white students. I felt a kinship with them even though I didn't speak Spanish.

It had taken months to adjust to Catholic school. In the beginning, I was very anxious and got nauseated in the car every morning before my mother dropped me off. The first few times I felt sick, she took me back home. After that, she pulled the car over to the curb so I could get out and vomit next to the palm trees before she dropped me off at school. I told her, "I hate school. I don't want to go," and she replied, "You'll get used to it." That was the beginning and end of the conversation. The odors of the cafeteria food or the stale milk that settled to the bottom of the milk crates stacked in front of the entrance to the cafeteria were enough to make me feel nauseated again. I had tried to eat at the cafeteria a few times, but couldn't swallow a bite. I told my mother I wanted to bring my own lunch to school. It consisted of a peanut butter and honey sandwich wrapped in a waxed paper envelope, slipped into a small brown paper bag.

I ate the same sandwich every day from the third grade until the eighth. I sat with mostly Chicano students in the back of the auditorium, separated from the cafeteria by a floor to ceiling accordion screen.

This area with two picnic tables was for students who brought their own lunches, which, to us kids, clearly indicated a reduced social status. The students who brought lunch were the poorer ones whose parents were trying to save on the cost of cafeteria meals. This wasn't the case for me, but I was happy enough to sit there as long as I could be left alone to eat a sandwich and sip from a small carton of milk.

Not feeling I had a lot in common with any of the other children except the Chicanos seemed normal after a while. I was painfully shy and self-conscious, had a hard time making friends and didn't know how to play kickball, jacks or other schoolyard games when I first arrived. By the time I reached seventh grade I had become more sociable and had a clique of BFFS (best friends forever), Greta, Debbie and Nan, which made my life improve dramatically. Every morning I'd make the important decisions of the day – which pastel-colored blouse to wear with my plaid uniform, which color of ribbon to wear in my hair. Though the nuns preferred we wear white oxford blouses, they let us get by with pale yellow, pink and even blue. I now looked forward to going to school. Reading came easily to me and I devoured books and got As in my English classes. My foreign accent was long gone.

* * *

I'll always be grateful to the nuns at Our Lady of Perpetual Help. In fact, I would have probably remained a Catholic if my spiritual and intellectual development had been more in sync with the catechism classes I took. As my interest in Catholicism developed, I asked more questions. But the answers weren't in my catechism book, and it was bad form to query the nuns about sticky religious points like the Immaculate Conception of Jesus Christ, transubstantiation or the pope's infallibility.

My intellectual curiosity was unsatisfied and as I got older, even my considerable religious fervor wasn't enough to keep me in the flock. Nonetheless, the nuns at OLPH helped shape my youth and psyche. They were the early teachers of passion and unconditional love. Through the life and miracles of Jesus, I learned about transcendence, which had meant escape from my lonely childhood into a different, more spiritual realm. I poured my youthful energies into the mystical world of Catholicism. I studiously observed Sister Adele Clare, the nun who had befriended me on the first day of school. She seemed saintly and I imitated her, trying to hold my hands in prayer exactly the way she did. I wondered what her face looked like without a veil. Sister Adele Clare was my guardian angel. She took me under her wing, sharing and explaining to me an invisible world full of intangible saints, untouchable spirits and unknowable forces beyond the confines of the material world I inhabited.

It was ironic that while my mother was concealing her Jewish identity from me and the rest of the world, I was hiding my devout Catholicism from her. I didn't want her to find out about the hours I spent in my room kneeling on the floor and reciting the rosary.

When Sundays came around, it was time to go to the Greek Orthodox church again. I didn't like the long, drawn-out service that was different and more dramatic than the Catholic mass, and did my best to remain detached from it. I followed along dutifully with the motions of standing, sitting and kneeling, but my mind was a million miles away. I didn't acknowledge my Greek background and refused to learn the language. I didn't identify with my father's culture, but completely with my mother, who was the person I loved and admired more than anyone in the world. I thought religion wasn't important to her and that she went along with being Greek Orthodox one day a week to make my father happy. Compartmentalizing was normal and I didn't see a conflict in going to Catholic school during the week and Greek Orthodox services on Sunday.

Catholicism provided me with an emotional base and religious identity, since I didn't feel Greek, Chicano or much of anything else. I knew my mother was from a country called Poland (she never said Lithuania), but she rarely mentioned it. When she did, it was only to describe something from her childhood like a beautiful silk, pleated dress with handmade lace or a sleigh ride pulled by horses with tinkling bells attached to their harnesses, which felt, she said, "like we were flying across the snow." The details of her life were still hazy and unformed.

She continued to be a religious chameleon. At the Greek Orthodox church, she was Greek Orthodox. When she went to OLPH, she was Catholic. There is a photo of my parents and me in front of the church altar at OLPH on the day of my Confirmation, one of the Holy Sacraments. My mother is wearing a small straw hat with a garland of beige and pink silk flowers; her hands are clasped and she has a pleasantly inscrutable smile on her face. I had asked to take Veronica as my Confirmation name, but she insisted on Christine. "It sounds more like your father's name," she said.

I didn't give much thought to my parents' religious affiliations. To me, religion was like a hobby. It was something you could pick up and practice or drop for a new interest. There were still no prayers or religious practices in our home and we never once talked about what went on during the church service. Yet religion fulfilled my need for rituals and marking time. It helped my psychological and emotional development connecting me to a world outside of the narrow confines of Glendale, Arizona. In my dresser drawer were a small plastic crucifix and a couple of rosaries along with an impressive collection of holy cards secured with a rubber band, but my mother either never looked in the drawer or chose not to question me about the religious paraphernalia.

I still had no idea my mother had a secret identity. I was naïve, sheltered and assimilated. I thought the very definition of religion meant believing in the Trinity of the Father, the Son and the Holy Spirit, a doctrine that I later learned was solidified when Emperor Constantine I assembled the Christian Bishops in Nicaea in 325 CE to uniformly codify principle tenets of the Roman Catholic church. I knew Jesus was a Jew, but I didn't know my mother and I were too. I didn't know my mother had a profound knowledge of Judaism. It was her one true and steadfast faith – a faith she never abandoned.

I Am a Jew

My mother is on the phone speaking Yiddish to my grandmother, Esther, who lives in Montreal. I overhear her saying, "*Mir kumen bald af Peysakh.*" We're coming soon, for Passover. This is big news to me. I sit down next to her on the beige and brown tweed couch in the family room next to the kitchen, staring at her and impatiently biding my time until she gets off the phone. Before she has a chance to put down the receiver, I ask incredulously, "We're going to Montreal – *this* Saturday?" I'm twelve years old and in awe of my mother.

"*Far vos nit?*" Why not? she responds. "You have some time off from school, and your father doesn't want to use up his vacation days now. We'll go there and visit your grandmother," she says by way of explanation. My mother is spontaneous and brings excitement and adventure to our middle-class existence. This isn't the first time she's suggested spur-of-the moment trips, but they've always been closer to home. We'd been to Montreal a few years ago, but this time we're going without my father. He drives us to the small airport. In the terminal is the already-famous mural of a huge, soaring red bird that greets travelers, painted by the artist Coze in 1962. It's the symbol of Phoenix, a bird rising from the ashes.

The long flight from Phoenix finally over, we land at Dorval Airport in Montreal and take a taxi to my Uncle Leo's and Aunt Berna's house on Hudson Ave. in the nearby suburb of Cote St. Luc. All the signs are in both French and English. Even the stop signs have *arrêt* and "stop" written on them.

Uncle Leo owns Provincial Home Furnishings, a store that sells carpets and furniture to homes and large institutions like hotels. I know from my mother that he is "*zeyer klug*," very smart. This must account for his large, elegant, multi-level house in Montreal with its carved Chinese carpet in the living and dining room and grouped paintings and needlepoints over the couch. The homes here look totally different from the flat, sprawling ones in Arizona. Leo and Berna also have two children. Iona is one year younger than me and Perry, five.

My aunt readies the guest room for us and opens the fold-out bed. It's nestled between the room with the ping-pong table and a short hall that leads to my grandmother's door and residence. Her home is furnished tastefully, without knick-knacks, and on the wall are a few framed pictures of needlepoint landscapes that she's done. My grandmother doesn't resemble my mother very much. She has light olive skin, brown eyes, brown hair and a subtle, warm prettiness. She wears bright tropical colors. In her closet are a gold lamé and black fringe evening dress and some others with oversized red floral prints. Her taste in clothes is different from that of my mother's, who favors beige and solid colors.

There's a faint lingering smell of Bengay and furniture polish in the apartment. A memorial candle with Hebrew lettering is always on the kitchen counter. There's a Yiddish newspaper on the table. Since I don't know Hebrew, I can't decipher any writing in Yiddish, which borrows the Hebrew alphabet, though it is an entirely different language. I listen to my mother and grandmother talk as we sit together next to a large window from where we can look out directly at the bright green front lawn. My grandmother calls me by a new name, which everyone uses now, "Helinke," a Yiddish diminutive of Helen.

We go upstairs to the kitchen, where dinner preparations are already in full swing. The atmosphere is *freylekh*, full of chattering and laughter. The overpowering scent of chicken in the oven is mixed with the freshly baked desserts cooling on the counter. "Rasia, we have your favorite," Aunt Berna says. "*Mon strudel!*" my mother exclaims with a big smile. It's a perfect spiral of poppy seeds contained in a sugary roll, a desert she often bakes at home. In Arizona, nobody calls my mother her real name, Rasia. There she's known as Rena, and sometimes Renée. My mother calls Leo by the Jewish diminuitive of his name, Lebele. Everyone's name seems to be interchangeable. Again, I don't give it a second thought.

The kitchen door swings directly into the formal dining room with the longest table I have ever seen at anyone's house. It's already set with a white tablecloth and cloth napkins, silver-plated bowls, gold-rimmed dinner plates, crystal stemware and foods I don't recognize.

A new ritual begins. My uncle and cousin put on a *yarmulke*, and the dining room atmosphere immediately changes and becomes solemn, as though we're sitting in church. My uncle begins reciting from a book in an unfamiliar language.

"What language is that?" I whisper to my mother.

"Hebrew," she says.

"Why is there grape juice in my wine glass?" I continue. She shakes her head slightly. I'll have to ask later. Soon the Passover recitation is over. Everyone starts talking at once and helping themselves to the food.

"What was he reading?" I ask.

"It's the Haggadah. He was reading about the Jews' exodus from Egypt."

"Oh. What are those big crackers?" I ask.

"It's *matzoh*. Here, take a piece. Try the matzoh ball soup and taste a little of the gefilte fish," she offers, ladling a spongy looking piece of food on my plate. "See if you like it."

"Why did Uncle Leo put a piece of parsley in the water and eat it?"

"It's a tradition for Pesach. I'll explain it to you later," she says.

"What's in the little silver bowl?"

"It's *charoset*," my mother says. "It's apples, nuts and cinnamon. It represents the mortar that was used by the Jews for building at the time they were in slavery."

I've heard of Jews before in Catechism class, though they were quickly glossed over. There's a lot to take in at the dinner. New food. New atmosphere. Something is different about my mother, too. She seems like another person here. She's carefree and laughing. She jokes with her brother exchanging *khokhmes*, witty repartie, and the two of them are so funny I feel I could fall off my chair laughing. I've never seen my mother alone with her family. For the first time, I realize she was once a girl like me. She seems so much happier here. Back home in Arizona, it's just my parents and me at the dinner table; we never laugh as much. I like having my cousin Perry to play ping-pong with. I wish he was my brother; I wish we could live here.

The next morning, when I wake up, my mother has already left the room. She's with my grandmother, drinking Earl Grey tea and having toast and home-made blueberry jam for breakfast. I walk over to join them at the round Formica table, and my grandmother asks if I'd like some Ovaltine. I notice my mother's eyes are red and my grandmother is crying. "*Far vos veynstu?*" I ask, Why are you crying? "We're talking about something that happened a long time ago," my grandmother says, "during the *milkhome*." It's a new word. I turn to my mother. "It's a Hebrew word. It means, the war," she says. "We Jews were persecuted during the war."

I'm only slowly putting the pieces of the puzzle together. "But I'm Catholic. You and Dad got married in a Catholic church."

"The Greek church wouldn't marry us because I wasn't Greek Orthodox, so we married in the Roman Catholic church instead. In the Jewish law, if the mother is Jewish, so is the child. So, you're Jewish. But you were baptized as a Catholic. You have a choice."

"I don't get it," I continue, more perplexed than ever. "So am I Catholic or not?"

"You can be whatever you want."

"What do you mean?"

"You can choose whatever you want. I wanted to wait until you were old enough to understand. The Jewish people have been a persecuted minority for over two thousand years and they'll continue to be persecuted. Why should you be Jewish and suffer? I didn't have a choice. You do." I look at my grandmother's tear-streaked face as she nods at my mother's words.

If my mother was Jewish, I wanted to be Jewish too, though I wasn't quite sure what to make of my new-found identity. In Montreal I felt newly connected to my relatives in a more profound way, and back home I felt exotic and different from my friends at the Catholic school. I had a foot in two worlds. In Montreal, I absorbed the elements of Jewish life; I was engulfed in yidishkayt. In Arizona, I didn't know a single person who was Jewish.

When my mother and I returned from our trip, life went on as it had before. But now I had a new secret identity. My mother said there was no reason to "advertise" my Jewish background to anyone. It was family information. "*Private*," she stressed, "Don't tell anybody. They won't understand." She told me it was possible they wouldn't associate with us, as the world was a place full of prejudice. I liked the fact that being Jewish was something only my mother and I shared. Since my father was Greek

Orthodox and not a Jew like us, I had yet another convenient reason to deny my Greek heritage. I had never felt connected to being Greek and now I felt less so than ever. Most important of all, my mother stressed, "Don't ever tell anyone at the Greek church that we're Jewish. There's no need to. It's our business."

In the meantime, I had started asking my mother questions about our recent trip to Montreal. "Why does grandmother cry so often?" I asked. I learned it was because of "*a groyser umglik dos hot pasirt,*" a big tragedy that had happened. My mother never used the word "Holocaust." She referred to it as the *groyser umglik.* I didn't know about Hitler. I didn't know that most of our extended family had been killed. I assumed the "big tragedy" was the war they talked about, and I thought it wasn't at all unusual for people to be persecuted and killed during wars. Wasn't that, after all, what the nuns taught us in history class?

Whenever I questioned her, my mother would tell me little bits of the past. She gave brief answers, but didn't volunteer any extra information. Only later did I learn the full tragedy of what had happened to her family.

Life went on as usual and daily routine took over. I was still a Catholic. I didn't think much about being Jewish, and didn't associate it with religious worship, as I had never been to a synagogue. I felt being Jewish was part of my cultural heritage and nothing more. I had no internal conflict. Catholicism and Judaism were in their neat compartments, and in my mind one didn't have anything to do with the other.

When I graduated from OLPH, I had the choice of attending the local public high school, Apollo High, or continuing a parochial education and going to Bourgade High, the private Catholic high school in Phoenix. This time my parents let me decide. I agonized and weighed the pros and cons. I didn't want to wear a school uniform again and going to Bourgade High meant I'd have to take a school bus to and from school. On the other hand, the public school, Apollo High was only a short, ten-minute walk from my house. But at Apollo High, the girls had to shower after physical education class. At Bourgade, there were no showers, and after sweating in our PE clothes, we'd just change back into our uniforms. I was painfully shy and self-conscious and hated the thought of enforced nakedness in the locker rooms. For that reason alone, I chose to spend Freshman year and half of my Sophomore year at the Catholic Bourgade High School.

At Bourgade High, uniforms were mandatory. The girls were required to wear white blouses and generic-looking navy blue plaid jumpers with two large strips of cloth that formed a large V-shape from the waist up and were strategically draped across our blossoming chests. Unlike OLPH, Mass was no longer a daily event, but we had religion class every afternoon. Our religion teacher, a young nun, was particularly fond of the musical *Jesus Christ Superstar*. She conducted our class like a study hall period and played the album *Jesus Christ Superstar* every afternoon. We kept ourselves busy at our desks, whiling away the time and listening to the music or doing homework. I knew all of the words to the musical by heart, and especially liked the song, "I Don't Know How to Love Him," sung by Mary Magdalene to Jesus. I had a school-girl crush on Steve Brown, a tall fellow with shoulder-length, wavy sun-bleached surfer hair, blue eyes, and a staccato laugh who was in my art class, but I had still never kissed a boy.

Every Sunday I attended the Greek Orthodox church with my parents. There, whenever my mother spoke to church members, she'd resume an alternate persona, one that was distinctly different from her private identity. One of the first questions people often asked her was, "Where are you from?" She always said Vienna. They never asked about her religion, assuming the wife of a Greek man must have converted and be Greek Orthodox too. I know she felt like an outsider in the Greek community, even though she had started taking Greek lessons and had a conversational grasp of the language. The other female church members were polite to her, but distant. My mother wasn't one of them, and they didn't go out of their way to include her in church activities. After a couple of attempts to bake cookies and volunteer for events, she stopped trying. "I'm an outsider," she said. "Those women will never accept me."

I didn't approve of her made-up identity. It seemed like a lot of trouble pretending to be someone else. I'd never contradict her in public, but at home I'd often say, "Why do you care so much about what those people think? What's wrong with telling them we're Jewish or that you're from Vilnius?"

"I don't think they'd even let us into the church if they knew."

"I don't believe it," I responded.

"I'm sure it's true," she confirmed.

Her comments didn't endear me to the church. In my eyes, my mother was faultless, but it was still hard for me to reconcile the idea of her double life. I didn't want her to be one person at church, the place where my parents' social life was centered, and another person the rest of the time. I didn't want her to be ashamed of who she was. It didn't take long for me to start wondering if there really was something very wrong about being Jewish, and if it wasn't such a bad idea to keep it hidden. Next, I started resenting my father. I reasoned: if he were Jewish and not Greek, we wouldn't have to be ashamed of who we were in the first place.

With my mother's relatives on the Sabbath and *Pesach* (Passover) in Montreal, there was laughter, good food and the feeling of belonging with people who cared about you. No one in Montreal denied being Jewish. On the contrary, it was a way of life to be celebrated. My mother's false identity at the Greek Orthodox church was making me feel increasingly uncomfortable. It was all I could do to sit by passively and observe her as she took on a different role like an actress on Sundays. I, too, played a role of the smiling and dutiful daughter – but inside I was neither. I didn't want my mother or me to be at the church where I was always on guard, afraid of accidentally saying the wrong thing, resenting the chatty Greeks who my mother had assured me wouldn't speak to us if they knew our secret. I felt there were places in the world where people would love my mother for who she was. That's where the two of us belonged.

CHRISTMAS

"Come on. Help me decorate the tree," my father says.

"I told you already, decorate it yourself!" my mother answers with a not-very-subtle inflection of annoyance and finality. It's not that she's hostile to the idea of a Christmas tree, but it doesn't interest her either. She's not the decorating type. My father likes to choose items for the house decor and rearrange furniture. The Christmas tree also falls under his jurisdiction.

"Helen, come here. Right now! Put the ornaments on the tree!" he calls out angrily.

"I'm not decorating a piece of metal. Maybe I would if you got a *real* tree!" I shout back. It's a typical Christmas season for us. My father mutters under his breath while he decorates the tree by himself. Busy in the kitchen, my mother doesn't pay any attention to his exertions. I follow her lead, retreating to my room where I close the door and pick up a book to read, indulging in the private world of one of my favorite pastimes.

I'm seventeen and a junior in high school. The year before, I transferred from Bourgade High to the local public school, Apollo High. My new friends at Apollo High are hippies with long hair and tattered jeans who smoke pot in the parking lot and play in bands. They're particularly fond of playing blues and "Derek and the Dominoes" cover tunes. Ever since I watched an anti-smoking movie in a third grade science class that compared a healthy non-smoker's bubble-gum-pink lung alongside a smoker's lung that looked like a piece of dun-colored tripe, I don't like cigarettes and don't smoke marijuana for the same reason. Still, I'm accepted in the clique and have a small, close-knit circle of laid-back friends.

My mother loves to bake. She's making spritz cookies, sugar cookies pumped out of a small, metal cylinder syringe, then decorated with chocolate sprinkles. She's an alchemist who uses an assortment of metal cookie discs to transform the dough into flowered shapes, diamonds, clubs and hearts. Soon the house will fill with a wonderful buttery aroma I associate with holidays like Christmas and Easter. On some Easters, my mother boils eggs that we paint and decorate. Then we all follow the Greek custom of ramming the eggs together, to see who will be the winner or loser. The winner's egg remains intact, while the loser's egg is dented or cracked. An Easter ritual and life lesson at the same time.

I'm eating lots of butter cookies these days, though it wasn't so long ago that I was anorexic. The year before, as a sophomore in high school, I had whittled my weight down to 89 pounds, a number I was extremely proud of. I was a serious and dedicated ballet student with dreams of becoming a professional dancer. Leslie Browne, who later became a principal dancer for the American Ballet Theatre was in my classes at the Phoenix dance studio owned by her father, Kelly Brown. Leslie and I performed together (though she was a soloist and I was in the corps de ballet) in her father's fledgling ballet company. All the other dancers I knew were exceedingly thin. Anorexia was just a bit further down the slippery slope of the physical "perfection" we were striving for, constantly and critically checking ourselves in the mirror with zealous narcissism. When I shared my aspirations with my mother, she scoffed, "Dancing isn't a profession! It's a hobby! It's good for your posture."

Though I wasn't consciously aware of it, I was still trying to piece together an identity for myself. I was trying to find meaning in my life. In ballet class, religion, ethnic background and other identifying factors fell to the wayside. I felt solidarity with the other dancers and had a stronger identity in class than anywhere else. There I felt in control of my life and learned first hand that it takes determination, hard work, time, and patience to achieve goals and inner satisfaction.

* * *

As always, my father centers the tree in the window and draws the drapes open so it can be viewed by anyone who drives by. To me it shouts, "Let all who pass by know that Christians live here."

As usual, we don't do anything much different on Christmas than on any other day. "Let's go to the church service," my father says, referring to midnight mass at the Greek Orthodox church.

"I'm not going," I say. "I made other plans."

"It's too late at night," my mother adds. The church service is a social event for her. She prefers to attend on Sunday mornings, arriving in time to catch the sermon and chat with people afterward over coffee.

The year before, I'd vowed never to go back to the Greek Orthodox church after an experience that was irrevocable. On that Sunday the priest had said in his sermon, "The Jews are responsible for killing Jesus." It's not the first time he's made negative remarks about Jewish people. But this time, it's the last straw for me. Sitting next to my mother in the pew, I nudge her with my elbow and we exchange glances. As we exit the church after taking communion and leave the darkened interior, spilling with other parishioners into the halogen-bright sunshine outside, my mother turns to me and says partly in Yiddish, "The priest, *er iz a yold.*" The priest is a fool.

"I know. Why would you even want to come back here when he says things like that?" I ask.

"He's an ignorant man. He's from a *dorf.*" A small village. "Not everyone thinks the way he does."

"But he's said stuff like that before. How can you just sit there and listen to him say negative things about Jews?" I respond, both incensed and humiliated at what I misjudge as her passivity.

"You don't understand. Everybody needs to belong somewhere," she says.

"But you said they wouldn't even let us past the front steps of the church if they knew we were Jewish."

"You're baptized," she says to me pointedly. "Anyway, if we didn't come here, we wouldn't have any social life at all. Everyone needs to belong somewhere."

"It's not where I belong!" I say.

* * *

I don't care if my father threatens me. I'll never go back to the church. It's my way of standing up for my mother and me, standing up for being

Jewish. When my father shouts, his face turns red and his eyes start to bulge, but at a certain point I disassociate and feel like a thick piece of invisible glass rises between us. I'm watching him on the other side of the glass. I hardly even hear him. I feel nothing. Only apathy. It's one of the preferred states of my adolescence and I try to cultivate it. I welcome it as a diversion from depression.

"You're coming whether you like it or not!" he commands, shouting through my locked bedroom door, menacingly rattling the knob. In spite of myself, I'm holding my breath. I'm afraid he'll use a credit card to unlock the door like he has before and burst into my room screaming.

"See what you did to her?" he accuses my mother who is now also at the door, in what I interpret as an attempt to rescue me.

"Forget it. I'm *never* going back. Leave me alone!" I shout at the top of my lungs. I put a Moody Blues album on the turntable. My mother recently bought me a new stereo system, which I listen to for hours at a time. It's my pride and joy: a Garrard turntable, Pioneer receiver, Advent speakers and Shure M91ED needle. I select my favorite song and turn up the volume to drown out my father's voice. "Knights in White Satin" starts to carry me away to a different and better place. "Nights in white satin, never reaching the end. Letters I've written, never meaning to send..." I lie down on the bed and stare at the ceiling. I wonder if other parents with different religious backgrounds argue the way my parents do. I have no idea. I don't have any friends in the same situation I can talk to.

It will be many years later, not until 2007, that I read an article in the *New York Times* that says the stresses holidays bring "are a familiar problem: the annual conflict faced by millions of adults in interfaith marriages over how to decorate homes, how and when to give gifts, and which rituals to celebrate." The article, "A Holiday Medley, Off Key," says "as of 2001, more than 28 million Americans lived in mixed-religious households."

My feelings are hurt by what the priest said. If he doesn't like Jews, then I don't like him either. I resolve to never go back to the Greek Orthodox church again. And I never do. The matter is settled. Tomorrow is another day and soon the holidays will be over.

My days as a Christian are over too.

Stories My Mother Told Me

Even as an adult, when my mother talked to me about her childhood, I felt like I was a child again and she was reading one of the wonderful fairy tales to me from the stack of books in my room. I could picture the forests, fields of yellow wildflowers, blueberries, and romanticize the kind peasants she told me about. I felt like I could get lost in the green magic kingdom that she experienced as a girl. I can't help idealizing her childhood. It's a time when I imagine she was the happiest.

I always felt that no matter how hard I tried, I could never do enough to compensate for all the suffering my mother went through. The enormity of her loss was something I started to resent. I felt powerless against it. I didn't want to be reminded of how vulnerable and helpless my mother and Jewish relatives had been. In the back of my mind, I always believed that if I had lived during the Holocaust, I wouldn't have had the wit and will to survive like my mother did. My mother says, "You never know how strong you are until you're tested." Her suffering and loss only made me try all the harder to make her happy. If she was angry or disappointed in me, I felt like there was a dark cloud hovering over my world. Her approval made the sun come out again.

Not unlike many Jewish mothers, mine thought I was a genius and often told me so. I knew I was far from being a genius. Nor was I even a serious student. I liked subjects that came easily and was lazy when it came to studying. My strengths were very limited: I could read novels all day long and got As on English class compositions. It was getting harder for me to live up to my mother's expectations. She wanted me to go to law school, something

189

I had zero interest in. I'm reminded of the superb Japanese film by Yasujiro Ozu, *Tokyo Story*, in which a parent remarks, "Maybe we expect too much from our children." In all fairness, the reverse is also true. I basically had two talents: one was writing, the other was parallel parking. I joked to my mother that I should get a job as a parking valet and write about it.

It was difficult to separate my needs and identity from my mother's. She was my backbone and strength. She always told me how important I was to her. "You are my reason for living," she'd say. But that kind of love was a burden. It involved too many obligations. It carried the weighty risk of failure. I didn't want to feel that I was responsible for my mother's happiness, but I did.

For many years I felt I wasn't fully alive. I felt I wasn't my own person, because I was living my life for the two of us.

* * *

The story my mother told about Hans Geisler, the German officer who attempted to help her, always fascinated me. How much did he actually help her? He tried, but largely failed. I played the scene of my mother and Hans sitting on the spavined leather couch together in the empty house over and over in my head as though it were a memorable scene I had watched in a movie. I added romance where there was none. I imagined my mother smiling and chatting with him, even flirting, when, in fact, she told me they sat together mostly in silence on the couch. She said she was so afraid they'd be caught that she could barely speak, though Hans told her about his life, children, and unhappy marriage. Was he trying to sleep with her?

I wondered about the details. Why did he risk everything to help her? Was it only for a gold watch? If they had slept together, would she even tell me?

Perhaps Hans Geisler was one more mercenary person trying to profit from the misfortune of the Jews. Or maybe he really cared about my mother. He was sent to the Russian front, so it's possible he survived. His children would probably be in their seventies now. What would I say to them? I would like to thank your father for helping my mother. I hope you're proud of him. Like a message in a bottle tossed out to sea, maybe one day my words will reach them.

* * *

I recently watched a documentary on TV about the Jewish mathematician, Benoit Mandelbrot, who is the father of fractal geometry. Mandelbrot was from a Lithuanian family who moved to Warsaw and then fled to France in 1936 to escape Nazi persecution. He said, "There's nothing more hardening in life than surviving as a hunted civilian. I lost my trust in people, in other people's wisdom." Mandelbrot's comment sounded like something my mother would say. She doesn't trust anyone outside of our immediate family. Even though she's warm and emotional around family and friends, when it comes to strangers she's suspicious of their motives and there's a toughness that underlies her charm. I don't know if this toughness is something she was born with or if it's a result of her life experience.

During the Holocaust she took chances when the odds against her were enormous. She never cracked under pressure. At her friend Regina Szewczykowna's party she waltzed with a Nazi officer while posing as a Polish woman. She looked people straight in the eye, and "without any emotion, trying to act like I didn't have a care in the world," lied about her identity, lied more than once to save her life, not to be found out as a Jew and taken to a concentration camp or "shot on the spot," as she'd often say. There were many close calls.

I've often dreamed that my mother is an Israeli spy. I'd wake up and say to myself, "Of course she is! Now it all makes perfect sense." It wouldn't surprise me. On a certain level she'll always be a stranger to me – like a spy with a hidden identity, with an unknown past. I wonder if there are parts of her life that she's locked away in her psyche and will never share with me. I suspect there are. I recently read a newspaper article about returning soldiers from Iraq who had suffered posttraumatic stress syndrome. The article made me think of my mother since the recovering soldiers shared thoughts so similar to hers. It said the soldiers created a new belief that the world is not safe – they have a combat mentality that works in combat, but when it comes time for them to come home, they can't make the transition to civilian life. I also read a new study written on PTSD that says people with the disorder "are unable to see the event as time-limited and assume that it has larger implications for the future… they overgeneralize from the event and begin to assume that normal activities are more dangerous than they actually are."

My mother believes the world is unsafe; people can't be trusted and they take advantage of others whenever they can. She thinks it is an evil place, but we can choose to try and live a righteous life. Even though I never wanted to accept her assessment of human nature, her beliefs left a deep impression on me. Not only did I assume everything she told me was true, I even took it a step further. When I was younger, I had devised my own theory and believed people didn't reveal their true selves and thoughts, but said the opposite of what they meant. I thought this was the way of the world. I didn't realize that I had incorporated my mother's divisiveness. Like her, I found ways to divide my psyche. (It wasn't until I entered psychotherapy years later that I learned about the unhealthy repercussions of a divided self.) There was the outside world of pretense and the inside world of my true thoughts. There was the outside world of presenting a Christian identity and the inside world of my spiritual and cultural ties to Judaism. I lived with this duality, which seemed normal to me. I was raised with it. But I didn't know what a big price my mother had paid to stand guard over her deception. Nor did I understand that living a dual life could be an isolating experience.

There was something missing that I couldn't pinpoint or define. One of the things lacking in our lives was a connection to a community. Our family didn't have roots in any group. My mother had tried to dig roots in the Greek Orthodox world of my father, but they never took hold. Even my father couldn't be totally accepted in the Greek community because he had married a non-Greek. At the church, my parents developed a deeper friendship with a couple who also had a mixed marriage, a Greek man married to an Anglican English woman. But like everyone else at the church, this couple didn't know my mother's true background. She was flawless in her deception. I both admired and resented it.

I never doubted my mother would have made an excellent spy. She can juggle two identities. She has incredible nerve and is a person to rely on when times are difficult. She's not the type of person one can depend on only when things are going well, as the Yiddish expression puts it – somebody only good for dancing at weddings, *Er toyg nor tsu tantsn af khasenes.* When I was in New York on 9/11, stores and restaurants started closing and the afternoon took on a slightly surreal feeling as normal activity came to a halt. A fleeting thought occurred to me, what if food supplies became scarce? What would I do? Of course, I'd call my mother! I knew my thoughts were completely irrational, but after all, she was an expert in finding food during World War II. If grocery stores shut down and food supplies were limited, she'd help me. She'd teach me how to barter, how to secure bread.

Although my mother is elegant and worldly, she reminds me of the Israelis, with their tough, abrasive, take-no-bullshit personalities. When I told her that her sentences have a rising inflection and she gestures in the same way and sounds like Joan Rivers, with arms raised and palms turned up toward the ceiling, she said, "Me? I can't stand the way Joan Rivers talks. I don't really sound like that, do I?"

There's a huge chasm that separates her private Jewish inner life from the Christian face she still presents to the outside world. She is still two people. But because I grew up with both of these people – the Jewish mother and the Christian one – I made the instinctive bridge between them as a child and her dual life didn't seem unusual to me.

The other day, we were on the phone having a conversation about religion, and she made a remark about the superficiality of her relationship with people at the Greek Orthodox church.

"They're not *real* friends," she said.

I asked her again, "Why don't you and Dad try going to a synagogue? You've been going to the Greek Orthodox church with him for so many years, couldn't he go with you just once?"

Her reply surprises me. "I can't go. I don't want to. It reminds me of my childhood. It touches something deep inside of me." She pauses. "It's too real."

"Can't you just try it *one* time?" I ask. Even though I should know better, I'm foolishly trying to use reason to win over an emotional decision. I don't want to give up. I think I know what's best for her, and am trying to find a way to make her happy. I'm certain she'd be happier if she went to the synagogue and connected to her own people. Our people.

"I'll never go," she says. "The thought is too depressing."

WHAT DO YOU KNOW ABOUT BEING JEWISH?

The protective cocoon of being a Catholic lasted while I was in grade school. But as my mother gradually revealed more about her life, as I became aware of the atrocities she had experienced during the Holocaust, a new development started taking place inside of me. Attached to my mother, and as protective of her as she was of me, I started feeling that her pretense of being anything other than Jewish was false. It was a betrayal to my relatives who had died in the Holocaust. It was a negation of who my mother was, and by extension, who I was.

In Montreal, my grandmother, uncles, aunts and cousins' lives were paper-weighted with Jewish tradition and ritual. They attended synagogue and observed the holidays. My mother and I continued to visit Montreal every couple of years, but my father rarely came with us, preferring to stay in Arizona. In Montreal, we'd come together as a family for the Friday night Sabbath or religious holidays, joining Uncle Leo and Aunt Berna, my cousins Iona and Perry, and my grandmother, Esther. We'd also visit my mother's older brother Benjamin and his wife Inez, who lived about a ten-minute drive away in the nearby suburb of Hampstead.

Benjamin and Inez had lived in Rome for many years before moving to Montreal. In Rome, Inez's family owned retail clothing stores where both she and my uncle had worked, and Benjamin managed a clothing store on Via Nazionale. I thought my Uncle Benjamin was wonderful. His personality was different from my mother's and Uncle Leo's. He was witty like they were, but wry and less sociable. When we said goodbye, instead of the customary, *zayt gezunt*, his departing words to me were always, "Enjoy life."

In Montreal, I started feeling connected to my mother's world, to the Jewish world. I didn't fit in the Greek Orthodox world of my father or Catholic school, where my faith in Catholicism had long ago peaked and fizzled out.

Though I had a strong yearning to be Jewish when we were in Montreal, as soon as we returned to Glendale, everything changed again and religion became a non-issue. It was on the back burner, or to be more precise, on no burner at all. It was a schizophrenic religious identity based on geography. In Glendale, I still didn't know a single Jewish person. My parents didn't have any Jewish friends. Though they continued attending the Greek Orthodox services on Sundays, I refused to go with them after I had made up my mind at age seventeen never to return there and be subjected to the Greek priest's anti-Semitic remarks.

In my quest for religious identity, I latched on to the *zeitgeist* and Eastern philosophy. I was searching for a personal creed, and was drawn to Buddhism and non-dogmatic expressions of spirituality, but not enough to devote myself completely to any one religion or practice. Instead, I burrowed further into the comforts of a middle-class suburban life. I was self-involved and mired in my own narcissistic adolescent concerns, interested in ballet, books and boys, more or less in that order.

* * *

When I was eighteen and a freshman in college, I bought a very small gold pendant to wear on a necklace. The pendant consisted of two intertwined Hebrew letters that spelled *chai*, the word for life. My parents and I had recently returned from a trip to Montreal, where I developed a sudden, strong yearning to study Judaism. I was curious about the traditions and rituals I saw my relatives observe on weekends. I asked my cousin Perry why he didn't turn on the television set from sundown on Friday to sunset on Saturday. Though he was five years younger than me, I considered him worldly, and it seemed an anachronism for someone like him to step into what I perceived as the ancient world of Jewish observance. I was intrigued. With the pendant around my neck, I felt I was connected to other Jews.

But wearing the chai pendant was a secretive and subversive act, which I tried to hide from my mother. In an ironic twist, I was mimicking my mother and hiding my Jewishness – not from the world, but from her. Wearing the pendant gave me a connection to something greater than my immediate surroundings. It gave me the feeling of belonging somewhere, though I wasn't quite sure where that was, and a sense of identification, though I wasn't entirely clear as to what I was identifying with either, other than my mother and her people. In the library stacks at Glendale Community College, I had pulled a lone, yellowed book on Judaism from the shelf and sat on the floor reading about Kabbalah, which intrigued me mostly because my mother once remarked that in Vilnius, "Only scholars who studied for years were allowed to read the Kabbalah." I got to a section where the author explained that God is referred to as Hashem, Who was, is and will be. I was accustomed to praying to God the Father, an image I still comfortably envisioned as one third of the Trinity (though I had conveniently deleted the other two thirds – Jesus and the Holy Spirit – when I lost my faith as a Christian). After returning from the library, when I got home that night, I began a prayer of supplication: "Dear Hashem," but felt I was addressing a stranger. I tried again: "Dear God, dear Hashem, give me faith. Help me believe in You."

It wasn't long before my mother noticed the necklace. Never one to mince words, she immediately asked, "Why are you wearing that? What do *you* know about being Jewish?" I sensed her disapproval. "I see no reason to display your beliefs or associations on the outside." As though there were need for further elucidation, she added, "Whether it's a cross or any other trinket, it's nobody's business what religion you are or what group of people you belong to."

Ashamed, I respond, "I don't know...I just thought it would be nice to wear it."

"What do you know about being Jewish?" she repeats, more an accusation than a question.

"I speak Yiddish," I say, stating the obvious, trying to reason with her.

"Not really," she says dismissively. "It's more German than Yiddish."

It's true I studied German at Bourgade High School, where by the long arm of coincidence, Tamara Nijinsky, the daughter of the famous ballet dancer, Rudolf Nijinsky, had moved to the Valley of the Sun and had been my German teacher for two years. I also studied German for a year as an undergraduate at Glendale Community College. Then, as now, I spoke a combination of both Yiddish and German, borrowing at random from either language whenever I lacked a certain word to express myself.

"But I understand *every single word* you're saying when you speak Yiddish!" I protest, in a last futile attempt to assert myself. "And I've been reading a book about Judaism too." It feels like my mother is now talking to me from a parallel reality, and I'm dismayed she's refusing to acknowledge my fluency in Yiddish. This is a side of her I don't recognize. I thought I knew her better than anyone else in the world. Apparently, I didn't. I never imagined she'd flatly refuse to validate my interest in Judaism. Suddenly, the person in front of me is a stranger. The loving mother I know is replaced by a disapproving woman observing me from an unreachable distance, as though I were watching her from afar in a science-fiction time machine.

I glimpse a part of her personality that is new to me, a part that must have existed during the Holocaust while she pretended to be Catholic and buried her Jewishness so deep inside that no one could even suspect it. I know by heart the many stories about her survival, but I've never once before experienced, not even for a second, the kind of person she must have been during the Holocaust. Now I know. She is formidable. The forbiding remoteness, the strangeness of it frightens me. Admonished and embarrassed, I took the chai pendant off the gold chain and put it away somewhere deep in my dresser drawer. Perhaps it got lost or maybe my mother took it away because I never saw it again.

* * *

After the discussion about the chai pendant, life in Glendale continued as always – suburban, sheltered and bland. At the time, moving to New York wasn't even on the radar screen of my wildest dreams. I was focused on finishing college and had no idea what I'd do afterward. I wanted to complete my Associate's Degree at Glendale Community College and then transfer to Arizona State University, where I'd major in English, and get a Bachelor's Degree of Arts. I didn't think about studying for a profession. My mother repeatedly suggested I apply to law school after I graduated. But all I wanted to do was read novels and write poetry forever. I had taken the Yiddish expression to heart: *a mensch tracht und got lacht*, a person plans and God laughs. I didn't plan. Maybe I was waiting for an aleatory event to change my life. As my mother often said, "We'll see what happens when the time comes." It became my mantra too.

ON THE LONG, WINDING
ROAD TO NEW YORK

While I was at Glendale Community College for two years study-ing to get my Associate's Degree, I didn't meet anyone Jewish. None of my friends ever discussed religion in a meaningful way. It was a non-topic and didn't play a role in how we defined ourselves. We cobbled together our identities from the books we read, the clothes we wore and the music we listened to. It was considered "cool" to wear inexpensive cotton clothing from India, make references to Hermann Hesse's *Sid-dharta*, and own Keith Jarrett's "The Köln Concert" or a Ravi Shankar album.

When I graduated, the next logical step for me was to attend Arizona State University in the suburb of Tempe. The tuition for an in-state resi-dent was less than a thousand dollars a year and I never even considered going to an out-of-state university. ASU was a real eye opener after coming from a small community college. The campus was huge, over 700 acres, the sidewalks were swarming with people and the grassy green lawns on campus were overrun with sunbathers and Frisbee players, of which I was neither. By the time I was a junior in college, I had already developed an aversion to sun tans. I dyed my waist-length hair with red henna (popular at the time), wore black clothing and long Indian-print skirts, and always walked in the shade. Nearby was the Grady Gammage Auditorium de-signed by Frank Lloyd Wright, which looked like a big salmon-pink layer cake with scalloped frosting around the edges.

A new friend entered my life. I was twenty years old when I met Karen Callahan, who opened up a new window on the world for me.

Karen came from an affluent Mormon home in Scottsdale, and much to my surprise, had a Jewish boyfriend. "I like Jewish guys," she said. I wasn't quite sure what to make of this, since I had never dated one. Karen and I met when we struck up a conversation in the women's bathroom in the English Department at Arizona State University. She was also an English major, and we shared a lot of the same admittedly quirky tastes and cultural touchstones: she, too, avoided the sun and walked in the shade whenever she could; one of our favorite books was Thomas Mann's *The Magic Mountain*; she was a fan of Federico Fellini and Ingmar Bergman films and loved the music of Leonard Cohen.

Karen had recently come back from a trip to Italy, where she had stopped for a few days in the small town of Riccione. Searching for something to read one afternoon, she wandered into a tiny Italian bookstore that had only one book in English, a novel by Yukio Mishima. Little did I know her purchase would be the catalyst for a major turning point in my life. Standing on the spotty grass and dirt lawn in front of the English Department, she pulled the thin paperback out of her fringed suede bag and handed it to me saying, "You've got to read this. It's so profound. It's made me see things in a different way." The book was *Forbidden Colors*. Written on the cover was a brief, enticing description: "A novel of love and sexual anguish by one of the great novelist of the modern era."

Soon I started what was to become a lifelong obsession with Japanese literature. It was like a drug. I read Junichiro Tanizaki, Yasunari Kawabata, Kenzaburo Oe, Matsuo Basho, Soseki Natsume, Sakaguchi Ango and other writers, working my way back to *The Tale of Genji*, by Lady Murakami, said to be the first novel ever written and composed in the Hein period (794–1185 AD). In my mind, Japan became a kind of Shangri–La, an idealized land of courtly rituals and endless cultivation of beauty. Dreaming of living in Japan, I sprinkled my own writing with references to pampas grass and cicadas. I wrote about samurais and the Osaka castle. My poetry professors said I had an original voice and suggested I publish a poetry chapbook.

Encouraged by my professors, Norman Dubie, Pamela Stewart and Roger Weingarten, who were themselves graduates of the prestigious Iowa MFA program, I applied to Columbia University's Master of Fine Arts program in Creative Writing. I did it on a whim, never imaging I'd be accepted, but much to my astonishment, I was. I deferred my enrollment for one year and at my mother's urging instead moved to Paris to study French. She had always wanted me to learn the language. "A cultured person knows more than one language," she'd say. She spoke English, Russian, Polish, Hebrew, Yiddish, German and now Greek. I couldn't argue with her.

I packed two suitcases, one for clothes and one for books. Though I didn't speak a word of French, I was ready for *La Ville-Lumiere*, the city of lights – aptly named, for around 1667 at Louis XIV's decree, it became the first European city to install hundreds of lanterns, lighting up the night skies and creating magic in the air. I spent two semesters studying French in Paris. Then it was time to say goodbye to my friends and move to New York to attend Columbia's MFA program in Creative Writing. Like the literary character, Tonio Kruger, who only anticipated a short trip to Davos in Thomas Mann's *The Magic Mountain*, but ended up staying years, I, too, expected to live in New York for only a short time, just two years of graduate school, and then I'd return to Arizona. However, it wasn't to be. Once I moved to Manhattan, I never left. I now understood what Isaac Bashevis Singer meant when he said, "Everybody needs an address." I had finally found mine.

THE NEW JERUSALEM

My tenuous need for a Jewish identity never entirely disappeared. It lay dormant inside of me until I moved to New York, to Manhattan's Upper West Side, a neighborhood awash in Jewish tradition, where I would make another attempt at being Jewish.

When I moved from Paris to New York to attend Columbia University, I was twenty-four. I lived on the Upper West Side on the corner of 89th St. and Broadway. I found the apartment share by responding to an ad posted on a bulletin board at a kiosk on campus. I moved into a large, rambling two-bedroom apartment with Rita, an actress of Italian heritage who did a daily Jane Fonda video workout in front of the TV, and most evenings went to her job as a restaurant hostess. She was the perfect roommate – gone most of the time, and filling the refrigerator with a steady supply of leftover restaurant food.

What astonished me most about the Upper West Side was the Jewishness in the neighborhood, in the air. No one seemed ashamed of being Jewish. It was a given, like having red hair or wearing glasses. I heard familiar speech patters with rising inflections like those of my mother and relatives in Montreal. There were accents from Brooklyn, Long Island and Queens that I couldn't distinguish between, foreign sounding to my ears accustomed to Arizona's primarily broadcast accent.

Soon I settled into the neighborhood rhythms and adopted the Saturday late-night ritual of buying the *New York Times* and freshly baked, warm bagels from H & H Bagels on the corner of 79th St. and Broadway. At the Jewish neighborhood institution, Zabar's, I shopped for whitefish salad, smoked salmon and herring. (When I was sixteen, I stopped eating chicken and meat, but still ate fish.) There were Kosher butcher shops with the stores' names decoratively inscribed in gold-colored Hebrew lettering on the window and numerous Kosher restaurants in the neighborhood, though I preferred a tiny macrobiotic restaurant four blocks away from my apartment that John Lennon and Yoko Ono had frequented. On Friday nights, sharply dressed couples in the neighborhood – men in well-tailored suits and women wearing fashionable clothes and beautiful, expensive-looking hats – walked together to nearby synagogues.

Even though I never met Isaac Bashevis Singer, just knowing he lived in the neighborhood gave me a feeling of belonging. I fantasized about running into him at a deli and chatting together in Yiddish. His world of displaced Holocaust survivors and Eastern European émigrés was a part of my world too. Singer's stories were translated from Yiddish to English, and he was one of the first Jewish writers to appear in the *New Yorker.*

I wanted to identify with being Jewish, but as always, I was conflicted. Culturally, I had always been Jewish, but I still knew nothing about the Jewish religion. To make matters worse, the Greek half of my heritage made me feel like an imposter, like I didn't fully belong with the Jews.

The Upper West Side had a large contingency of young, single Orthodox Jews. I had been working next to Sarah, a devoutly Orthodox woman, when I started a summer job at the midtown advertising agency Backer & Spielvogel. At the time I contemplated becoming a copy writer, though it didn't take long to change my mind and return to the academic world. Sarah gave me an almost daily report on Jewish single life on the Upper West Side, as well as breaking news updates on her own romantic involvements. She suggested I attend the Reform synagogue, Bnai Jeshurun, also known as BJ on West 88th St. She added it had a *freylekh*, upbeat atmosphere as well as a burgeoning singles scene with a plentiful supply of doctors and lawyers (which reflected her interests, not mine).

One Friday evening, I decided the moment had come. It was my first visit to a synagogue, and I was full of anticipation, my heart bursting with emotion and my mind filled with the self-importance of my quest. But at the synagogue, everything was unfamiliar and strange. I couldn't ascribe meaning to the rabbi's actions. I didn't understand Hebrew and felt self-conscious and conspicuous, not that anyone seemed to notice me. Matters only got worse when I joined a room full of singles after the service. I forced myself to mingle, making an attempt at small talk with a young woman standing next to me. "Hi, how are you doing? My name is Helen," I ventured. She smiled and politely answered, "I'm fine. I'm Janet." We both stood there awkwardly. "This is my first time here," I said. "Oh, really," she responded noncommittally, "Well, it's nice to meet you." Before I could utter another syllable, she dove into the crowd. I didn't have the wherewithal to attempt another round of conversation. With the knot of anxiety in my chest feeling like it would burst, I fled.

A new chapter in my life started when I met Steve Mass, who became the first Jewish person I bonded with in New York. He was my best friend and mentor for many years. Like my mother, he kept the fact that he was Jewish a secret. Steve reminded me of my mother in countless small ways. Like her, he had a totally different private and public persona. He didn't trust people and assumed everyone was out to take advantage of him, sounding again much like my mother, who had little faith in human nature. However, in public, his persona was completely different. He was gregarious and an iconoclast, so stylishly oblivious with his beard and plaid flannel shirts that he became the very essence of hip.

Steve owned the legendary Mudd Club, the *echt* Punk club. It was famous (and, of course, infamous) in downtown New York, as was its owner. The club was a place where the paths of many artists, personalities, writers and designers crossed, like Jean Michel Basquiat, Keith Haring, Andy Warhol, Anna Sui, Marianne Faithful, Jay McInerney and Marc Jacobs, just to name a few. Steve and I often visited his friend, John Cale, from the Velvet Underground (who was also a big Leonard Cohen fan) at his nearby Greenwich Village apartment. One year my mother and I were taking the subway to a Leonard Cohen concert at the Beekman Theatre on the Upper West Side, and ran into John and his wife on the #1 line, at the Sheridan Square Station in the West Village. They, too, were on their way to the concert

Steve and I regularly went out to clubs, and I became enthralled with listening to people talk about their lives in the wee hours of the morning. It was a relief not having to worry about being a witty conversationalist, since it turned out most people wanted nothing more than an appreciative audience. The later it got, the more people divulged secrets, sharing what they'd never admit in the light of day. It reminded me of a favorite line from a Japanese novel, "In the night, real things are no more real than in a dream." I was intrigued by the contrast of the outside poses people adopted and their inner selves. I still assumed everybody lived with a dual identity. I thought it was normal for people to do one thing and think another, or say one thing and believe differently. I had unintentionally learned from my mother that the self we presented to the world was a convenient and sometimes necessary shell that protected our inner life.

In the meantime, Steve had become a surrogate Jewish mother to me. He guided my tastes and made comments on my make-up (preferably none) and wardrobe (not long and baggy). About demeanor: "Slow down. Don't be such a busy bee. It's not attractive." He added, "You dress like a Jewish matron from Great Neck." Though I wasn't sure where Great Neck was, I knew it wasn't a compliment. I stopped wearing loose, black, silk clothing that "hid my body, but revealed the grace of my stride," a sartorial affectation I had picked up from reading *The Tale of Genji*, and found quite elegant at the time.

My disparate Jewish and Christian worlds were starting to slowly meld together, though it would take quite a few years until I could reconcile and mend the split parts of my psyche. I started feeling proud of my Jewishness. It was okay to be Jewish with my ally, Steve, at my side. We read stories translated from Yiddish into English by Sholem Aleichem, an icon of Eastern European Jewish folk language. At Katz's Deli on the Lower East Side, we ate bagels with cream cheese and lox. In Steve's ramshackle van, we drove to Boro Park in Brooklyn to explore the Hasidic neighborhood and eat at Kosher restaurants where most of the people I overheard speaking Yiddish had a Hungarian accent, different from the familiar Vilnius Yiddish I grew up with.

I was starting to put down roots in my private Jewish life. But in public, like my friend, Steve, and like my mother, it was perfectly normal – even prudent – to hide my Jewish self.

SYMBIOSIS AND SEPARATION

Concurrent with my great love for my mother was my great fear of losing her – the flip side of the same coin. I had enormous separation anxiety as a child, and on the rare occasions my parents left the house to go out in the evening, I stood peering out the window, waiting and crying, afraid my mother would never come back.

One evening she wore a beautiful Nehru-collared, shiny, gold-satin suit. (She was fond of suits, particularly in beige, and had at least half a dozen hanging in the closet that all looked alike to me.) To complement the gold suit, she wore black gloves and a long, envelope-shaped, black, patent-leather clutch purse. Her hair was teased up in a fashionable French twist. I thought she looked like a movie star. The hours seemed endless as I waited for her return, trying to ignore the babysitter, the intruder in our living room, who was as alien to me as the outer space creatures I watched on my favorite television show, "Lost in Space."

I didn't know my normal childhood separation anxiety was exacerbated by my mother's experiences in the Holocaust. I clung to her and she clung to me; she was always a watchful and protective presence. I didn't realize her over-protectiveness was one of the symptoms of survivor guilt, something I wouldn't have been able to comprehend as a child

Most Holocaust survivors have a hard time accepting anything good that happens to them. Either they don't trust it, feel they don't deserve it, or both. In the book, *Survivor Guilt: A Self-Help Guide*, the psychologist Aphrodite Matsakis explores the subject. She says, "People with survivor guilt often relate to others with a sense of protectiveness or urgency. They don't ever want to experience such loss again, so they are motivated to do everything possible to make the world safe, not only for themselves, but for those they care about." She writes that those with survivor guilt expect the worst to happen and are determined to be prepared for it. "'Never again' is the motto of many trauma survivors; deep in their hearts they have vowed to never again be unprepared or vulnerable to human or man-made disaster."

Matsakis informs survivor guilt victims, "A part of you trusts no one and nothing, so you check out people, places and objects for possible danger. You don't want any more mistakes, but your family members and friends may not appreciate your overprotective attitudes and behaviors." In my mother's case, her overprotectiveness didn't boost my confidence, but inadvertently served to lessen it. Though we were living in a sleepy desert-landscaped world in Arizona, my mother navigated through it as though it were a minefield and grave dangers still lurked outside at every turn. "Be careful," was her constant refrain. I heard it at least once every time I left the house.

Like separation anxiety, some of the issues I struggled with – depression, chronic anxiety and a symbiotic relationship with my mother – weren't resolved until they exploded full-blown in my adolescence. I adopted my mother's responses to the world and didn't trust in any future that could be guaranteed by an outline or bullet points on a piece of paper. In my own life, chance had led to some of my more satisfying experiences. I preferred chance to planning.

Like my mother, I, too, would worry about things only "when the time comes." I wanted to be uninhibited, spontaneous, and free to come and go for the sake of adventure. In other words, I wanted to be an entirely different person from who I was. It took a while until I realized I wasn't searching for something outside of myself, but for internal freedom – a space for my own psyche to develop.

It was a difficult journey, trying to find psychic freedom, learning to rely on my own instincts. My parents never missed an opportunity to remind me they knew what was best for me, often arguing about the subject while I stood on the sidelines, vainly trying to interject my own opinion on the matter. By constant repetition, they had convinced me I wasn't capable of making independent choices or decisions. I needed to listen to them because they had "more experience in life" than me. I needed their wisdom to guide me because people were out to take advantage of anyone they could. I couldn't argue with their logic. I gave up trying. As long as I listened to them my life would be a bed of roses. Without them, I would be treading on thorns; I could make fatal mistakes. The world was a dangerous place where people were waiting to pounce on the weak. In my mind, my mother was a Wonder Woman. She had special powers that made her different from ordinary mortals. I felt secure when I was with her. Nothing bad could ever happen if she was watching over me. Worshiping my mother was an unconscious way to repress my feelings of embarrassment for her, for the humiliation she suffered during the Holocaust. And I couldn't acknowledge I was ashamed of my feelings too.

It wasn't until I was in my mid-thirties that, one day, it occurred to me that my mother's set of experiences weren't mine, and by extension, her experiences weren't relevant to my life either. This was a mind-blowing epiphany. It came out of nowhere, and was like stumbling across a forbidden button I was now allowed to push to invalidate my parents' control over me. For the first time I saw that my parents came from a different background and a different era. The same cleverness, shrewdness, caution, distrust of authority – like an outmoded skill set that needed to be updated – were abilities that had once served them so well during the upheaval of a world war. But they weren't applicable to me. They were even a hindrance when applied to the unthreatened, middle-class, suburban reality that was my life. My parents admonished me for being so American – so trusting and naïve, and they conveniently overlooked the fact that I hadn't formed the willpower and self-awarness to assert myself and make choices. I needed to cultivate inner strength. Strength of being.

Over time I began to learn I could think for myself and trust my intuition, but it wasn't until my late thirties that I shed my cocoon of passive dependency and began to move toward autonomy and independence. By chance – like most good things that had happened to me – I came across the psychiatrist, Dr. Masterson, when I picked up one of his books at a bookstore. It was Dr. Masterson who tried to pry me away from my mother.

"THE HOLOCAUST IS NOT YOUR PROBLEM" — DR. MASTERSON

One late fall afternoon, I was standing in the Barnes and Noble book store on 18th St. and Broadway in Manhattan, browsing the shelves of the psychology section. Studying psychology was an obsession at the time. It came in a brief but intense spurt between reading novels – which I had done for the first part of my life – and reading history, biographies and memoirs, which will no doubt occupy the second part. At the time, I was immersed in reading everything I could find by Karen Horney, the famous post-Freudian analyst who wrote about feminine psychology, and countered Freud's theory of penis envy by positing that men had "womb envy" because they couldn't bear children. I had just finished an excellent biography about her life by Bernard J. Paris, *Karen Horney: A Psychoanalyst's Search for Self-Understanding*, and I was looking for something new to read, scanning various titles, when one caught my eye. *In Search of the Real Self*, by Dr. James F. Masterson.

I picked the book up and started skimming through it. Suddenly it felt like a searchlight was beaming into my very soul. The provocative chapter headings called out to me: "The False Self: The Internal Saboteur," "Fear of Abandonment: The Self Under Siege." I was searching not only for my real self – but my *own* self. I was forty-one years old and still hadn't found it. Maybe this Dr. Masterson could help me.

On the back of the book jacket, I discovered that Dr. Masterson, "one of the world's foremost psychiatrists," had a practice and institute in Manhattan. I bought the book, finished reading it the next day, and immediately looked up the phone number for the Masterson Institute.

I called and within minutes, much to my amazement, I had an appointment with Dr. Masterson himself, though I was politely forewarned that after the "intake" session, he might refer me to one of the psychiatrists-in-training at his institute.

The following week I met Dr. Masterson in his office. He was older than I expected, not tall, very thin with gray-flecked hair, and extremely serious. He didn't smile when we met and dispensed with the usual pleasantries, though I later discovered he had an excellent sense of humor. He sat across from me at a nondescript brown, wooden desk in a large, generic-looking office. He asked me the open-ended question that must be in every shrink manual: "What brings you here today?" "I read your book, *In Search of the Real Self*," I began, "and...uh, I really liked it," I said, sounding even to myself like a young co-ed trying to butter up her professor for a good grade.

My "presenting problem" for seeing him was chronic depression. I had been depressed for a good part of my life, but always took great pains to hide it as though it were a physical defect I was trying to conceal. I still mirrored the duality of my mother – on the inside I felt depressed, but on the outside I wanted to be perceived as normal and well-adjusted. Depression was a private subject I shared with only a few close friends. My good friend, Karen, and I had often talked about it, but we chalked it up to our anti-establishment posture and difficult childhoods.

There was no point in talking about my real feelings to other people. It would sound like I was complaining, *kvetching*, insisting on seeing the world as a glass half-empty. Talking about depression to anyone but a paid professional would be subjecting the listener to boredom – like recounting a dream in too great and lengthy detail. Who cares? Mostly I didn't talk about it because I didn't think anyone could help. However, now for the first time, I had hope. After reading Dr. Masterson's book, I was convinced he had the wisdom and power to "cure" me.

I didn't particularly like Dr. Masterson on our first meeting, though when I tried to come up with reasons to dislike him, I couldn't. He didn't have any mannerisms that annoyed me. Still, I couldn't say we "clicked." He was far from chummy, but there was something more important about the visit that made me want to return. I felt he understood me. Maybe he could help me unravel and free myself from years of brutal self-searching and self-absorbed worries. I had unsuccessfully tried to rid myself of my problems, but couldn't get beyond my own subjectivity and narcissism. I was frustrated with the familiar monologues turning like a Möbius strip in my head, convenient blaming of my parents, spinning my wheels, and the self-analysis that always led to the same dead end. Maybe this time things would be different.

On occasion, Dr. Masterson had a way of quizzically tilting his head and raising his eyebrows while I was talking, particularly when he didn't quite buy what I was telling him. Later on in therapy, he would even go so far as to sometimes roll his eyes at the things I said. It usually made me laugh, and I valued his directness and honesty.

"Trying to be normal takes up so much energy," I told him. I went on to reel off my well-rehearsed list of maladies: I was suffering from writer's block, I never felt "fully alive," I suffered from serious claustrophobia, avoiding the confines of the subway and rarely taking elevators, preferring to walk twenty or more flights of stairs if required. I had chronic anxiety, insomnia, depression and, last but not least, problems sustaining intimacy in relationships. I wasn't in touch with my "real self." In fact, I told him, "I'm not even sure if I *have* a real self."

I had dumped a lifetime of troubles on Dr. Masterson. He was unfazed. But what if my problems were the usual mundane problems that self-involved, overly-analytical women like me had? I wanted to be special. Appreciated. Admired, even. I remembered a *New Yorker* cartoon in which a therapist sums it all up for his client in three words: "Coulda, woulda, shoulda." I wanted to see Dr. Masterson again, so I pulled out all the stops. I swallowed my pride and revealed my shame. "My father used to hit me and my mother is a Holocaust survivor." It worked. I had an appointment to see him the following week – same time, same place – a small bedrock of stability in the ever-changing river of life.

The next week, Dr. Masterson and I began our session by talking about romantic relationships. I commented, "Relationships can be so painful. What's the point of them anyway?" I had asked a rhetorical question, but he paused thoughtfully and slowly answered, "Comfort." The older I get, the more often I'm reminded of his response. On the subject of men, I had told Dr. Masterson, "I like men, but I don't respect them. Maybe it's because I don't respect my father." For me, dating a new guy was the equivalent of taking an enrichment seminar. A new relationship meant a chance to learn about new things: new music, new books, new ideas, new restaurants, travel to new places, receive new gifts, etc. Inevitably, the relationship would run its course and it was time for the next learning experience to begin.

Dr. Masterson informed me, "You have 'arrangements' instead of relationships." And, "Your fear of intimacy is even bigger than you think it is." Of course, he was right. In a "relationship," if my feelings were actually invested, I would toggle between love – which became smothering, burdensome, a threat to my autonomy (the kind of love I had learned from my mother) – and panic, my fear of abandonment anxiety and being left alone in the world. I'd toggle from one extreme to the other and couldn't find a healthy balance in between.

I can't say I liked hearing what Dr. Masterson had to tell me, but more importantly, there was something about our sessions that rang true. I always looked forward to the next one. At every session with Dr. Masterson, I talked about my mother. And then, we started focusing on her even more. It seemed to be the only subject he wanted to talk about.

I was getting frustrated. "I'm just repeating myself over and over again like a cow chewing its cud and not being able to spit it out."

Though not familiar with a cow's behavior, it felt like an apt analogy. The sessions cost a small fortune; time was ticking away and dollars were slipping out of my wallet. I was spending most of my monthly salary on the sessions and sliding deeper into credit card debt which only increased my stress level. Therapy was really starting to bug me. I had talked about my mother plenty and there were other things on my mind I needed to clear up. I understood that Dr. Masterson wanted me to "individuate, separate," and to become my own person. As much as we both had the same goal in mind, I didn't realize at the time that I was unconsciously fighting it. The idea of separation was fraught with conflict and ambivalence. Even at the risk of harming my own capacity to grow, it was still more gratifying to cling to my dependent, infantile attachment to my mother.

During one session, the fog finally started lifting. Things became clearer. "What does it feel like when you're depressed?" he asked me. It sounded like an obvious question, quite unlike his usual ones. But by then I knew the simplest of questions could be the most challenging to answer. I was at a loss.

"Well…it's hard to describe. I don't know…it just feels…*bad*," I said finally, hoping I could breeze through this one and move on. No such luck.

"Obviously," he snapped back, not rolling his eyes, yet not about to let me off the hook either. "But what does it *feel* like? Try to describe what it's like when you're depressed," he asked again.

I was stumped. Only the night before I was sitting on the black leather couch in my living room feeling depressed, lonely and hopeless about the future.

"It's really hard to put into words," I said, trying to buy some time. "It's more like a physical feeling. My body feels really heavy. Like it weighs five hundred pounds."

Silence filled the room. He looked at me and I could tell there was something going on that I didn't get.

"How do you think your mother feels when she's depressed?" He was back to his favorite subject, talking about her again. I shrugged. "She doesn't get depressed. She won't let herself," I answered. "She blocks her feelings. She even says it's a skill she's developed, like she's proud of it." He put his hands on the arm rests of his brown leather chair and leaned back. Like a "give" in poker, it was a gesture I had come to recognize, one he made to punctuate an observation. All of a sudden, I understood. At a certain point when things were too painful, I hit a wall. I had emulated my mother and developed the art of detaching from my own feelings. Without consciously realizing it, I had learned to block my feelings the way she did.

I always felt too sorry for my mother to fully acknowledge the negative feelings I had toward her, and too overwhelmed by guilt whenever I did. Instead, harbored and repressed, those feelings manifested themselves in an insidiously silent way growing inside me. It was better to keep a lid on them so they would just go away. Dr. Masterson told me I had learned to disassociate. Feelings caused pain. Apathy had been my preferred emotion for many years – it was liberating, like meditating and reaching a zone where "the monkey mind," as it was sometimes called by meditation practitioners, didn't jump around. But the blank zone felt empty, not fulfilling. In his book, Dr. Masterson had written that a person without a real self, "Senses, but cannot understand, the hollow core at the center of his life."

"I don't want to sit around just *wallowing* in my feelings," I said with distaste, like I was spitting out a piece of gristle from a hamburger. "But I just can't get out of this rut."

Dr. Masterson had been working with me on trying to get some psychological distance from my mother. "Do you think your loneliness is connected to talking to your mother less?" he questioned.

"I'm not sure."

"Don't call her every day," he advised me. "Start by calling her just every couple of days, then let a few days go by."

I looked at him like he had to be joking. "It's not like she wouldn't notice. The first thing she'd do is ask why I wasn't calling her," I said.

"Then keep the calls shorter. Don't go into so much detail," he suggested.

I had a plunging sensation of loss, as if someone had died. I felt that if I couldn't talk to my mother about my life, it didn't count. I couldn't do it. In fact, I wasn't even sure if I wanted to. Just the sound of her voice gave me solace. Maybe I was wasting $180 a week. Debt was becoming a black cloud hanging over my head. I started adding up the cost of the sessions. Four times $180 was $720 a month. That amount could go a long way toward paying off my credit card debt – or, I couldn't help but think, maybe buying some new clothes. Just the thought of shopping at Macy's or Saks Fifth Ave. instead of paying for therapy instantly boosted my spirit. I knew I was trying to find reasons not to see Dr. Masterson. Typical patient resistance. A part of me resented his intrusion between my mother and me. I couldn't use him to replace my mother as my sounding board. Maybe that transference wasn't meant to happen. Things were more real – they only counted – when I told her about them.

For as long as I could remember, my mother was my best friend. I consulted her on any important decision. Even unimportant ones. She never tired of listening to me. She asked countless questions; no detail was too small. She always made me feel like I was the most important person in the world. Now I was talking about her behind her back to someone I wasn't even sure I liked.

"What are you feeling now?" he asked.

"Empty...sad," I said, "But I read that's a normal feeling for Children of Holocaust Survivors."

"What do you mean?" he asked.

"This article I read said that for Holocaust survivors even the smallest emotional loss is traumatic because any separation for them isn't like it would be for a regular person. For them it represents total loss, like death,

214

like what they suffered in the Holocaust. And their kids have the same problem, but not as bad."

I often read psychological articles, and tried to run them by him for discussion and feedback. I would plug myself into the latest theory, then wondered if Masterson would validate it for me. But he rarely indulged me in discussing theories. I thought he would jump on my readings about Children of Holocaust Survivors, but on the contrary, he didn't seem particularly interested. Not that he was entirely dismissive, but he was on a different track. He wouldn't let me intellectualize my feelings as I had always done in the past.

He nodded. "You were saying you felt empty..."

"Right. Empty...lonely..."

"What do you do when that happens?" he asks.

"I tell myself to just snap out of it. That I'm being self-centered and self-absorbed."

"That sounds harsh," Dr. Masterson said. "There's a difference between indulging yourself and feeling compassion for yourself."

"Oh...I thought compassion was something you felt for *other* people." I said.

Our time was up.

One day in another session, we were discussing a current relationship I was in. "Of course you can't get into a relationship with a man," Dr. Masterson told me. "You have an anchor around your neck." He had made other similar remarks about my mother. I felt a huge sense of relief when I was in his office, but with it an equal accompaniment of guilt and dread. I was betraying my mother. It seemed like the two of us were ganging up on the person I loved most in the world. I resented him. He encouraged me to say things out loud that I'd been thinking, but didn't want to accept.

"Do you think I have a borderline personality?" I asked him during one session.

"What do you think?" he replied in typical shrink fashion.

"Well, maybe...just a little. What do you think?"

"Tell me what borderline means to you."

"Well, in your book it says someone who feels inadequate most of the time, whose mother didn't nurture their independence. Wait, there's another thing. Oh, right. They feel hollow inside," I added with a short laugh.

He nodded, but didn't say anything.

I had rattled off the main symptoms of borderline personality disorder like I was ticking off items on a grocery list. There were no feelings attached. This was where Dr. Masterson and I had to do the work together.

One day, we had been talking about my mother again. "You know," I said, "I'm thinking of writing a book about being the daughter of a Holocaust survivor." No reply from Dr. Masterson. Interpreting his silence as a sign of encouragement. I continued, "I'd really like to go to Vilnius. I wish my mom would go with me. Maybe I could take a video camera and film us there."

He was silent. Then abrupty said, "The Holocaust is not your problem." It was the last thing I expected to ever hear. I was speechless.

"The Holocaust is not *your* problem. Your problem is you." I was trying to take everything in, but it wouldn't compute.

He sounded a little less harsh, "Your mother lived her life. You have your own life to worry about. You need to focus on *your* life."

"Oh…" I responded. I couldn't think of anything to say.

It was like someone had thrown a pail of cold water on me. After the initial surprise wore off, my most immediate thought was, he couldn't possibly be Jewish – a Jewish person would never say such a thing. But what if he were? I didn't know for sure. What difference would it really make? Next, I rationalized, "He just doesn't get it." But in spite of myself, it was finally starting to sink in. My life was separate from my mother's. I had to separate. I had always depended on her for continuity. I had looked to her to provide meaning in my life, to validate it and make it count. Without her, I felt I didn't count. I could float away; I had no anchor.

Masterson had written in an article, "The central goal of the therapy is what we call the flowering of the individuation – a feeling akin to becoming a new person. Breaking down artificial defenses can liberate the borderline's real self and enable her to complete her development." I had to arrive at my own identity, a basic confidence in my own continuity. I had to look forward, not back at my mother's life. I lacked that basic confidence. Dr. Masterson was telling me that was my problem. "You don't have confidence in your own emotions," he had said only the week before. I knew what was expected of me, but the big question was "how?"

I had to stop living under my mother's protective shadow. Due to her exaggerated fear of losing me (which actually made sense given her experiences in the Holocaust), her protection manifested itself in a peculiar kind of negative motivation and warning system based on her clairvoyant understanding of the dire circumstances to come if I didn't follow her advice. "I have more experience in life than you do," she reminded me, always trumping my arguments. But the end result of her warnings didn't motivate me. Instead, my internal compass was spinning. Her warnings only served to make me more frightened of life, reluctant to rely on my own judgment, more worried and anxious about my competence for the future.

My mother had surrounded my early attempts to venture into the world with an invisible electronic fence like the kind suburbanites sometimes use in their yards to keep pets on the property. As an adult, I still needed to stop believing that she always knew what was best for me. I had to stop living by her standards. I had to stop trying to rescue her from her life, and mend the emotionally abusive love-hate relationship she had with my father. Even though I was often the immediate cause of their disagreements, I hadn't realized their conflicts had nothing to do with me. I had to stop trying to make her happy. Trying to somehow make up for the enormity of the losses she suffered during the Holocaust was useless because it was impossible. Even though I knew it wasn't rational, my emotions didn't want to give up. I only became more depressed and helpless. Dr. Masterson was trying to liberate me from the shackles of the past so I could discover who I was when I stood on my own two feet.

"What do you think would happen if you spoke to your mother less often? Maybe just a couple of times a week?" Dr. Masterson asked me again in one session.

"I don't know. I guess I feel like she's a plant I have to water...and... if I don't water it..."

I couldn't continue. I looked at the table next to me. No Kleenex. I looked around. "There's no Kleenex in your office," I said. I was embarrassed that tears were running down my face. I hated having anyone see me cry. No response. He was looking at me intently. The missing box of Kleenex was a welcome distraction – did he forget to buy it? Did his cleaning lady forget?

"What do you think it means?" he asked.

"You don't want people to cry in your office?" I said, smiling through my tears.

217

"So…if you didn't water the plant…" he continued.

I tried to pull myself together. "If I didn't water the plant…it would whither away…and die," I said, tears now streaming unchecked down my face.

"So you're afraid your mother would die if you didn't talk to her?" he asked.

"Yes," I answered. He had acknowledged my deepest fear, losing her.

Dr. Masterson talked to me about the difficult process of separating from this symbiotic relationship. He explained to me that the more I tried to activate myself, i.e., become my own person, the more depressed I got, which in turn would start the vicious cycle and then my defenses against depression would surface. He identified the trap I had fallen into. With his help, I could emerge. Before then, I had felt that I couldn't live my own life until my mother died – which started another cycle of guilt and despair. I didn't want her to die. It was the last thing I wanted. What I was trying to do was "kill" my dependency on her. What Dr. Masterson had been trying to tell me was that the Holocaust wasn't my problem, because my problem was me. I had to find out who I was. I had to unravel myself from my mother. I had to pursue self-activation and self-expression for myself, not my mother's approval. Dr. Masterson was right. The Holocaust was a separate issue. On a certain level, my mother's past had nothing to do with me. It was her past. Not mine. This was a revolutionary idea.

"Finding meaning in life isn't easy for anyone." Dr. Masterson told me in one of our last sessions.

"Not even you?" I had asked him incredulously.

"Not even me," he answered, with a slight smile.

Eight months had passed and I decided it was time to stop seeing Dr. Masterson. As I walked out of his office for the last time, I thought of Anton Chekhov's renowned short story, "The Lady with the Dog," with its famous ending: *And they both realized that the end was still far, far away, and that the hardest, the most complicated part was only just beginning.*

ZAYT GEZUNT — BE WELL

There's a kosher restaurant called Diamond Dairy in the National Jewelers Exchange building on 47th St. in Manhattan, a street that's also known as Diamond Row, legendary for diamonds and jewelry. Whenever I find myself in the midtown area, I'll often go to the small restaurant where I order vegetable soup and cheese blintzes. It's nice to hear people around me speaking Yiddish. The restaurant is on a mezzanine at the back of a huge room filled with rows of booths. You can sit there and watch the hustle and bustle of commerce on the ground floor below you.

Diamond Dairy was mentioned in the *New York Times* for having the best cheese blintzes in New York. I think of blintzes as the Jewish equivalent of the more elegant-sounding French crepe suzette that is also a paper-thin pancake often rolled around a soft cheese or sweet filling. The restaurant has been there since 1955. Because it's a kosher restaurant, it doesn't allow the mixing of meat and dairy products. As a vegetarian, it's convenient not to have to ask if there's chicken stock in the soup.

Hasidim who work in the diamond district tend to frequent the restaurant. Still dressed in the garb of eighteenth-century Poles, the men wear tall fur hats and side locks, *peyes*, and women wear a *sheytl* or wig, and long dresses. I take a seat not at the counter, but at a table next to the edge of the mezzanine, hoping I can still overhear a conversation in Yiddish, though it's usually in a Hungarian dialect. I'm often the only person wearing jeans and a t-shirt, and don't want to appear disrespectful or sit in close proximity to any men. Hasidic men aren't supposed to look directly at women. Or is it unmarried boys who can't? I'm not sure. I was told it's not proper for a woman to sit next to a man in a car if she's not married to him.

Sitting at the counter I'm in a different world, but one that's nonetheless familiar. It's *nit aher, nit ahin* – neither here nor there, the place of belonging, but not belonging that I'm most comfortable with. The restaurant owner, Sam, who's been there since 1992, sits on a stool in front of the cash register, counting out change, making brief exchanges with the regulars. I once made a comment to him about the blintzes. Now he remembers me, gives a faint nod and smile when I pay the bill. I can't help but wonder, what would it be like to belong to his Hasidic world?

Sam and I have a short conversation in Yiddish. He asks if I practice Judaism. When I say no, he looks at me with an expression I can only interpret to be pity mixed with wonder, maybe disapproval, but I choose to ignore the latter.

"Why not?" he asks.

"I wasn't raised that way…in a religious way, I mean," I say, shrugging my shoulders. I don't mean to sound cryptic, but at the same time I'm not in the mood to explain my background either.

I'm hoping he won't take this opportunity to do *mivtzoim*, outreach, and invite me to his synagogue. Should I tell him about the few times I went to a synagogue and tried to fit in, but always felt like an outsider? Or admit I sat next to the exit sign, afraid an anti-Semite might start a fire or attack the synagogue while I was inside? I can't even look at Hasidim without feeling sad. They remind me of the Jews during the Holocaust, and I visualize them stumbling along in long, patient lines, praying on the way to their deaths. I had always pictured Hasidim on the streets of Vilnius, but I was wrong. My mother said, "I never saw them. There weren't any in Vilnius." She told me that if there were Hasidim in Vilnius, they dressed like everyone else. The renowned rabbi and Eastern European sage, the Vilna Gaon, (Gaon means genius) had decreed that they shouldn't distinguish themselves with different clothes. In 1777, he wanted to curtail the influence of the Hasidim and excommunicated them from Vilnius.

I know my restaurant visit will be short, a lunch snack, nothing more. There's not a bigger connection. I look at Sam's gentle eyes, remembering again what my mother often said, "The Hasidim are lucky people. They know what their place is in the world." For the first time it strikes me she's implying that we're not lucky; we don't have a place. I'll have to ask her about this, but for now I don't dwell on it.

Recently my mother and I went to a jewelry repair shop that's in the basement of the same building the Diamond Dairy is in. For as long as I can remember, my mother and I have gone out to lunch and shopping together. We traveled together too. To Asia, South America, and Europe. She is the most spontaneous person I have ever known, always saying "yes" to any travel suggestion, ready within minutes to depart for another continent with nothing more than a credit card and some cash, a change of clothing, a cheese sandwich, and a few toiletries in a carry-on bag. "If we need something, we'll buy it when we get there," she says. She told me she learned to make instant departures while on the run during the Holocaust.

We left the repair shop with a promise that my mother's ring would be sized and ready in a few days. It was lunchtime, and pointing to the mezzanine, I asked her, "Do you want to have lunch upstairs?" I smiled and added, "The blintzes are almost as good as yours." "Sure! I want to try them. Let's go," she says, always ready for a new experience.

We walk up the stairs, and sit down at a table next to a glass wall that cantilevers over the small jewelry booths snaking together in long rows that remind me of stalls in a medina or the Grand Bazaar in Istanbul. Both the buyers and sellers jostle for an advantage beneath the civilized veneer of negotiation and temporarily shared interests in much the same way people have for thousands of years. In the past, I've listened to my mother in awe as she's negotiated prices on a range of items, whether it be on our travels or for a household appliance. She seems to know exactly what to say at exactly the right time, like, "Come on, you're a good guy. We both know you can give me a better price." Much to my amazement, by the time a deal is struck both my mother and the seller will be smiling happily and joking together like they're the best of friends.

"If they're not embarrassed to ask for so much money, then why should you be embarrassed to try to pay less?" my mother reasons. It's hard to find fault with her logic. I once tried to describe a negotiating scenario to my husband, Tony, whose eyes only became wider as the story progressed. He'd never tried to bargain before. It wasn't part of his upbringing, though he's now tried it for himself and it worked. Even Dale Carnegie said learning how to ask for something is one of the more important life lessons to learn. Carnegie added that it's in most people's nature to want to give a positive reply – they'd prefer to say yes than no. Though I sometimes wonder if that's true.

After a filling meal of vegetable soup and blintzes, my mother and I walk over to the cash register to pay the bill. Sam has been speaking Yiddish to the last customer, and my mother mentions one of the items on the menu to him.

"I noticed you serve *cholent*," she says. "I'd like to try that next time." I've never heard of cholent before, and I learn it's a mixture of meat, beans and potatoes usually prepared for the Sabbath meal. My mother and the owner discuss various ways of preparing the dish. When he inquires, she tells him she's from Vilnius. They continue chatting for a few minutes in Yiddish about recipes, and then the conversation moves on to a discussion about the Vilna Gaon, who was the first scholar to try and bridge the gap between Talmudic studies and secular intellectual life, and helped turn Vilnius into a center for Jewish learning.

In spite of myself, tears start welling up. As I listen to them reminisce about the rich culture of Eastern European Jewish life, all I can think about is that it's lost forever. The world they're talking about has disappeared. I don't want my mother to see that I'm crying, so I turn away. As I turn, I notice a small group of Hasidic men *davening* in a narrow room adjoining the restaurant. I wonder why they bow back and forth when they pray.

Out of nowhere a different thought occurs to me: even the seven wonders of the ancient world are lost. I try to list them – the pyramid of Giza, the hanging gardens at Babylon, something in Alexandria. It's as far as I can get. Dissolution. Genocide. Hasn't it always been this way? It's not only the Jews who suffered throughout history. Tony is a history buff who mentioned that in *The History of the English-Speaking People*, Winston Churchill described the Anglo-Saxon takeover of Britain as genocidal. In 1492, King Ferdinand and Queen Isabella expelled the Moors from Spain, soon after the Jews. There's a new biography on Chairman Mao, *Mao, the Unknown Story*, which claims he was responsible for the death of 70 million Chinese. My mind wanders to the war in Iraq and Afghanistan, to the conflicts in Africa today. Aggression is a primitive instinct common to animals and man – if it weren't for aggression we wouldn't have the biological need for friendship, I remind myself, recalling the words of the Nobel Prize winning scientist, Konrad Lorenz, in his book, *On Aggression*.

I look around the crowded room that's buzzing with activity like a bee hive. My eyes pan across it like a camera lens taking everything in. I look left and right. Up and down. It occurs to me that every single person I see right now will be dead one day. I find the thought strangely consoling. I'm forty-five years old, and in another forty-five years, chances are I won't be here either.

"*Zayt gezunt,*" the restaurant owner says to my mother. "*Zayt gezunt,*" she responds, then turns toward me, interrupting my thoughts. "That was *really* an excellent meal!" she says, a big smile on her face. "We'll have to come back here soon."

As we leave the restaurant and walk down the stairs, I ask her, "Why do people sway back and forth when they *daven*?"

"I'm not sure…" she says, "but there's something about it in the Old Testament." When I go home I find the answer in a book on Judaism. The reference is to Psalm 35: "All of my limbs shall declare, 'O L-rd, who is like You?'"

SECONDARY SHAME

Being half Greek wasn't something to be proud of. As far as I was concerned, it signified second-class citizen. The Greeks I had known from church were friendly enough, but loud, emotionally gushing and gaudily dressed. My mother, ever the sober judge of human nature, said, "They're false people. They'll smile at you and then talk behind your back." The women wore too much perfume and makeup. The men tossed about *komboloi*, worry beads, in their hands, which struck me as a child-like and unseemly habit. Ever since I'd heard the priest make anti-Semitic remarks in his sermon, I didn't have to look hard for reasons to dislike them.

I blamed having to hide my mother's and my own Jewish identity on the "Greek mentality." More specifically, on my father's mentality. Wasn't he the one who insisted I answer that my mother came from Vienna if someone inquired about her origins? In case anyone at the Greek Ortho-dox church asked about her religion – though no one did, thinking she had converted – I was told to say she was Catholic. Even though it wasn't true, I tried to tell myself it wasn't much of a stretch, since she had lived for years in Vienna disguised as a Polish Catholic.

I knew there'd be dire consequences if I revealed my mother's true identity. My father warned me: we wouldn't be able to show our faces at the Greek Orthodox church; we'd never be able to see our Greek relatives in Athens again. As much as I hated going along with my parents' story, it would be worse, unimaginable not to. Their fundamentally untruthful connection with the world was something I had not only to accept, but perpetuate. It felt dishonest, but I didn't think about it much because I was too wrapped up in my anger. I didn't know I was reinforcing my "false" self, one that made me feel estranged from others, and that there'd be psychological repercussions later on.

I flatly refused to believe that being Jewish meant we were outcasts. But deep down inside, I couldn't help but wonder – what if it were true? This led to deeper concerns and I questioned the sincerity of my connections to people. Was I only accepted and liked for the image I presented? I was torn between two possibilities, unable to find a middle ground: my naïve instinct of accepting people at face value or the opposite, not believing a word they said. If I were presenting a false self to others, who's to say they weren't doing the same? This dance of duality was too complicated. It was easier to keep an emotional distance from people. Whenever we visited our relatives in Athens as I was growing up, I was always on my guard. Like my mother, I was playing a well-rehearsed role. Around my relatives I was the dutiful Greek Orthodox girl who listened to my father's every word with admiration and respect, when in fact, the opposite was true. I was afraid of my father and disliked him.

* * *

My mother isn't the only one who hid her Jewish identity. Many Jewish people, whether in show business or not, hid their backgrounds or anglicized their names. Though he didn't hide it, even Elvis Presley never talked publically about being Jewish. In her biography on Elvis, Elaine Dundy writes that both his mother and grandmother were Jewish, and his parents told him not to mention his Jewish ancestry because many people hated Jews. I was incredulous when I first realized my mother was choosing to hold on to her camouflaged identity.

"But why?" I'd try to reason with her. "Don't you think it's unhealthy to go on living like it's still WWII and you have to hide being Jewish?"

"That's how it is."

"But you could change it if you wanted to."

"We can't change anything now."

"Why not?"

"It's too late. We can't change our story now."

I was baffled and frustrated. I tried to see the situation from my parents' point of view without much success. I tried to adapt to their faulty logic. In spite of myself, I always sided with my mother because – who could blame her? After all, she had suffered through the Holocaust. How could her own daughter betray her to relatives and friends and reveal she is a Jew? Unknowingly, I had been pulled into the dynamics of the Holocaust – my mother and I had to conceal our identity.

I was trapped in a no-win situation. The more I perpetuated our false Christian identity, the more frustrated I felt. I wondered why my father, who took such great pains to hide my mother's Jewish identity, had even married her in the first place. I resented people who I thought wouldn't accept me if they knew I was Jewish. Most of all I was angry at myself for not finding a way out. I didn't want to live a double life like my mother, but I couldn't find an alternative. My resentment turned to anger, then depression.

I was locked into my parents' story, into their world. But the worst part was the question I was afraid to ask out loud: "Is my father an anti-Semite?" One day, I finally asked my mother.

"Do you think Dad is an anti-Semite?"

"Of course not," she answered adamantly.

"Then why is he so afraid of anyone finding out you're Jewish?"

"The Greeks wouldn't understand."

"Oh, so you mean *they're* all anti-Semites, but he isn't?"

"I'm sure not everyone is. Anyway, this is the way things are," she says, avoiding a direct answer. She repeats the familiar phrase, "We can't change our story now."

"Oh…so then maybe he is…just a little?" I ask, not bothering to hide the sarcasm in my voice.

"No, he's not at all," she answers firmly.

I'd like to believe her, but I don't. I think she's incapable of accepting the truth.

* * *

When Tony and I visited my father's family in Athens together for the first time, he, too, became an unwitting accomplice. After a painful and heated conversation, I had promised my parents – I had sworn – ahead of time that Tony wouldn't reveal anything about my mother's true background.

"Forget it. I'm not involving him in this!" I fumed. "It's 2003. The Holocaust is over!"

"You have to," my father said. His face is starting to turn deep pink, the first stage of an escalating anger I know only too well. Using my mother's nickname, he turns to her in desperation.

"Rachele, you talk to her."

"I understand how you feel," she says. "You don't have to lie. Just change the subject right away if it comes up." Now she's the good cop. I'm already beginning to soften. I can't say no to her.

"Why do we have to keep hiding things – like we've done something wrong?" I protest.

"Please. Just do this for us," she says.

"*Fine!*" I shout at them in frustration, "I'll do it." I'm starting to cry, angry and ashamed of myself for shouting at my parents. Like my father, I'm on the verge of losing control. I want to tell them that not hiding my mother's identity will validate her, will validate me, will somehow help erase all the injustices of the past. I want my mother to re-claim her identity and be proud of who she is. But it's not so simple.

"Promise us! Swear!" my father commands. He's never trusted anyone except my mother. He's a shrewd man, but he doesn't believe in people. Not even me. He's right. I wouldn't do it for him.

"Promise," my mother says.

"Okay! I promise." A dark cloud of depression and futility hovers over me. I feel beaten down with the false self of my childhood re-awakened again and reinforced. My father is finally satisfied. He knows I'd never break a promise to my mother. My senses are dulled. I feel like I've stumbled out of a brain-washing session.

"We should be proud of who we are," I say, looking at my mother, feeling she's betrayed me.

* * *

Tony and I arrive at the Eleftherios Venizelos International Airport in Athens. Built in 2001, it's a state-of-the-art facility, open and airy, with natural daylight streaming in. As we're waiting for our luggage to come off the carousel, I can't delay any longer. I've been dreading this conversation.

"I know this might sound a little strange, but my parents asked me to make sure you don't mention anything about my mom being Jewish. Also, the relatives think she's from Vienna. Not Vilnius. My parents said if the subject of religion or my mom's background comes up, just change it immediately." Tony looks at me and doesn't say anything for what seems like an eternity.

"Okay, I'll do whatever you want," he responds.

I can't shake the resentment I'm still feeling toward my parents when the exit doors next to the baggage claim area slide open and I spot the happy, expectant faces of my cousin Efie and her husband, Nick, who have been patiently waiting for us. We wave enthusiastically. Within minutes we're hugging each other. Efie and her husband live in Iloupolis, a hilly suburb of Athens. When I was fourteen, Efie gave me a bottle of Miss Dior perfume. I had never received such a grown-up present before. Sometimes when I walk by a perfume counter in a department store, I'll spray a bit of Miss Dior on my wrist and indulge myself in the past: I'm swinging on a wooden bench on Efie's white marble porch filled with large potted red geraniums, purple petunias, pink and orange zinnias. She's a few steps away in the kitchen, preparing a multi-course dinner, while I snack on a bowl of pistachios from the island of Aegina, waiting for her to say, "*Ela*," come, so I can help set the table.

As much as I would like to, I wonder if I can ever build a truly meaningful bond with my Greek relatives. In the back of my mind, I question how they'd react if they knew we were Jewish. It pains me to deceive them. It's easier to keep a distance, not to get too close and complicate the lie. I like to imagine Efie would embrace me and say *then pirazi*, it doesn't matter. But my father's words echo in my mind, "They'd have nothing to do with us if they knew your mother is Jewish. They'd never talk to us again." No. I refuse to believe it. But then again, I'll never know for sure. The damage is done. He's planted a seed of doubt in my mind.

WHAT IS FAMILY?

Families were something other people had – like a country house or a swimming pool. Of course, my parents and I constituted a "family," but to me it felt more like three people just living under the same roof. After Uncle Papu in Arizona died when I was five, our extended family in the United States diminished from one to zero. But if the Harvard epidemiologist who discovered that friendship and social connections aid heart patients' recovery said that "friends substitute perfectly well for family," perhaps my parents' move to Arizona wasn't so bad after all. Most immigrants cling to their own people, but not my parents. They seemed to be happy enough secluded from other ethnic groups, except for their Sunday forays to the Greek Orthodox church. They carried on with the American dream on their own.

In the English literature and composition classes I've taught over the past twenty years, I've read innumerable essays about my students' families. In English as a Second Language classes, the students are from all over the world. The countries they represent in one classroom would make a colorful Unicef greeting card. Students often write about their close-knit gatherings like holiday parties, picnics together with extended relatives in city parks, and helping each other out with personal and financial problems. When I read their essays, I can't help but notice how different their parents are from mine.

I rarely mention more than some obligatory and academic details about my background, preferring to focus on my students. The class is about them. I always remember a professor I once had, a doting grandmother, who took up class time sharing anecdotes about her four grandchildren and showing photographs to her less-than-delighted captive audience. I always feel close to the Jewish immigrants, especially the ones I've taught at the Flatbush campus in Brooklyn. I'm fortunate to be an English professor, and it's a rare class that I don't leave the room smiling and in an even better mood than when I walked in. The college where I've worked for over twenty years has become a second family to me. The dean of my department and I share a similar background; her parents were from Poland and survived the Holocaust. Though the college is founded by Orthodox Jews and has a campus for religious studies, the school is geared toward all students, both Jewish and non-Jewish alike.

* * *

When I was growing up in Arizona, my grandmother, Esther, was the only relative who came to visit us. Once every few years or so, she'd arrive from Montreal and occupy the third bedroom in our house, which doubled as a guest room and small library with its orange tweed daybed and large mahogany bookcase against one wall. To me, Esther was exotic. Unfamiliar scents like lavender perfume permeated the room and unusual objects I'd never seen before, like a wooden needlepoint frame or a loofah appeared in the house. She spent hours on needlepoint, sitting on the patio in the backyard with the strong rays of the sun on her back, and taught me how to do needlepoint too. She showed us photos from Africa. She gave me presents of small, hand-carved, wooden deer with tiny, ivory horns and elephants with tiny, ivory tusks from Johannesburg. Her only surviving sister lived in Johannesburg and my grandmother had traveled there a few times to see her.

After my grandmother's visit was over and she returned to Montreal, it never occurred to me that my parents and I led fairly isolated lives. Daily concerns took over. Our situation seemed normal. I didn't give the subject of extended family and relatives much thought until after I got married. When my mother-in-law (Tony's stepmother) told me William Bradford – who was elected the first governor of Plymouth in 1621 and wrote a famous account of life there in his book, *Of Plymouth Plantation* – was her eleventh great-grandfather, I thought to myself, only in America could an immigrant like me suddenly become related to a founding leader of the United States.

When I first met Tony, our religious backgrounds weren't even a subject of discussion. We were introduced at a small gathering given by a mutual acquaintance at an Irish bar in midtown New York. We clicked immediately and talked about architecture (I mostly listened), travel and current topics. After dating for about a year, we decided to get married. We were welcomed equally by his father and step-mother as well as my parents. When my mother told Uncle Leo I was getting married, he responded, "So? Is he Jewish?" He was the only person who even thought to ask.

My mother is a voracious reader and has always been interested in religion and history. When I told her Tony was Episcopalian, she said, "Isn't that the same church Henry VIII created? What are the tenets of their faith?" I answered, "Yes, it's Henry VIII's church. In England it's called Anglican, but here it's called Episcopal. Tony said it's close to Catholicism, but I don't know anything else about it. I'll find out." I had an excellent source. My father-in-law is an Episcopalian priest who taught at the School of Theology at The University of the South for many years. He's the go-to person on the subject of religion. When Tony and I listened to a CD of *The Da Vinci Code* on a car trip to Montreal, we later asked my father-in-law if the book's premise that Jesus had children could be true. "It makes for a good story, but absolutely not," he said, and explained why the theory wasn't plausible.

I've finally been able to ask my father-in-law all the questions I could never ask the nuns in catechism class. The last time we visited him in the Episcopal retirement community where he and his wife live in Asheville, North Carolina, I inquired about something that had puzzled me since grade school.

"Do you think original sin in Christianity is really the sin of incest? I mean, if we're all the offspring of Adam and Eve's children and there was no one else around in paradise, then their kids must have had sex with each other. Right?"

"Hmm," he responds tactfully, raising his eyebrows just a little, "I've never heard that one before."

"In the Midrash it says the twelve sons of Jacob were each born with a twin sister who they married," I offer, trying to be helpful. "King Tut's parents were brother and sister too, so maybe incest wasn't always a taboo."

For the next ten minutes, my father-in-law launches into a detailed explanation of the "history" of sin. He mentions that St. Augustine was the first theologian to teach we were born into the world with original sin.

"And what about Lilith?" I continue, still imagining sex in paradise and intent on pursuing my incest theory, "Do you think maybe she had children with Adam?" Again, my father-in-law cites references and explains the mythical Lilith was only folklore, not mentioned in the Bible, not Adam's first wife. His erudition has piqued my curiosity, and when I get back to New York, I do a search on the internet to learn more about the Episcopal faith and how it diverges from Catholicism.

When my father-in-law taught at the Episcopal theological seminary in Sewanee, one of his students was Dan Mathews, who later became the Rector of Trinity Church near Wall St. in Manhattan, where Tony and I got married. George Washington once worshiped there and it's one of the oldest churches in the country. Dan performed our wedding ceremony in the small, ornately decorated All Saint's Chapel alongside the nave of the church. Tony and I wanted the most private wedding possible – so, our small group consisted of Dan, two required witnesses recruited at the last minute who worked at the church, and the two of us.

Before our wedding day, we needed to meet with Dan and receive his counsel on marriage. Though I looked forward to it, at the same time I couldn't help feeling like a teenager obliged to listen to a parent's lecture before being allowed to take the car out for the evening. I half-expected a sermon in which I'd want to roll my eyes to the ceiling as he advised us to be all the things to our partners suggested in self-help manuals: caring, respectful, patient, attentive listeners and so forth. But much to my surprise, Dan didn't say a word about the institution of marriage. I wondered whether he'd ask about my religious background, but the subject never came up. As we were turning to leave he smiled and said, "I almost forgot. I have just one piece of advice for you. Make sure to surround yourselves with other happily married couples." We took his words of wisdom to heart, though they turned out to be a lot harder to follow than we expected.

LIKE AN ANTHROPOLOGIST
IN TENNESSEE

When Tony and I visit Sewanee, Tennessee, where he grew up, I feel I have a lot in common with my mother – I'm a Jew posing as a Christian. Here, I'm in an insular world that feels frozen in time. It's like being in the middle of a John Cheever short story, a world of Wasps. Ironically, even Cheever, the urbane and brilliant chronicler, had a dual identity and hid his bisexuality for many years. I imagine Tony's childhood was full of adult martini drinkers, loud laughter at parties, cars pulling up pea gravel driveways in lawns full of towering oak and maple trees. Of course there'd be all kinds of illicit and discreet activity going on behind polished smiles and locked bedroom doors.

Tony tells me while he was growing up, there was only one Jewish couple in the community. Everyone here assumes that I, too, am Episcopalian. Since people are far too discreet to ask direct questions, which is still a refreshing novelty for me, there are few inquiries as to where I'm from or what I do. It's fine with me. When I meet someone new, I'm always curious to hear the details of his or her life, finding it far more interesting to listen to someone else than tell them about myself – a life I already know all too well. I contrast the lack of inquiry with my Jewish relatives who will politely barrage someone with questions and learn their cv within the first acquaintance. In Sewanee, I'm married to someone from "the mountain," as they say, and that's enough for admission to their club. Clubs of any type, I also learn, are of utmost importance in the South.

Years ago when I was composing poetry at Arizona State University, I had heard of the *Sewanee Review*. It's the oldest continuously published literary quarterly, one of the esteemed literary magazines our professors encouraged us to send poems to. I would have never imagined the *Sewanee Review*'s home was in a small university perched on a mountain amidst 10,000 acres of pristine, rolling green hills and forests. The University of the South in Sewanee was built so affluent Southern families had a place to send their children and rest assured their values and religious affiliation would be honored. They didn't want their offspring going to schools in the North, a place where Yankees might corrupt their sons' fine minds and Southern gentility. The school has a strong, inescapable Anglican influence and a bell tower that rings the Westminster Chimes.

Daily chapel, once mandatory, was no longer required by the time Tony attended the college. However, the professors wore gowns unbuttoned to class as did students who acquired a gown if their grade point average was high enough. It was considered admirable for students to wear their gowns to class with rakish indifference. They brought their dogs and smoked cigarettes in the classroom. Both hound dog and master received a top-notch education.

"It was dog paradise," Tony said.

"Didn't they bark or disrupt class?"

"No, they just sat at our feet. Our dogs went everywhere with us."

"It's a Southern thing, right?" I ask. I'm still learning the subtleties of being Southern.

Southerners have a strong devotion to tradition and the closest thing to ancestor worship I've seen in this country. Proud of their heritage, many of the Southerners I met still clung to the faded glory of the past, and to my chagrin, I found myself begrudging them their hold on times long gone. "Get over it," I wanted to say. When I saw old family pictures in silver frames, worn Persian carpets and wingback chairs, sets of matching china and large chandeliers suspended over dark wooden tables that could seat an extended family, I felt like an anthropologist observing another species. I couldn't help but note the differences in their lives and mine. Worst of all, I found myself feeling a clearly irrational and illogical envy. Not of any one individual, but of everyone who lived in the South. I didn't envy their material possessions. It was more abstract: I envied the pride and confidence these people derived from their heritage.

I was struck with the difference between being rooted to a place for many generations and being an immigrant. I noticed how the Episcopal religion united the community in Sewanee. It occurred to me that an immigrant's life could be lonely and empty – the transition to a new country, a new language, sometimes few relatives or friends to buffer hard times, often without material objects to lend a feeling of home and place. But my parents' lives didn't seem empty. I had believed that for them, being immigrants represented freedom from the past and a clean slate in a new place. What constituted a home? Was it family and relatives or was "home" just a state of mind? I had always felt the latter, but now I saw how nice it could be to have a place where someone had already not only paved the way, but supplied the furniture too.

Historians often point out that one of the results of the Holocaust is the disruption of family and continuity. Yet I had never wanted to think of being personally victimized by the past before, telling myself the Holocaust was an event that happened long before I was born. Being a victim translated as being weak. But for the first time, while visiting Sewanee, I wondered what it would be like to grow up in a place where my family had always lived. I tried to form a collage in my mind of the photos I'd seen of relatives and assemble them into some kind of imaginary house. But the image didn't take shape. I remembered a remark made by the writer, Helen Epstein. She said, "Our handicap, that of the Second Generation, is that we were not given any memories."

My mother's lost family had built an invisible world inside of me. The psychotherapist Tamar Shosan has explained about children of Holocaust survivors that there is "sadness concerning the memories they do not have, and their longing for people from their family's past, whose identities are too unclear and too wrapped in horror for them to feel connected to. The members of the Second Generation suffer from a kind of inborn nostalgia, very similar to a depressive state, which seems to have taken the place of the continuous mourning of their parents."

"We each have our own karma," is a notion I took to heart long ago. It never made sense to compare my life to someone else's. So I'm surprised at myself now. Why do I begrudge these friendly Southerners their ties to the past? Why do I make fun of their Anglophilia, noting with disdain every wooden duck decoy placed on a table, or silver tea service or knick-knack with an equestrian motif?

"Southerners aren't very original," I say, venting to Tony in a rambling monologue. "All they're doing is copying the British! Edith Wharton said something like that too – why bother coming all the way over here from Europe and creating a new country just to copy the old one you left behind? Oh, and you know who else noticed that? Emerson. He said we have to get the tapeworm of England out of our minds and hearts. Southerners are just creating a second-hand version of England. I'm surprised women around here don't wear Hermes scarves on their heads and walk around with a pack of corgis trailing after them like Queen Elizabeth. They're just a bunch of copycats!"

I say this partly in earnest, but also partly in jest since Tony knows I admire Queen Elizabeth's wardrobe. It would be fun to wear jumbo-sized hats and brightly-colored, meticulously tailored suits, let alone all the magnificent jewelry. I, too, like frame handbags that snap shut with a neat, reassuring click, like the small bags from Launer London in England that Queen Elizabeth favors. In addition, I see no reason why women can't start wearing gloves all year round if they feel like it. I once even checked out Launer London's website to look into ordering a handbag like the Queen's.

But why should I resent the Southerners? What have they done to me? They invite us into their homes and serve food and drink. Albeit significantly more drink than food, another difference from my Jewish relatives that I can't help but note. I simply begrudge these people their ties to the past. I begrudge their effortless connection to their parents' heritage. Where is my heritage? My mother's past? Her family's past? It's one more tragic story among millions of other tragedies of WWII.

Just the other day I read about an artist, Carroll Dunham, who said he takes his grandfather's desk with him every time he moves. "The fact that I know this was in the personal space of someone I have some familiar connection to makes me feel connected to something bigger than me…It's being part of the chain of things." Recently, I also read an article in the *New York Times* about Newport, where my father-in-law is originally from. The piece was called "Updating Newport, Ever So Gently" and featured decorators who "preserve Newport's high-Wasp style." One of the decorators complains it's hard to update the interior of a house because, "In many cases the house has never been owned by anyone but the family. They are very aware that a table or painting was bought by their grandfather. You have to be careful if you're going to suggest moving it." The article connected home decoration and family values in a way I hadn't thought about before. In the past, I believed that owners who kept old furniture were too strapped for cash or just too frugal to buy something new – it never occurred to me that the continuity of having furniture, artwork, and other leftovers from previous generations gave people a sense of security and comfort.

My parents brought only a few possessions with them from Europe to Montreal, which they'd acquired in Vienna after World War II. Everything in our house was brand new – bought by them. As a child, I assumed everyone's furniture came from the Levitz Furniture Store. Until recently, I used to love frequenting antique stores. Maybe I was trying to restore a part of the past for myself. My main interest was collecting Japanese porcelain. I favored Nippon which was made from about 1890 to 1920, the more recent Satsuma of the 1930s, and also the inexpensive ceramics made in occupied Japan (the end of World War II until April 18, 1952). I bought porcelain vases and platters laden with gold beading and bright pastel flowers bursting with life that would look right at home at the Chateau Versailles. I could easily imagine the porcelain pieces on a heavily carved wooden bureau in my grandparents' living room in Vilnius. Perhaps my mother grew up surrounded by beautiful objects like these. Perhaps, if I *really* stretched my imagination, I could believe the items I bought in antique stores came from my grandparents' house.

Just as my collector's urge once surfaced years ago, it quite suddenly and entirely disappeared after a trip to my parents' house in Glendale. My mother had stacked the dining room table with items she now needed shipped to New York. After Tony and I got married and moved to a larger apartment in the same building, my parents took ownership of my former alcove studio apartment. They now had a small apartment in Manhattan and Montreal and a house in Glendale.

Ready to be shipped to New York were a few copper pots and pans, a twelve-piece place setting of twenty-year-old unused Oneida flatware and other odds and ends. I added a 1970s streamlined, white metal lamp from my old bedroom desk. By the time Tony and I hauled all the items to the UPS store, it occurred to me that objects (and certainly moving them) could be a big burden. Nor did possessions give me a feeling of protection or stability. In the back of my mind, I couldn't forget that during the Holocaust my mother and her family had lost everything they owned.

I took it a step further and envisioned all of my painstakingly collected objects, salvaged from thrift shops and collectible stores or bought online on E-bay auctions, being scattered to the winds after I die or just cycling back to thrift shops again. If I were an ancient Egyptian or a Chinese emperor (who commissioned the famous terracotta army in Xi'an to accompany him into the afterlife) and believed I could take everything with me, it might make sense. But it didn't – I didn't want or need so much. At first, I dismissed my change of habit to Tony's influence and minimalist proclivity, but instead what was taking place was a developing aversion for material possessions. I was coming to dislike "things" because they outlasted people. (Though conversely, I can understand this is part of their appeal.)

Our uncluttered apartment is spare, with clean lines and modern furniture. Attached to the living room is a small solarium where we grow flowering plants, herbs, and Saguaro and Barrel cacti. Tony designed our apartment, which we renovated before we moved in. Our bedroom is inspired by our love of Japan, and we humor ourselves by wearing yukatas around the house and sleeping on the floor, the bed covered with a black-and-white patterned Marimekko duvet – Japanese and Finnish design our favorite influences. Though the rest of the apartment is sunny and bright, the bedroom is painted a dark charcoal, almost black, with sound-proofed windows and a black-out shade. Even though we're in the middle of Manhattan, it feels like we're sleeping in a peaceful, primitive cave. The room reminds me of the Japanese writer, Junichiro Tanizaki's thoughts in his famous book about wabi sabi and darkness called *In Praise of Shadows*.

These days, I often take a short walk with my mother to the Farmer's Market in Union Square to buy local fruit and vegetables (within a 250-mile radius from the city). On occasion, I'll buy a bouquet of wildflowers, though each time without fail, my mother shakes her head disapprovingly and says, "It's your money, but why waste it on flowers that are going to die in a few days?" Back home, I'll fill a vase from my collection – a diminishing collection, since I've begun giving pieces away to friends. For special occasions, I'll set the dining room table with the sterling silver, floral-patterned flatware my mother bought at Sears in the 1960s and a set of Minton china given to me by a friend when she moved to Australia.

Though it wasn't intentional on her part, I learned from my mother not to get attached to material possessions and also not to trust people. Lessons once learned that are difficult to unlearn. Sometimes I wonder if my life hasn't also been one long lesson in reluctant trust: trust the surgeon operating, trust the anesthesiologist whom you pay not to put you to sleep, but, as my mother says, to wake you up again, trust the pilot flying the plane, trust a driver to stop at a red light, trust that your spouse will love only you forever, trust that people have virtuous intentions, not selfish ones. And I learned from my mother about irreparable loss. In spite of my mother's efforts, my childhood had been shaped around what she had lost. Nothing can or ever will replace my grandparents' heirlooms nor the past they represent – everything stolen and forever gone from their home in Vilnius.

Kleyne Pekelach – Small Packages

There was a Broadway revival of *Fiddler on the Roof* at the Minskoff Theatre. Tony and I joked about going to see the play, saying our excursion was part of his "continuing education" on Jewish culture. The last time I saw the play was in high school, when it was performed by a repertory company in Phoenix, and I remembered it as a joyful production full of spectacle with a dramatic dream sequence and soul-stirring klezmer music. I was looking forward to an uplifting experience, already humming "Sunrise, Sunset," "If I Were a Rich Man," and the play's other famous melodies to myself as I got ready to take a seat in the theatre. But this time, at the end of the play, I was sobbing.

Fiddler on the Roof is based on a Sholem Aleichem story called "Tevye and his Daughters," written in Yiddish and originally published in 1894. As I watched the play, as Tevye and his family's simple life in Anatevka unraveled and they exited the stage with their small bags, *kleyne pekelach*, I began to cry uncontrollably. I wasn't crying for the fictional characters in Czarist Russia, but for my mother and our relatives who were forced to leave their homes with only the few possessions they could carry.

My mother had described walking around Vilnius for hours, circling the streets on the way to the ghetto, with hungry and exhausted people eventually abandoning even the small bundles and pieces of luggage they had hurriedly put together. Some of her recollections are so vivid and painful they've become seared into my brain. Sometimes if I'm shopping and see a large, leather purse that looks like a satchel, I will think of my grandmother. My mother told me how my grandmother had collected

240

all the family documents, identification papers, photos and money in her purse right before leaving for the ghetto. When she turned her back for a second, the purse disappeared. Strangers had swarmed into the house grabbing whatever they could carry, and had stolen her purse, too. Now her husband had been taken away, documentation of her former life gone and she was alone with two children to protect.

When I think about my mother and grandmother's anguish, the pain registers inside of me with a physical sensation that feels like the weight of a small animal has landed on my chest. Whenever I see a long line of people carrying suitcases – at an airport, even in a hotel lobby – I am reminded of the poor Jews walking to the ghetto. I don't wear striped clothing because it reminds me of concentration camps. When I step into a shower and the water isn't adjusted right, I think of concentration camps. The list goes on. I try to force myself to let go of these thoughts. I don't want to be held hostage by the Holocaust. But sometimes I can't help it. My emotions win out.

Now for the first time, at the age of forty-eight, watching *Fiddler on the Roof*, I began to cry for my grandmother and my relatives – the unknown ghosts – who had aborted lives and tragic deaths. I was mourning for my extended family and the continuity of family that I will never know. The characters in the play could have been my ancestors as far as I was concerned. I felt the loss of lives that were gone forever, and of a cultural devastation that could never be reborn. Even in Vilnius, the vibrant Yiddish-speaking community of my mother's memories is no longer there, though I've heard that recently a few stores in the old Jewish quarter have posted Yiddish lettering on their signs. "To increase tourism," someone cynically said.

While I was watching *Fiddler on the Roof*, I was faced with the unsettling paradox: how important we are to the people who love us, but how insignificant we are in the course of time. How many other billions of Homo sapiens (with emotions not unlike ours) have existed on the earth in the last 195,000 years, each with his or her own concerns about survival? Still, the grim statistics of the Holocaust wouldn't budge from my mind: Of the 250,000 Jews in Lithuania in 1939, about 12,500 to 17,000 survived. Those numbers are too numbing and abstract to grasp, but watching the play made them somehow more real to me.

I was ashamed to be crying in public, afraid I'd lose control and wouldn't be able to stop. A few other people were sniffling, holding crumpled tissues in their hand. But the majority were smiling, as though they had just exited a comedy club.

Tony put his arm around me. It reminded me I wasn't alone, and of how insular and lonely sadness can be. I made a supreme effort to control my emotions. If I couldn't do it for myself, I'd do it for him. I've always felt there's no reason to burden him with my inherited past. Still sitting in my seat, I tried using a technique for blocking out negative thoughts a friend who'd taken a bio-feedback class told me about. "Just keep repeating the word 'cancel' to yourself," she said, "until it goes away."

"Cancel," I repeated over and over to myself. It wasn't working. Try to spell it, I thought, and focused on spelling c-a-n-c-e-l until my normal self gradually started to return. "Let's go," I said to Tony. We left the theatre and walked into the glittering New York night. "That was a great play," he said, with earnest appreciation. "Yes, the music was amazing," I responded. I felt a sense of relief, like I was in a Yasujiro Ozu film where human tragedy is balanced with the reassuring pleasantries of small talk and comments about the weather.

After watching *Fiddler on the Roof*, I realized I'd never be able to disinherit myself from my mother's past. But there was a delicate balance that involved inheriting and holding on to her past, while letting go of her life as the benchmark for my own. And, aside from her losses, the enormity of the Jewish people's sorrows was too much for me to comprehend and absorb. It overwhelmed my emotions. I had to step away from myself and simply make a life-affirming choice. So, I reasoned: Aren't I happy a lot of the time? Isn't that enough? Why be greedy and ask for anything more?

Yom Kippur – Praying With Strangers at a Grave

It was 1991, and I was in Zurich, Switzerland when my mother phoned from Montreal to tell me my grandmother had died. The funeral would be the next day. I was on a two-week summer vacation, staying with Dara, a Swiss friend I knew from New York. Zurich intrigued me because it seemed like two cities rolled into one. A genteel bourgeois demographic typically encountered by tourists on brief stopovers was counterbalanced by an anarchic and artistic underground scene. Dara took me to art galleries, the Kunsthaus Museum of Fine Arts, and her (mostly photographer) friends' parties.

Though I didn't feel like leaving, when my mother told me the news, I immediately offered to get on the next plane to Montreal. But she insisted, "There's no point in coming back just for the funeral. You don't need to." "Do you really mean it?" I asked, relieved. "Yes, I really do," she said. "Don't come." I was happy not to cut my vacation short and to avoid a depressing event. Only years later did my mother admit she was trying to spare me the sorrow of going to the funeral.

After her phone call, instead of heading to the airport, I was eager to go for a walk and window shop on Bahnhofstrasse, the stately main street. I felt sad for my mother, but distant from the event. I told myself, "*You should be crying now.*" But I wasn't. The distance was both geographical and emotional. I had never felt very close to my grandmother. I liked her because she was nice to me and because my mother loved her, but we had never spent much time together.

My grandmother, Esther, had gotten re-married in Montreal to an older gentleman who was a widower, but he died before I met him. Her second marriage gave her a new last name, Kayler. Mr. Kayler was rarely mentioned and I had never seen his photograph. Though my grandmother had friends and family in Montreal, she had always struck me as a lonely, melancholy person. She said to me in Yiddish once, "*Itst bin ikh a tsebrokhene mentsh.*" I'm a broken person now. I had been asking her questions about the past, curious to hear about my mother's childhood in Vilnius and the factory my grandfather owned. The life of luxury and comfort my grandmother recounted to me surpassed even my mother's recollections. I always felt both sorry for my grandmother and detached from her at the same time. There was something about her grief that instinctively made me want to distance myself. As a child, I thought she cried at the drop of a hat, and I shied away from her sorrow.

* * *

It is 2007, a couple of days before Yom Kippur. I call my mother in Montreal. She's about to leave for the cemetery and visit my grandmother's grave. She's going there by herself. My father is staying home because there is a brisk wind on this crisp fall day and he says his tendonitis is acting up.

"I wish he'd go to the cemetery with you," I say. "If I was there, I'd go with you." Even though I try not to, I'm feeling sorry for my mother again. I don't want her navigating graveyards by herself. And I don't remember her having gone to the cemetery before – why now? "Is this what people do before Yom Kippur?" I ask her. "It's in the Jewish tradition to visit the graves of relatives before Yom Kippur," she says.

"It's so sad to go by yourself. Why can't Leo or Benjamin go with you?"

"They already went a couple of days ago," she says. "There was a man praying at the grave next to mother's. He had a prayer book and asked if they'd like him to say a prayer, and they prayed together with him. Yes, of course, it's very sad. But it's reality. It's part of life."

* * *

Tony asks me, "What's Yom Kippur about?" He's become interested in Judaism. It's still a relatively unknown faith to him, one he's encountered from the Episcopal point of view in which Jews are referred to as the "elder brothers in faith." He's an intellectual, interested in ideas and theories, and now Judaism has piqued his curiosity.

I'd like to explain what Yom Kippur means, but I can't tell him much. All I know is, "It's the holiest day of the year. The Day of Atonement. People fast and ask for forgiveness." That's it. I've come to a halt. "I have to look it up," I say, and take out the book I often refer to, *The Idiot's Guide to Being Jewish*. There I read that Yom Kippur is a day when people go to the synagogue and pray to God for forgiveness for the sins they committed either consciously or unconsciously the previous year. I learn that "the Jews made a golden calf and worshiped it, and Moses prayed for God's forgiveness for forty days and forty nights. God forgave the Jews for their idolatrous worship and sin on the Day of Atonement."

I call my mother up and say, "I was just reading about Yom Kippur. Did you know that pious people wear a white robe called a *kittel* that's symbolic of a shroud? It's to remind them of their mortality."

"I never heard of that," she says.

"Remember that old custom in Vilnius you told me about where people empty their pockets in the river on Yom Kippur?"

"It's not Yom Kippur. It's for Rosh Hashanah. It's called *tashlich*."

"Oh," I say, "Did you do that?"

"No, not our family, but the Orthodox Jews walked to the river and emptied their pockets into the water."

"Everything in their pockets or just some things?" I ask her, always interested in the details.

"I don't know," she says. "It's meant as a symbolic gesture to cast away your sins."

* * *

Recently, an Israeli student who was in my College Writing class told me, "Two universities in Tel Aviv are offering free tuition if you study Yiddish. People want to learn it now."

"Is that right?" was all I could say, trying to process this new information. I was totally surprised. General opinion held that Israelis didn't like speaking Yiddish because it reminded them of the German language. I had also read Harold Bloom's review, "The Glories of Yiddish," in the *New York Review of Books* (November 6, 2008), in which he said the scholar, Max Weinreich, noted "the scorn for Yiddish of many Israeli Zionists, for whom Yiddish was the language of victims and not of self-reliant soldiers." In his moving review, Bloom wrote, "Yiddish has suffered near annihilation; its fate is dark...Endlessly metamorphic, like Franz Kafka, Yiddish survived by its openness, but no language can survive the destruction of the small children who had begun to speak it."

Tony and I are planning to travel to Israel next year for Yom Kippur. He'd like to take a Christian tour and follow in the footsteps of Jesus. In Jerusalem, which King David made the Jewish people's capital in 1003 BCE, for the first time I'll meet my mother's Aunt Basia, and first cousin, Rosa, who survived the concentration camps. I'll speak Yiddish with them in the holiest of cities on the holiest day of the year.

OUR VILNIUS

I developed a taste for herring, dill and beets from my mother. When I was little, she would often bring home silvery shards of pickled herring in a jar.

"This is good, but *matjes* herring is the best. Too bad I can't get it here," she would say.

"*Mat-jes*…what's that?" I ask, sounding like a tourist.

"It's the more fatty kind," she tells me. "It used to be my favorite."

My mother's European childhood has always sounded like a myth to me. Though I know the story of her childhood, I still can't imagine what growing up in Vilnius was like for her. I can't picture the clothes she wore, the city, her house, the sleigh rides she loved in the winter, nor do I understand Polish, the language she spoke at school before WWII started. When I was little, it was almost as if my mother had stepped out of the pages of an N. C. Wyeth illustration from one of my favorite bedtime stories. With her green eyes and long, pale blond hair in glamorous waves, painstakingly created by pin curls, she was far more beautiful than any of my friends' mothers. She was my own blond fairy princess.

My mother was never like any of my friends' moms. She has never been to a senior prom, worn bobby-socks or sipped a soda in a bowling alley. She has never belonged to a country club nor did she ever own a tennis racket or golf club. And, even though she has lived in Arizona for so many years, she still sounds like Zsa Zsa Gabor. "Really, I have an accent? I don't hear it," she always says, sounding surprised.

* * *

My mother and I both love the cold and snow. In fact, she often flies to Montreal (after stopping to see me in New York) in the dead of winter for a week or two just to trudge in the snow and ice, saying that she needs to collect the mail and check up on the apartment. This continues to baffle her relatives who have fled like geese to Florida, not to mention my frazzled father who has resigned himself to berating her with stern warnings of slippery ice and broken bones.

He doesn't go with her on these wild winter sojourns. He simply stays home in Phoenix and relents, "What can I do? She won't listen to me." My mother answers each time, "I can't help it. I love the snow. It reminds me of when I was a girl in Vilnius riding to school in a sleigh with the bells ringing and a fur throw pulled up to my chin."

Vilnius. That fabled hometown of her fairy tales. And nightmares during the Holocaust. Even though I've never been there I feel like Vilnius is my hometown, too. My mother has her Vilnius of the past – a place she often tells me she'd never return to. "For what?" she said, "To visit a cemetery?" But, I, too, have my own Vilnius – the Vilnius from the stories she's passed down to me. Our Vilnius.

Because my mother said she'd never go back, I thought I'd never go without her. Instead, I'd have to settle for just trying to imagine the city she knew so many years ago. For me, Vilnius was a complete mystery. A big blank.

But one day I changed my mind about going there.

* * *

I've been poring over a map. Vilnius, Lithuania is part of the Baltics and just across the Baltic Sea from Finland. Tony and I have been planning a trip to Helsinki, practically next door to Vilnius. It's about an hour away and only $186.20 round trip on Finnair. But I'm still undecided – if we go to Vilnius, what will we see there? We'll be two tourists who don't speak the language in a city totally strange, yet familiar. I have mixed feelings. I call my mother on the phone to talk it over; maybe it will help me decide.

"You know, Mom, I've been thinking about our trip to Scandinavia. When we go to Helsinki, maybe we could fly to Vilnius for a couple of days. It's so close." I say this hesitantly, half-afraid to hear her reaction. I'm like a penitent in the confessional box revealing her subversive desires.

There's a long gap of silence, unusual for my mother. "You're not serious, are you?"

"I don't know. But we could squeeze it into our trip. I could go to the building where you grew up on *Breyte Gas*." I use the informal, Yiddish name which means "wide street."

"The apartment building where we lived is completely erased from the map," she says flatly, dispassionately, like a tour guide. "It was bombed during the war. But the apartment building my parents owned at 8 Subocz is still there."

My Uncle Leo and cousin, Perry, who is a lawyer, started proceedings years ago to try and reclaim the family property in Vilnius, but have made little progress so far. "They're in the European Union now. Don't they have to return it?" I asked. "They so don't want to give anything back," Perry said. Now the restitution issue in Lithuania has become worse. My Uncle Leo recently forwarded a letter to me from the lawyer in Vilnius who has been trying to reclaim my grandparents' property:

I am fighting for the Jewish private property restitution many years. The situation is that the Jews (among them survivors) who emigrated to Palestine or Israel were not able to become citizens of Lithuania, because according to the law on citizenship they were considered to be repatriated. After my petition to the Constitutional Court about the definition of repatriation in November 2006, the Constitutional Court passed the ruling that I am right and that the definition of "repatriation" is against the constitution of Lithuania.

At the same time, the terms to apply for the property are over. All citizens of Lithuania according to the law have the right to apply to the court and to extend the last deadline, but not those (mostly Jews) who were not citizens up till December 31, 2001. But they were not able to become citizens, because the illegal law on Citizenship was in force. Therefore, I am now asking the Constitutional Court why only citizens of Lithuania are eligible to obtain the nationalized property, because I think that it is against the constitution and EC regulation.

Lithuania is the only country that links property to citizenship. If nobody helps me, I will not be able to win. By the way, you would help not me personally, but all the Jews.

I'm afraid to go to Vilnius. It's too abstract, too emotional, too laden with ghosts from my mother's past. It exists like some dark dream, like a city in a film noir movie. I was surprised to find out we still have two relatives living in Vilnius. My mother's second cousin, Suze, lives there. She proudly told my mother that her son is "the Bill Gates of Lithuania."

I dismissed the idea of going to Vilnius. I rationalized we didn't have enough time; the trip would be too depressing. Sweden and Finland would be enough for now. A few days later, I'm at the computer researching our trip. Tony recently installed Google Earth with its aerial views of the globe. I zoom in on Finland, happily plotting our summer trip to Turku, Porvoo and then on to Stockholm. I feel like I'm on a magic carpet as I navigate over rooftops, circle around a little more, then float through the heavens over rivers and forests that head straight into Vilnius. I see the Neris River that runs through the city, and a small maze of buildings near the Vilnia River. That must be the old city, where the ghettos were. I zoom around and see the big, green parks and forests, the roads my mother traveled many times during the war, escaping from the ghetto out of the city to the farm-land beyond. Suddenly, something clicks. I *must* see Vilnius for myself.

I indulge myself in researching a trip, one of my favorite pastimes. First, I look up Vilnius on the TripAdvisor website, a site for hotel infor-mation and all kinds of other useful travel tips. Soon I discover there's more than one Vilnius. There's the Christian city and the Jewish city. I learn that after Waterloo, Napoleon's troops managed to disperse as far as Vilnius. Czeslaw Milosz, the Nobel Prize-winning poet, got his law degree at The University of Vilnius and lived there for many years.

As if by coincidence, a travel brochure from Smartours arrives in the mail. I'm about to throw it in the trash when the "special offers" for a trip to the Baltic states catches my eye. There it is – Vilnius. I see my city. The tour goes to Vilnius, Riga, Tallin and other smaller cities. On "Day 3" of the itinerary, I read, "Boasting some of northern Europe's most impressive baroque architecture, the central Vilnius skyline is adorned with domes and belfries. On the ground, you'll discover a maze of winding, narrow alleys lined with eighteenth-century buildings with archways leading to cobbled yards…Afternoon is at leisure and you may wish to visit the old Jewish Quarter, former home to one of Europe's largest, most prosperous Jewish communities. You may also relax at one of the many outdoor cafés and admire Vilnius' thriving cultural diversity."

I put the brochure down on the table. Then I pick it up again and re-read the sentence. "Former home to one of Europe's largest most prosperous Jewish communities." I sit there for a few minutes with the brochure in my hand, staring at the wall and feeling numb – not even numb really, something beyond numb. I'm stunned by the brevity and matter-of-factness of the sentence that glosses over any mention of the Holocaust. I recall the maze of winding alleys and hear my mother's voice dictating to me as I type her memoirs – how she, my uncle, my grandmother and the other Jews were herded into these "winding narrow alleys" on their way to the ghetto. Mention of the cobbled yards brings flashbacks of my mother's near escapes from death. I remember sitting at the computer, typing as she deciphered and dictated to me the cramped writing in her notebook. Tears ran down my face as I tried to sit as silently as I could, like a typing statue, so she wouldn't notice I was crying. Sometimes it felt like there wasn't enough air in the room, not enough oxygen to breath.

"It's not me. It's like this happened to a stranger, to someone else," she says as we work. I don't believe her, but I'm grateful to hear the words.

I recall a remark Helen Epstein made in one of her notable books, *Children of the Holocaust*: "I set out to find a group of people who, like me, were possessed by a history they had never lived." I picked her book up reluctantly, only after a friend insisted I read it. I wasn't interested in reading stories about other children of Holocaust survivors. I was afraid their words would intrude upon mine, on my life and privacy, as if their thoughts could invade my own. I hadn't realized how closely I had guarded my own private vigil over my mother's past. Perhaps going to Vilnius would pop the bubble I had formed in my psyche. But now that I'd seen an aerial view of Vilnius on Google Earth, my desire to go there only increased.

I continue searching on the internet. I type in "Vilnius Ghetto" and the site "death camps" appears. I force myself to read it. I skim a few paragraphs afraid of what I'll see next. Then I read, "On the morning of September 6, 1941, all Jews were ordered to leave their homes and move to the ghettos. Three thousand of those unable to find shelter in the ghetto were taken to Ponary for execution." "No other Jewish community in Nazi-occupied Europe was so comprehensively destroyed." I feel like a huge weight is inside my body and dragging me to the floor. I can't stand reading anymore. I don't want to have nightmares or flashbacks, which often happen after I read about the Holocaust or watch television documentaries showing Hitler and the Nazi swastika. But I continue.

I read about Ghetto 2, where my mother stayed. "Two ghettos were installed, separated by Niemiecka St. This street was outside the limits of both ghettos and served as a barrier between them. A wooden fence enclosed each ghetto, and the entrances of houses facing the outside were blocked off. Each ghetto had only one gate for exit and entry, placed at opposite ends of the enclosed area, so that it would be impossible for those entering and leaving to cross paths. At first, people were moved into either ghetto at random. [About] twenty-nine thousand people were incarcerated in Ghetto 1 and nine thousand to eleven thousand in Ghetto 2. The living conditions were those common to the ghettos of countries under Nazi occupation – dilapidated housing, lack of sanitation, unbearable congestion…The killing never stopped."

My body feels heavy and slow, like a poisonous serum has been injected into my veins. I skip a few pages and read the last couple of paragraphs. "Between two thousand and three thousand of the original fifty-seven thousand Jewish inhabitants of Vilnius survived, either in hiding, with the partisans, or in camps in Germany and Estonia, a mortality rate of approximately 95% – almost exactly corresponding with that of Lithuania as a whole."

My mother's words come back to me. "I don't know why I survived. I wasn't a good person. I was selfish. Spoiled."

"But you were so young," I said. "It's normal for teenagers to be selfish." I'm hoping this pat remark will put an end to the painful conversation.

"I don't know why God spared me," she says, still questioning the reason for her survival after so many years. "I think he kept me alive just so I could save my mother and Leo. But I know there is a God who watched over me and wanted me to survive."

* * *

Now that I've decided to see Vilnius, my mind is filled with all sorts of dreams and images. I can't go there soon enough. I want to go tomorrow. Today even. I can't wait to tell my mother. I call her and say, "Mom, I talked to Tony and we decided. We're going. Why don't you and Dad come meet us in Helsinki for a few days, and then we could all fly to Vilnius together?" Silence. I know my father hates to travel, but I'm still pushing the idea. "You know, it's not fair. You've gone to Greece with him so many times, but he's never been to Vilnius with you. He won't even go to Poland with you!" I say, petulantly. I know fairness has nothing to do with the subject, but it's an emotional one, so my negotiating tactics are skewed.

"Speaking of Poland, I just got off the phone with Nina," my mother tells me. "She invited us again to stay with her at Maryla's house on the Black Sea in Bulgaria." Maryla Rodowicz, her daughter, is one of Poland's most famous singers.

"That sounds wonderful," I say. "Why don't you go?" My father has never met Nina, the woman who saved my mother's life when she gave her the ID that belonged to her sister who had died of tuberculosis.

"You know he hates to travel. I don't want to go by myself."

Even when my father was younger, travel was more punishment to him than pleasure. He hated to disrupt his clockwork-like routine; he wasn't fond of sleeping in unfamiliar beds, of eating meals at unpredictable times. Now that he's elderly, he often uses his age as an excuse to bow out. "Sure, go to New York – leave me here," he once told my mother when she came to visit me for a week. "You'll come back to find my skeleton."

"Mom, you know, I just thought of something." We're still on the phone. "Planning this trip to Scandinavia was just a way for me to get to Vilnius. I kept telling myself, '*It's so close. It's so close.*' Now I realize I must have wanted to go there all along. I just wasn't ready before." I get straight to the point. "So instead of stopping in Helsinki first, we'll connect there and go straight to Vilnius."

"Mom?" Total silence, as if the line has gone dead. "Mom?"

"I didn't think you were serious," she says finally.

"Well, I wasn't. Not until the other day."

"I don't know what it is..." she says, after a long pause. "It's so strange. I feel like it isn't safe for you to go there."

"But, it's a safe place, Mom," I say, wanting to add the word "now."

"I know, it's ridiculous," she says. "But I feel afraid. What airline are you flying? Is it from the country that's having all the problems with the Muslims? It might be dangerous."

"No, that's Denmark. We're flying Finnair."

A student in one of my classes at Touro College is from Vilnius. She's the first person I've met in New York who's lived there. She's a polite young woman who wears a short gold chain with a crucifix around her neck. She was surprised when I told her of my interest in the city. "Not too many American tourists go there," she said. I didn't tell her about my mother's past. The next class, she gave me a DVD to take home. I went straight home after class and put the DVD in my computer, a sense of dread and anxiety coming over me.

There it was – Vilnius, another aerial view of the city like the one on Google Earth, only this time, much closer. The camera slowly panned across the city to the gothic St. Anna's Church, Cathedral Square, eighteenth-century buildings with archways and cobbled courtyards. I clicked on the next tab and saw Vilnius at night. The camera wended its way across the eerie, darkened city with its lantern-lit sidewalks and winding streets. I immediately superimposed a picture of my mother as a young woman surreptitiously walking down these dark streets, almost trapped, trying to hide, to outwit the Nazis, to stay alive.

"Don't go out alone at night," Mom says. I hear the concern in her voice.

"You know I won't go anywhere without Tony. Don't worry." How many times in my life have I told her not to worry? A million? Maybe more?

I can hardly believe we're going. I recall the statistics in the article: 95% of the Vilnius Jews were murdered. "You didn't get them all," I say to myself with grim satisfaction.

Minutes later I dial Finnair's number. I listen to the recording in Finnish, then a brief English translation. I press the number to speak to a reservation agent in English.

"Can I help you?" a woman with an unfamiliar accent inquires.

"Yes," I say, "I'd like to book a round-trip ticket for two, please. From Helsinki to Vilnius."

New Roads to Old Places: My Trip to Vilnius

Tony calls this trip the "Baltic roots" journey. I've started packing, bought token presents for our two relatives in Vilnius – a turquoise silk chiffon scarf for Suze, and for her son, Garik, a black t-shirt from the Strand Bookstore with the logo on the front and "18 miles of books" printed on the back. I've gone down the checklist of preparations for the trip including trail mix to eat on the plane, dark chocolate, organic instant coffee for Tony's breakfast, organic Matcha green tea for mine, Ambien, a container of Pro Greens, Milk of Magnesia, and our memory foam travel pillows. There's still room in the suitcase, so for good measure, I toss in a few small cartons of rice milk.

As a prerequisite for the trip, I think it might be a good idea to watch a documentary Uncle Leo recommended. It's called, *The Last Kletzmer*, a 1994 film about a Jewish man, Leopold Kozlowski, who survived the Holocaust by entertaining and playing music for the Germans while he was in a concentration camp. Tony and I start watching the film and by the time the last kletzmer, now an aged and renowned musician in Moscow, returns to his village in Poland for the first time since WWII and visits the spot where his father was shot, I am sobbing. I imagine that the place in Ponary where my grandfather and members of our family were killed looks very much the same. A peaceful, green forest. Tony turns to me, and concerned by my crying, puts his arm around me and says, "But going back is a positive experience for him. It's closure." I'd like to think of it that way, but I can't.

Uncle Leo phones me from Montreal. He's in touch with Suze and Garik, and says they'll be picking us up at the airport. "Are they involved in the Vilnius Jewish community?" I ask, wondering what it's like for them to live in a city once vibrant with yidishkayt.

"I have no idea," he answers. We continue talking, and then there's an unexpected pause in the conversation. A too-long silence. "You're the only one from our family who's gone back after all these years." Suddenly he's crying. I'm thrown back to childhood, to the familiar feeling of helplessness I had when the adults talked about the past and wept. The same thing happens again when I'm on the phone with Uncle Leo. I don't know what words to use. For lack of anything better to say I tell him, "Please don't get upset." This is so inadequate, so superficial. But I want to say something to make him feel better. I've always loved my mother's younger brother who entertains everyone with his vast repertoire of hilarious jokes in Yiddish. The talk with him saddens me. It reminds me again of how little, even with compassion and empathy, we can enter or ease another's pain.

Sometimes when teaching a literature class and talking about a story from another time period, I'll say to my students, "Take off your 2010 glasses and put on your 1884 glasses for a moment and try to see the story through Chekhov's eyes." Now I tell myself the same thing. "Put on a different pair of glasses. Try to change your perspective. Re-frame it. Make the trip to Vilnius a positive experience."

My uncle gives me the phone number of the lawyer in Vilnius who's trying to reclaim my grandfather's apartment building and land in the old part of town. "If you have time, go see her," he says. I ask him, "Is there anything specific you'd like me to say?" He replies, "Ask her if she can push the process a little bit and make it faster. Another twenty years and not one of us will be left."

Tony enthusiastically researches the Baltics in preparation for our trip. He e-mails me his finds on the internet, and sends a few poems by Czeslaw Milosz, a celebrated personage from the city. I'm not familiar with Milosz's work, but remember Joseph Brodsky often mentioning him with admiration in the poetry workshop I took at Columbia University. My mother tells me Nina once mailed her a poem that Milosz wrote for her daughter, the singer, Maryla. The next time I go to the literature section of the New York Public Library in midtown (which has a collection of documentaries that I sometimes borrow to show in my English classes), I notice the title of a film about the poet from my mother's hometown. It's an interview and poetry reading that Milosz gave in California, where he lived for many years. I check the DVD out from the library and immediately call Tony on my cell phone to tell him about the cosmic coincidence of this finding so soon before our trip.

Later that night, as we're watching the DVD, I'm struck by some of Milosz's comments. Like my mother, he talks about Vilnius like it is an enchanted city, something out of a storybook. A week later, I return to the library and start skimming through some of his poetry and essay collections. I pick up *To Begin Where I Am*, and the title of one of the chapters jumps out at me, "The Streets of Vilnius." I don't know what I'm expecting to find, but I feel like an archaeologist trying to dig through whatever layers are available, to go back in time, to find something from the past that is real and true.

As I'm scanning the introduction to Milosz's book, I see the word Wilno. This is the Polish spelling of the city. I'm unbearably curious and eager to read about his impression of Vilnius. I hungrily start reading the section on Vilnius streets, skipping from street to street, until I realize what's happening. I am searching for my mother. I feel like we co-exist in mythic time. I half expect to find her somewhere, stepping out of his writing as though she's rounding a corner about to meet me. I'm looking for our relatives, for our family. How little there is left of my mother's past, I think. A few photographs. My grandfather's scarf. Memories.

Milosz mentions a green bridge. This must be the same green bridge where a Lithuanian policeman stopped my mother and asked for her ID papers, the bridge where she was almost apprehended and had another close brush with death. Milosz writes about the bridge, "The sawmills where the 'flats' tie up, so that sometimes the Wilia [river] would be completely covered by them, were somewhat farther downstream, past the green bridge, across from St. Jacob's." What are flats? Where is this green bridge? Where are the places my mother walked? I have to see them for myself.

* * *

The nine-hour Finnair flight from Kennedy International Airport briefly makes a stopover at the Helsinki Vantaa Airport before we connect to the short flight to Vilnius. I learn the Vantaa Airport was rated

257

the most punctual in Europe by the Association of European Airlines in 2005. Soon Tony and I are on board a 113-seat Baltic Air 32S airplane for the flight to Vilnius. I'm sitting toward the back of the plane lightly bobbing along with the bumpy weather in a fog of jet-lagged anticipation, too tired to even flip through a magazine. Mindlessly, I watch the black coffee in my cup swirl around, rise near the rim, but never quite spill out of its small white plastic container.

The one-and-a-half-hour flight seems interminable. As the plane slowly starts its descent, I lean across Tony's seat straining to peer out the window at the lush, monochromatic green expanses of field and forest below me. I look out the window at the ribbons of river, the small homes dotting the countryside. I can see the "beautiful countryside," the term my mother always uses when she describes the land she loved so much, with its birch trees and fields of Queen Anne's lace. Recently, the Scandinavian countries have helped raise environmental consciousness in the Baltic area, and Denmark contributed 48 million euros to Lithuania between 1991 and 2002. The environmental standards are very high, and I imagine the land is as pristine now as it was when my mother lived there. Looking out of the airplane window, I wonder which of these roads she traveled on as a child to the country house in Czarny Bor, which forests she picked wild berries and mushrooms from, and later as a teenager, which path she took when she escaped the Vilnius ghetto and hid in small towns and villages.

Now we're here. "New roads to old places," I say to myself, the line sounding like something out of the country lyrics Tony and I listen to on WSIX when we're driving through Tennessee. Without realizing it, I immediately conflate my mother's Vilnius and my own. Tears well up in my eyes when I ponder the thought that we're the first ones to return since WWII.

But here on the plane, from seemingly out of nowhere, a new, unexpected, even unwelcome side of me is starting to surface. This new side is not only my mother's daughter, but a separate person – an American tourist eager to see the city she's pored over in guidebooks. Now I'm not the daughter of a Holocaust survivor. Tony and I are simply travelers, strangers visiting a lovely Baltic town, about to land in a city with a World Heritage Site of renaissance, baroque and medieval buildings, famous gothic churches, shops chock full of local crafts and resin jewelry native to the Baltic area, picturesque narrow winding streets and welcoming outdoor cafés and restaurants. At latitude of 54.38N, the sunny summer days will be extremely long with up to eighteen hours of daylight. We haven't even landed, and there are already two cities inside of me – my mother's Vilnius and my own. The past and the present.

The plane lands and quickly reaches the gate in the small, efficient airport. Within a matter of minutes, our bags appear on the carousel. I'm impressed by how smoothly things have run in both Helsinki and Vilnius. Walking out of baggage claim, we wonder how we'll recognize Suze and Garik. Luckily, Garik is holding up a piece of loose-leaf notebook paper with our last name scribbled on it in pencil, as though he's a driver from a car service. Tony spots the paper first. We wave at each other. Suze, who is in her early sixties, has light brown eyes and chestnut colored hair in a blunt, shoulder-length cut. She reminds me of the models in Breck shampoo ads and looks much like the photographs of my grandmother when she was younger. Garik, in his thirties, is slim and has piercing blue eyes that belie his open smile and easygoing personality. Neither of them speaks Yiddish, but Garik is fluent in English, Russian and German. Suze speaks some English too. We greet our only relatives in Vilnius, eagerly but gingerly embracing them. They're our family and intimate strangers at the same time.

We all step out of the airport and my travel-weary eyes are blinded by the bright sunshine and clear, blue sky. I make a mental note to order prescription sunglasses when I return to New York. This is not at all what I anticipated. I'm reminded of a book I read called *Stumbling on Happiness*, in which the author, Daniel Gilbert, a Harvard psychologist, says humans are the only animals that can "prospect," that is, imagine the future. He notes in his numerous studies in the book how mostly wrong we are when we try to predict what our feelings will be. I'm already wrong and I've only just left the airport.

Already, Vilnius is not how I imagined it. The part of me familiar with my mother's past expected to step into a scene from a stylish film noir movie like *The Third Man*. Even though the 1948 movie takes place in post-war Vienna (where my parents were living in 1948), there's a similar stateliness to both cites. I somehow thought we'd be immersed in a black-and-white world, with women wearing seamed stockings and laced-up shoes that clicked when they walked on the murky cobblestones still slick with raindrops. I half-expected men in hats to leave long shadows and trails of smoke behind them as they rounded sharp corners into the dark recesses of the night. I imagined Vilnius would be hushed and urgent, dark and elusive. But it's the opposite. It's bright and clean, relaxed and welcoming.

Over and over again, the bleak tragedy of my mother's family is forgotten as Tony and I walk the city streets in the glory of peak summer days. I catch myself feeling guilty as I stroll the narrow streets of the Old Town, enjoying the sights, holding a copy of "Vilnius Now" in one hand and a bottle of Evian in the other. The rich aroma of coffee and potted flowers wafts in the streets. There is a faint breeze. The light is golden.

"Did you know," I say to Tony, who likes travel minutiae as much as I do, "that amber comes from the vascular tissue of trees?"

We stop for a minute while I read from one of our guide books, "Baltic amber is approximately forty- to sixty-million years old. It was one of the first commercial products and was found in the form of pendants dating from the Paleolithic Era (c. 12,000 BC)."

The next day, while Suze, Garik, and Tony wait outside, I pop into one of the numerous jewelry stores overflowing with this ancient vegetal gem. One piece immediately catches my eye. It's a necklace of clustered amber millions of year old that looks like golden chips of ice strung together, priced at eighteen dollars. A few minutes later, I'm outside the shop, a content tourist holding my purchase in a shiny brown paper bag tied with a rustic straw ribbon.

The self-satisfaction of the amber necklace purchase feels frivolous, and the pleasure quickly fades when Suze and Garik lead us a few blocks away to Subocz 8, the apartment building on Subocz St. that belonged to my grandparents. I can't believe my eyes. The building is much bigger than I imagined and, except for the color, seems like it could easily blend in with the architecture on the Rue Montaigne in Paris. It's four stories tall, painted a dusty pinkish terracotta with tall, narrow, arched windows and delicate ironwork framing the balconies. I wonder how many families live here. We all look at each other without having anything to say. Then it dawns on me they must be waiting for my response.

"It's a beautiful building," I say laconically. Tony's suggestion to take a photo in front of the wrought iron gate is a welcome distraction from my emotions.

In my childish fantasy a tenant walks out of the courtyard and I say to him, "You can't live here. It's not your building. It's ours. It belongs to my mother and her brother." But no one walks out, and I would never say such a thing. It's not the tenants' fault. Now I'm glad my mother isn't traveling with us. Unlike everything blown away by time and lost in the Holocaust, this building is still here, a sturdy and tangible reminder of the past. There's no pride of ownership. There's only the discouraging knowledge that we might never be able to reclaim it. A recent letter Uncle Leo received from Ambassador Eisenstat in Washington informed us Lithuania still hasn't established any legislation for restitution of private Jewish property confiscated during the Holocaust.

The Conti Hotel where Tony and I are staying is in a nineteenth-century building at Raugyklos 7/2. The rooms are elegant with dark woods and warm peach colors, and the modern Grohe bathroom fixtures are from Germany. The desk clerk informs us the Old Town is only 500 meters away.

"How far is that?" I ask Tony.

"Approximately five times three, so roughly 1,500 feet," he responds. He's amazingly quick with metric conversions, one of the many bonuses of traveling with an architect.

My parents are now in Montreal, and I call my mother from the Conti Hotel. I tell her where it's located. She doesn't recognize the street.

"All of the street names were changed after the war," she says. I look at the hotel map that shows the immediate landmarks in the vicinity and read, "The sixteenth-century All Saint's Church is just a few blocks away."

"Oh, of course," my mother says, "I know exactly where it is now. The church is on Rudnicka St. close to where the entrance to the ghetto used to be. I went into that church many times when I had no place else to go."

The next day we ask Suze and Garik if they want to come with us to the Ponary Forest where my grandfather and many members of our family were killed. Suze offers to drive us there, saying we can even go right after lunch. This jolts me out of my superficial touristy observations. I can hardly eat. I ignore the intensely scarlet beet soup with a ball of sour cream floating on top and the freshly baked loaf of dark bread rubbed with butter and chunks of garlic. Suddenly the past feels like it's all around me.

Our short ride in Garik's van starts out pleasantly enough, as though we're all going on a picnic. Though Ponary is located just 3.7 miles from town, neither Suze or Garik have ever been there before. Since they don't know exactly where the Ponary Memorial is and the roads through the countryside and dense forests are sporadically marked, while we're driving Garik makes a number of calls on his cell phone to ask a friend for directions.

At last, we find the Ponary Monument in the midst of the forest, surrounded by nearby bucolic villages that look untouched by time. The forest has tall pine trees that reach to the sky and form a leafy canopy that almost block out the fierce summer sun, and there is a seemingly endless stretch of deep green carpet beneath us. It's peaceful and beautiful. How could so many atrocities have happened here?

We're the only visitors. The site looks deserted. The words "Paneriu Memorialas" are carved on a simple stone wall about six feet high. On the other side of the pavement is a memorial plaque that states the grim numbers and facts of Ponary in Lithuanian and Russian. The Lithuanian government didn't allow the stone to be engraved in Yiddish. A memorial in English reads, "External memory of seventy thousand Jews of Vilnius and its environs who were murdered and burnt here in Paneriai by Nazi executioners and their accomplices." According to Yad Vashem, "between seventy thousand and one-hundred thousand Jews, including fifty thousand to sixty thousand from the Vilnius Ghetto" perished there from July 1941 to July 1944.

Prisoners first took their clothes off and handed their valuables over, then were marched naked holding hands in groups of ten or twenty to stand at the edge of a large pit where they were shot. Or they were shot as they walked on a plank stretched across the pit. As the killings progressed over days, the executioners (many of whom were drunk, according to accounts by witnesses) complained of shoulder pains from the continuous shootings, and took less aim or deliberately shot at the victims' legs and stomachs, leaving the wounded to be buried along with the dead. A few of the wounded managed to escape. Of the twelve pits, three still remain open. The pits are filled with ashes, as the Germans, later trying to hide the evidence, forced Jewish prisoners to burn the bodies left in the pits.

Tony and I walk hand in hand through the endless tall trees behind the memorial plaque. We wander for a while on the graveyard of dense green forest floor. The wind is gently blowing through the leaves and birds are chirping. I say a prayer for my grandfather and silently speak to him. I tell him I hope I can meet him one day in the place we call heaven.

* * *

The next afternoon, Tony and I take a walk to explore the area around the Conti Hotel. We're drawn into mysterious courtyards. We venture under small arched passageways linking buildings on opposite sides of narrow cobblestone streets, and wherever else the winding sidewalks lead us. We admire fanciful white plaster moldings and gilded rococo motifs on the facades of buildings painted in pastel Easter-egg colors. The courtyards and the squares are adorned with wrought-iron palings and *rocaille* embellishments, the design motif sometimes described as the crest of a wave frozen in time. It feels like we're walking inside a fairy tale.

A few people pass by speaking Lithuanian, a language entirely unfamiliar to me. In the middle of a narrow street, a wedding party is posing for photographs. Laughter and voices are coming from deep within some of the cobbled courtyards.

That evening we meet Suze and Garik in a trendy coffee shop. It's in the open courtyard of a renaissance building. The blue summer sky is framed by the massive neoclassical architecture of the rectangular courtyard that's surrounded on all sides by long arcaded balconies. I feel like we're on a set from Romeo and Juliet. We order ice cream, and again my thoughts turn to my mother. Maybe she walked past this building or was inside this very courtyard herself? Suze and Garik don't mention the ghetto or anything else that happened during the Holocaust. Garik was raised under the Soviet rule, and Suze and her family were arrested by the Soviets and shipped to Siberia in 1941 where they survived the war before returning to Vilnius. Though Jewish, they are now assimilated into the Christian world.

Suze and Garik don't even mention Jewish life in Vilnius, but talk about other things. Garik informs us that the Lithuanian language is one of the oldest in the world and distantly related to Sanskrit. He's brought us a tourist magazine. It includes a brief introduction to the country's tumultuous history, which I start reading when we get back to the Conti Hotel. I'm particularly interested in the period of time when my mother lived in Vilnius. I read:

In 1939, the Molotov-Ribbentrop Pact of 23 August 1939 initially relegated Lithuania to the German sphere of influence; however, on Lithuania's refusal to attack Poland as a German ally, it was transferred to the Soviet sphere of influence in a second secret pact signed in Moscow on the 27th of September that same year. On the 10th of October

1939, Vilnius was returned to Lithuania and Soviet military bases were established within the country. In 1940, Soviet forces occupy Lithuania in June. Formal annexation into the Soviet Union was made in August, following a bogus parliamentary election. In June, 1941, the Soviets carried out the first mass deportation of the Lithuanian people to Siberia, with approximately thirty-five thousand deported within days. Later that month Germany attacked the Soviet Union. Several days later, the Wehmacht had occupied the whole of Lithuania. A massive elimination of the Jews was launched, one that would claim two-hundred thousand lives by 1944.

My head is swimming with numbers and dates.

* * *

I have come to Vilnius wishing to pay homage to the past, expecting to cultivate a personal shrine in my heart for my murdered relatives and my mother's lost world. But the long summer days and warm weather, the shops, museums, cafés, restaurants, Tony's knowledgeable insight and commentary on the architecture – all of it is like an enormous magnet whose pull I can't resist. It drags me out of the past, out of the dark days of WWII and into the sunny, glorious July afternoons. I feel like a swimmer persistently trying to dive into the ocean of the past, only to have the waves toss me back each time on shore – back to the present.

I have an epiphany. How natural it is to let go of the past and make room for the present. How instinctive for our memories to fade, to eventually forget even the details of a loved one's face if we don't have a photograph. I had always thought just the opposite was true, that we were programmed to remember, to reminisce. But now I realize for myself how fragile and selective memory is. I don't want to think about it. I bury the thought immediately because I still want to hold on and give my relatives who died the only thing I can – remembrance. My mother and I are witnesses, each in our own way, who have chosen the task of preserving the memory that our relatives once existed in this world. Even if forgotten by the rest of the world, we can at least offer them something concrete: black type on a page, words in a book that confirm both their brief existence and eternal absence from our lives. They, too, once lived. They, too, once mattered. Though my words aren't nearly as eloquent, my mission is the same as the famous Greek historian, Herodotus. When he started traveling and chronicling the known world twenty-five centuries ago in *The Histories*, he said his purpose in writing was "to prevent the traces of human events from being erased by time."

The past and present form a symbiotic wholeness and neither one can shut the other out. William Faulkner's well-known dictum comes to mind: "The past is never dead, it's not even past." Both the past and the present tug at me. But while I'm in Vilnius, I feel myself being torn away from the tragic associations of the Holocaust by the pleasant reality of the moment. "Remember, be here now," I had read so long ago in Ram Dass's famous counterculture book of the 70s. After all, isn't this what I had always been aspiring to – accepting the here and now fully? With unusual gusto, I throw myself into the role of a tourist. My journal descriptions even read like a visitor's guide from the Chamber of Commerce meant to enhance tourism to the city. I leave out private thoughts that are too painful to put on paper. By not writing about my feelings, I can keep them safe and guarded inside of me. Only when I return home to New York, do I realize that lingering on the superficial beauty of Vilnius and filling the role of a besotted tourist was a way to distance myself from my mother's painful past. It was a cheerful armor I had unconsciously donned to shield myself with.

Our visit to Vilnius is soon over. We say goodbye to Suze, and Garik offers to drive us to the airport the next day. He arrives early in the morning at the hotel in his late-model, blue mini-van, punctually on the dot, and smiling, as always. When we pull into the airport parking lot, my eyes start watering up. We've grown close to our relatives in this short time. We say our goodbyes to Garik. I hug him. Tony shakes his hand. I do my best to feign cheerfulness. I don't voice my first, unbidden thought at airport departures, "What if this is our last good-bye?"

* * *

Back home in New York on sleepless nights, a slide show of images of Vilnius and the Holocaust replay themselves in my mind. Now I have real places that I've seen with my own eyes to fill in the abstractions of stories I once heard from my mother. Traveling to Vilnius was a way to own the past, to somehow put my arms around it, embrace it and then leave it behind. Or so I thought. Instead, I learned I could never leave the past behind because the lost world of ghosts became real to me. Through my mother's stories and my own visit to the city, the relatives in old photographs became like friends I had once known. I had walked the streets where they lived. I saw the same buildings, the same parks and the same countryside. I was a witness to their past. The world of Vilnius materialized before me, and I realized the sorrow I feel for my relatives and the other innocent people who perished long ago has become a part of me that I'll never lose.

On those nights when I start thinking about the Holocaust and can't fall asleep, I'll fix a cup of chamomile tea, go into the living room and lay on the couch, where I read a book until the ghosts recede and the contentment and immediacy of my own life return. William James, the philosopher and psychologist, said many years ago, "My experience is what I agree to attend to," and I make an effort to turn my attention to the present. I want to live in the moment as much as possible, not in a rear view mirror. I'll slip back into bed and put my arm around my husband, knowing in the morning everything will be fine again. The present is here, the future awaits – and so does happiness.

MY GRANDFATHER'S SCARF

All that my mother has left of her former life in Vilnius is a navy blue wool scarf with gray stripes that belonged to her father. She carried it with her throughout the war, and it's now carefully folded and stored away in a plastic bag with moth balls in the closet. My mother and I rarely speak about my grandfather, and I deliberately don't mention him more than absolutely necessary while we're writing our book, knowing when we talk about him she'll start to cry.

My mother tells me about a dream she just had about her father. It's the first dream in years she remembers having about him. "He was running away from me and I was chasing him. He turned a corner and I could only see the edge of his jacket. I was running as fast as I could. I wanted to see him again."

"Did you see his face?" I ask her, with a sense of foreboding. I usually find it boring when people recount their dreams in detail, but not my mother's.

"No, I tried to, but he was running too fast," she says. There's sadness in her voice. I know she's a little superstitious about dreams and thinks dreaming about relatives who have passed away might be a sign of impending death for someone in our family. I feel the same way, but I'm reluctant to say so and verbalize my concern. I'd like to dream about my grandfather, but I never have. Not even once. I have a vivid picture of him in my mind from the photographs I've seen. I'd like to meet the man with the sharply tailored clothes, the blond hair, blue eyes and my mother's nose.

"Have you been thinking about death recently?" I ask her. I don't really want to talk about the subject, but there's a worried tone in her voice. I can't think about my parents dying. The more we've all grown older together, the more I'm used to having them in my life. The older I get, the more I appreciate them being here. I look out the window at the large mulberry tree growing on the roof of the building across the street. The green leaves are brimming with life.

"Yes, of course I have. But no more than usual," she answers. I'm relieved when she says she'll call her brother; she can get his feedback. "Leo told me he had a dream about mother a couple of nights ago too. It was the same night I dreamed about my father. I'm going to call him again and talk to him about it."

"Do you think this is some kind of message?" I ask. I'm remembering my friend who committed suicide and the many dreams I had about him after he died. I felt they were messages from him. We laughed and had conversations together in those dreams and I believe his spirit still wanted to keep in touch.

"I don't know," my mother says. "In the Jewish religion, the Mishna says not to pay attention to dreams. They have no meaning."

"When was the Mishna written?" I ask.

"I'm not sure," she says.

"That's okay. I'll look it up."

"But don't worry," she says. "The dream happened on an 'empty' day." Then she adds, "Anyway, it's just superstition. Folklore. It doesn't mean anything."

"How did you learn this system for empty and full days?" I ask.

"The maid taught it to us," she says. The elaborate system for dream interpretation is one of the pieces of Eastern European superstition that my mother halfheartedly believes in. When a dream falls on any day but Tuesday or Friday, it's considered an "empty" day, meaning the dream is empty, it doesn't count. On the contrary, if a dream happens on Tuesday or Friday, a "full" day, then it's a precursor of things to come. The time of day that a dream occurs is important too. If it happens early in the morning before waking up on a full day, the event dreamed about is imminent.

Though I don't believe there was any connection to my mother's dream, sadly, within the year there were two deaths in our immediate family. My mother's older brother, Benjamin, diagnosed with lung cancer, died in Montreal. Then a few months afterwards, my father's congestive heart failure quickly worsened. He was admitted to New York University's Tisch Hospital and died four days later.

Living in the Present, Juggling the Past

"When I die, I want my ashes to be scattered in Israel."
I'm eavesdropping on my mother. I'm in her apartment and she's on the phone with Vera, a friend she met in New York who's from Vilnius, also attended the Epstein Gymnasium and is a year younger than her. I've never heard my mother talk of her funeral arrangements before. In fact, she doesn't plan for the future unless it's absolutely necessary. "I'll worry about it when the time comes," is her standard response.

I walk into the kitchen to hear more. There she is, sitting casually on a stool holding the bright yellow phone and chatting about death as if it were on a menu. I look at her quizzically, my eyebrows arched. Without skipping a beat, she switches into Polish, a language I don't understand.

As soon as she hangs up, I say, "I thought cremation isn't in the Jewish religion."

"Of course it's not," she answers, continuing in Yiddish, but I don't want to *ligen in drerd*." Lay in the ground.

"I didn't know you felt that way about Israel. You've only been there twice since 1948."

"I didn't before. I think it happens when you get older," she replies. "You want to go back to your roots. I want to go there soon and spend some time with my cousin Basia. We were like sisters."

"Why now? Don't you think it's dangerous?"

"If I waited for a time when it's totally safe, I'd never go. Anyway, it's not dangerous. Over seven million people live there."

269

I think because she survived the odds in the Holocaust, she believes they will always be in her favor. Maybe that's why she buys lotto tickets too. It seems to separate the optimists from the pessimists.

"But, Mom, don't you feel this is your home? Here?" I say, gesturing to the room around us. I ask the rhetorical question, realizing midway through the sentence that I already know the answer.

"Not really," she says. "This is where I live. Israel is my home. It's where we Jews belong."

* * *

In the years my mother and I worked closely on this book, not only did I learn more about her life, I learned more about myself, too. And finally, after all this time, I resolved the nagging questions that had been troubling me for so long: Why did my mother hide being Jewish after the Holocaust? Why did she baptize me as a Catholic? Why did she forbid me to tell anyone I was Jewish? Was she living a lie in order to feel safe and protect me from anti-Semitism or was it simply a ruse to appease my Greek Orthodox father?

Gradually, I realized my mother's denial was the only way she could cope. It was the only way she could get through the day without the ghosts of the Holocaust haunting every minute of her life.

"I couldn't go on. I couldn't stand it, if I thought about it all the time," she once said, safely using a pronoun to abstract reality. My mother didn't want to live her life labeled as a Holocaust survivor. She didn't want to be the object of people's curiosity. She didn't want their pity. She didn't need to be reminded of her horrible past. She could never forget it.

Even today my mother continues using her Christian identity whenever she feels it's necessary. But I know – we both know – that it's an obsolete safety net from the past that she hasn't been able to completely rid herself of. For me her double identity had always been a contradiction. A lie. It didn't feel right. For me, that is. But, for my mother, there was never a conflict. Both identities, Christian and Jew, co-existed, just like the two cities of Vilnius. Her Vilnius and mine. Only now can I begin to understand the sad dichotomy of her life.

As the years passed, I discovered that I, too, didn't want the Holocaust to define me. It conferred a distinction and gravitas I hadn't earned and didn't deserve. It was one that I'd only experienced second-hand through my mother's recollections. Though I didn't hide that I was Jewish, only my closest friends knew about my mother's background. I didn't want to be identified as a token COS – the acronym for Children of Survivors. I didn't want to represent any one group or anything else. Perhaps, self-ishly, all I wanted was to lead a happy life with Tony. That was enough for me. I pushed to the back of my mind the Buddhist teachings I had stud-ied: that one must not become attached to things because everything is impermanent and fleeting. And the only constant is change. I didn't want anything different from the life I was already so attached to. It had all the components of happiness I needed. I just wanted more of the same: more good health, more creative projects, more dinner parties with family and friends, more travel, more events on a calendar to look forward to.

And though it was difficult to put into words, I sensed that the abyss of the Holocaust, which had taken place so long ago, still had the power to entrap me. A friend, the psychotherapist, Marlene Teichman, also a Child of Survivors says, "I always felt there was a place for memorials and museums and archives, but I also felt that the gift of life and the life within the Jew that was lost is what was never sufficiently balanced with the pain because of the time needed to grieve by Holocaust survivors."

Every day my mother's biggest challenge is a juggling act – to re-member and honor the past while living fully in the present. As she's often said, "I acknowledge my past, but I don't want to dwell on it." Like my mother, I want to be free to walk in both worlds, the Jewish and the non-Jewish one – to be accepted by both my Jewish and Christian rela-tives. And like my mother, I, too, finally know who I am and where I belong.

During the Holocaust, my mother was brave enough to step out of the line of ghetto workers marching down the middle of the streets of Vilnius and slip off her jacket with the Star of David sewn on the front and back. At that instant, she shed her skin as a Jew and became a Christian. "To join the free people," she said. Now she's a "free" person, but as a Holocaust survivor, her freedom will always be curtailed by her memories. Ever since that fateful day in Vilnius, living each moment has been a renewed act of courage for my mother. And, now that we've trav-eled through the past to write this book together, I've finally been able to understand the loss around which my mother's life was formed.

But what I learned from writing this book is not at all what I ex-pected. During the many hours and days my mother and I sat next to each other in front of the computer, while she read out loud from the tiny script in her spiral notebooks and I transcribed her words, I learned I had always viewed her life through the limited prism of my own sheltered, comfortable, middle-class life. I didn't know I had unfairly been judging her by my standards. The more I discovered her past, the more I under-stood her as a separate person – a person who once lived in a world in which I did not exist. The understanding finally allowed me to break our symbiotic bond. I was separate from her. I, too, was now a free person.

Only when I stopped judging my mother was I able to stop judging myself. The more I think about it, I realize – who am I to question how she has chosen to live her life?

Photo Album

Cover of Rasia's Workbook for Foreigners

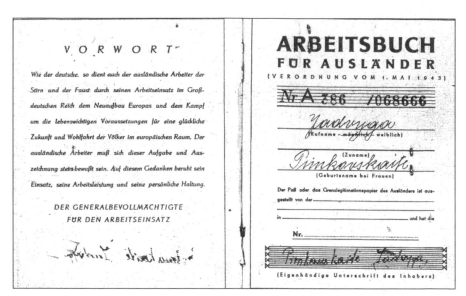

Cover page of Rasia's Workbook for Foreigners. The text reads as follows:

FOREWORD

Like the German, so, too, the foreign worker served the Stars and the Fist through his participation in the larger German Empire in the new construction of Europe and the fight for the vital requirements of the happy future and welfare of the people in the European realm. The foreign worker must be conscious of his task and proud of the distinction of his assignment. His participation, his work performance and his personal behavior should be based on these thoughts.

THE GENERAL AUTHORITY RESPONSIBLE
FOR THE RECRUITMENT OF WORKERS

Second page of Rasia's Workbook for Foreigners

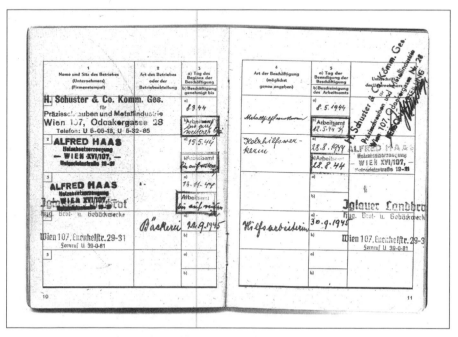

Page inside Rasia's Workbook for Foreigners

Rasia's fake ID in which she lists her occupation as a peasant. She intentionally spilled liquid on the ID to obscure some of the information.

Left to right: Leo, Hershel, Rasia and Benjamin in Czarny Bor

Left to right: Esther, Benjamin, Hershel, Rasia and Hatzkel, 1928

This photo was taken in the village of Czarny Bor on August 14, 1939, not far from Vilnius, where Rasia's family spent every summer. In the group photo are Rasia's aunts, uncles and cousins. Esther, Leo, Rasia, Viera and Leon survived the Holocaust. Top row from left to right: Aunt Manya and her husband, Uncle Leon; Esther Kliot (Rasia's mother); Uncle Solomon and his wife, Aunt Viera; Hatzkel Kliot (Rasia's father) and Rasia. Bottom row, from left to right: Cousin Ida, Cousin Ruvele, and Rasia's brother, Leo.

Left to right: Mira from Poland, Jane from France, Rasia, and Maria from Russia in Mr. Haas's work camp; Vienna, 1944

Rasia in Vilnius; high school photo during the Russian occupation

Antosia and Wladyslaw Januszkewicz with their daughter in Becoupe. These are the farmers Rasia worked for when she was hiding out on their farm and pretending to be a Catholic peasant laborer, 1943.

Rasia in Vienna, 1945

Rasia and Chris in Wienerwald, 1946

Vienna, 1948

*Chris, Rasia, and cousin
Schmulik as a soldier; Ir
Ganin, Israel, 1949*

Helen and Rasia

Rasia, Helen and Esther in Montreal

Dolly McCall gave a framed photo of this family gathering to Rasia and Chris on the last day of their employment.

Nina (right) in 1962, who gave Rasia her deceased sister's ID. Here with her husband and daughter, Maryla Rodowicz, one of Poland's top singers.

Helen and Uncle Papu in the backyard on Osborn Rd. in Phoenix

Rasia, Chris and Helen in the front yard on Osborn Rd. in Phoenix

Helen and Sister Adele Clare

Helen's Confirmation Day at the age of eight

Garik, Helen and Suze at the Vilnius Airport, 2007

Apartment building 8 Subocz St. in Vilnius

The new, brown building in the middle stands where Rasia's house used to be, across from Rotuse, the town hall.

Helen at the Ponary Memorial

The Ponary Memorial; In this area, about a half-hour drive from Vilnius, seventy thousand Jews were killed between 1941 and 1944. The memorial plaque is translated into Polish, Hebrew and Lithuanian. Here, huge pits dug by the Soviets to hold oil are where the Jews were shot and buried.